Allah
in the West

for Blanche

. . . quae nunc abibis in loca pallidula, frigida, nudula . . .

Allah
in the West

Islamic Movements in America and Europe

GILLES KEPEL

Translated by Susan Milner

Polity Press

This English translation copyright © Polity Press 1997.
First published in France as *À l'Ouest d'Allah*, copyright © Éditions du Seuil 1994.

First published in 1997 by Polity Press in association with Blackwell Publishers Ltd.

Published with the assistance of the French Ministry of Culture.

Editorial office:
Polity Press
65 Bridge Street
Cambridge CB2 1UR, UK

Marketing and production:
Blackwell Publishers Ltd
108 Cowley Road
Oxford OX4 1JF, UK

ISBN 0–7456–1557–0
ISBN 0–7456–1558–9 (pbk)

A CIP catalogue record for this book is available from the British Library.

Typeset in 10½/12pt Sabon
by Wearset, Boldon, Tyne and Wear.
Printed in Great Britain by Hartnolls Ltd, Bodmin, Cornwall

This book is printed on acid-free paper.

Contents

Acknowledgements

The research on which this book is based was made possible by the support of the Centre for International Study and Research (Paris) and the generous help of friends and students. In the United States, Yvonne Haddad, Beverly McCloud and Larry Mamiya helped me to get to know the world of the Black Muslims, and Eric Fassin and Denis Lacorne gave me the benefit of their exceptional knowledge of American society. In the United Kingdom Danièle Joly and her colleagues at Warwick University's Centre for Research on Ethnic Relations, as well as Jörgen Nielsen, director of the Islamic–Christian Centre at Selly Oak College, Birmingham, gave me access to many ideas and important sources of information. Neil North and Philip Lewis were invaluable guides, and Jacques Leruez helped me to understand the way British society works. In France, I am indebted to the contributions made by doctoral students researching into the Arab world at the Institute for Political Studies (Paris); many of them published their first research work in *Exils et royaumes*, a collection dedicated to our mentor Rémy Leveau and which I found extremely useful. They are a remarkably talented group of researchers and I greatly enjoyed working with them and benefited from their comments and their rigorous criticisms.

Finally, I would like to thank all those Islamic activists and observers of these movements who spoke to me and presented their views. What I have to say (based on analysis rather than views) may not always agree with their opinions, but I hope that it will contribute to a debate in which they are actively involved.

My thanks go also to Michel d'Hermies, who kindly checked through the manuscript, and to those close to me, to whom the time spent on this book prevented me from showing my affection as much as I would have liked . . .

Introduction

With the fall of the Berlin Wall in November 1989, an entire way of conceptualizing the twentieth-century world disappeared. At a stroke not only the confrontation between East and West, but also conflicts between social classes expressed politically in the left–right opposition became obsolete. From the United States came the message that 'the end of history' had arrived, together with the advent of a new world reconciled under the favourable auspices of capitalism allied with democracy.

However, along with the end of the old order symbolized by the wall, 1989 also brought events which signalled new divisions reflecting some of the contradictions of the world to come. From Tehran, Ayatollah Khomeini pronounced Salman Rushdie's death sentence, whilst in Britain's rundown inner cities working-class Pakistanis burnt copies of *The Satanic Verses*. France, instead of uniting in celebration of the bicentenary of the 1789 Revolution and the values it proclaimed, was rent by divisions as it had not been since the Dreyfus affair, over an apparently trifling incident: could French society allow three Muslim girls (living in an underprivileged city suburb) to wear an Islamic veil to attend state school? The incident was all it took for Islam, in its militant version, to replace the moribund Soviet Union as the new 'evil empire', embodying the demonized figure of the barbaric Other against which all civilizations tend to define their own identity.

Reaching beyond such stereotypes, the present book seeks to analyse and contextualize the assertions of Islamic identity we see in the West today, of which the Rushdie affair, the 'veil' incidents in France, or the 'Islamization' of American black ghettos under the banner of the Black Muslims are the most spectacular and controversial expression. Behind the headline events, new social, cultural, political and religious fault-lines have emerged around a specific version of Islam activism which functions right at the heart of postindustrial modernity. These changes operate at various levels of meaning. As we might expect, the new Islamist movements reflect wider changes affecting contemporary Islam throughout the world. Establishing themselves outside the areas where Islam has traditionally been present, using universal Western languages (primarily English), having ready access to radio and television and evolving in a democratic political system, the proselytizing Islamist movements of Europe and America form the avant-garde of the faith's international expansion.

But, in an unexpected way, this phenomenon also has considerable significance and instructive value for the Western societies in which it has developed. Over and above the Islamic question itself, the claim to a community identity expressed in Muslim discourse constitutes a prism through which we can observe how, and around which constructions of identity, our postindustrial societies are structured. In this last decade of the twentieth century, the labour movement and declining trade unionism are no longer capable of assuming the demands and the social future of this new proletariat of 'black-and-white-*beur*'[1] youths living on the fringes of the labour market, in the rundown housing projects of French city suburbs or British and American inner cities. By laying claim to Islam, which they load with extremely diverse meanings, a certain number of young Blacks in the United States, Indians and Pakistanis in Britain or North Africans in France are seeking to construct a community identity and are thereby making a deliberate cultural break with the dominant values of countries of which they are for the most part citizens in law, but which in their view exclude them in fact.

This separatism is as much a means of defence against a dehumanized or hostile social environment as a way of mobilizing 'brothers' and negotiating collectively in their name with the authorities. In their fight against drugs, violence and all forms of exploitation, the protagonists are at the same time constructing an alternative identity, thanks to specific teachings, modes of behaviour and attitudes which heighten difference and 'otherness', among which the strict observance of all religious rules and prohibitions plays a fundamental role.

In the 1990s, such movements, organizations and currents of thought are far from having a dominant influence on the social behaviour of the majority of people of Muslim origin living in the

West, let alone on the expression of their faith. There are a thousand ways of being Muslim in everyday life, just as there are a thousand ways of being Christian, Jewish, Buddhist or atheist. This book does not aim to be an exhaustive sociological study of Muslims in Europe and the United States. Rather, attention is focused on groups which are tempted to go to the limits, even when they find themselves (temporarily?) in a minority. The book seeks to identify the social contradictions such groups exacerbate, sometimes in an extreme and outrageous fashion. It attempts to understand what their viewpoint reveals to us about the structures of the new order – or disorder – of postindustrial societies as experienced by the groups' followers. The method of analysis used here owes much to Weberian sociology in the importance given to the construction of ideal types which are not necessarily representative of the whole of society, but which reveal underlying patterns and enable us to interpret changes within society which we find difficult to perceive spontaneously, precisely because we are living within society and are actively involved in its conflicts of interest. Serious attention to these movements does not however mean excluding the possibility of other ways of interpreting the social changes in question, from different standpoints; on the contrary, it is the debate between different standpoints which moves knowledge forward.

Our analysis is prompted by the desire to throw light on a series of paradoxes which have guided the choice of the American, British and French contexts examined here. Not the least of these paradoxes is that assertions of community identity are taking place within societies which are moving in the opposite direction: that is, towards a growing indistinctiveness of inherited cultural identities, their dispersion in the universal consumption of standardized 'products' and, following the erosion of the great divides between left and right, 'exploiters' and 'exploited', 'bourgeoisie' and 'proletariat', the search for a consensus around values acceptable to everyone. The aim is therefore to examine more closely these calls to an Islamic community identity. Who are the activists and supporters? What are their demands? What are their priority fields of action? Why do they choose to identify with Islam in open societies where individuals have much more freedom in their allegiances than in the 'traditional' societies of the Muslim world, where the predominance of the inherited culture retains a determining influence on social identity?

In this respect, the action of the Black Muslims in the United States is particularly significant. Their identification with Islam has nothing to do with an inherited culture; rather it stems from a free choice and the invention of a genealogy which through the slave trade and slavery restores a collective history and therefore personal dignity. In this process the hierarchy of values of American racism is inverted with the demonization of white people, and calls for the construction of a community identity are pushed to their extreme form, that is, separatism.

The Black Muslim movement founded by Elijah Muhammad, then made famous by Malcolm X and Louis Farrakhan successively, was initially extremely heterodox, but has gradually ironed out its 'deviations' through increased contact with Saudi Arabia. Above all, it has invented the modes of social action and mobilization which we find among a good number of Islamic groups in Western Europe in the 1990s: the fight against drug dealers and addiction, the 'rehabilitation' of gangs by converting their members, the break with dominant norms in order to mark out a strong community identity, and the autonomous assumption of responsibility for the protection of those living in the ghettos who remain marginalized from the labour market without any hope of integration and who face only poverty and exclusion.

They reject integration into 'white America', seen as the source of all evil, as a deadly trap. Claiming the status of the ultimate victim as descendants of slaves, they have clashed violently with members of the Jewish community who feel that this status belongs first and foremost to them because of the Nazi genocide. Beyond the polemics (for instance, 'the Jews' have been accused of playing a major role in the slave trade), the tensions caused by the growing fragmentation of contemporary American society into juxtaposed communities may be observed here in exacerbated form. In this respect, the development of the Black Muslims represents a major contribution to the worldwide expansion of Islam at the end of the twentieth century, but it is also a symptom of the disintegration of the US social system in the postindustrial age. Significantly, the Black Muslims have taken over mass modes of cultural expression, such as rap or film, making the group Public Enemy or the figure of Malcolm X into universal, televisual Muslim heroes in the dispossessed urban areas of Europe and the Third World alike.

The Rushdie affair likewise took on universal significance thanks to the strength of televised images which broadcast across the globe the burning of *The Satanic Verses* in the centre of Bradford. But before it was appropriated by Ayatollah Khomeini for his own ends, the affair brought to a head the contradictions within the British model of systematic community organization (communalism). The roots of the Rushdie affair go right back to the first time in history when Islam had to face both the situation of being in a minority and a loss of power: in the British Empire of the Indies. It was then that, in the face of this unprecedented challenge, Islamic modes of resistance against the onslaught of foreign modernity were developed; decades later, they were transposed almost intact onto the situation in the Muslim districts of British industrial cities. The model of withdrawal into the community for fear of adulterating religious identity within an open society was congruent with the doctrine of Margaret Thatcher's Conservative governments, which sought to relieve the state as much as possible from responsibility for dealing with social problems, but it was also able to adapt to the electoralism of the Labour Party, some of whose MPs saw the mosques' imams as efficient suppliers of votes. However, the coexistence of Islamic communities and postindustrial society could not withstand the publication of Salman Rushdie's novel.

Many Muslims felt *The Satanic Verses* to be an insult to their beliefs, and it prompted religious leaders, who saw an opportunity to unite the Islamic community under their leadership and in a radical direction, into an increasingly vocal condemnation of the book and mobilization of the faithful. The most extreme consequence of this mobilization was the symbolic proclamation of a 'Muslim Parliament', intended to sit in opposition to the Westminster Parliament. This largely unrepresentative initiative was meant to be provocative, but it merely pushed to the point of absurdity the contradictions inherent within a political system giving priority to the existence of separate communities over individual integration.

France, on the other hand, has based its policies on principles which categorically reject the formation of separate communities and favour their withering-away within secular society. Nevertheless, French society has had to face a widespread assertion of Islamic community identity. This phenomenon first excited attention in 1989, the year France celebrated the bicentenary of the Revolution. The assertion of community identity, symbolized in the case of Muslim schoolgirls who insisted on covering their hair to attend school, marked the meeting point between the network of Islamic associations of the 1970s and 1980s and a section of young people of Muslim origin who had been born and brought up in France and who felt disillusioned by the anti-racist mobilization and the *'beur'* movement of the previous decade. At the same time, following the collapse of the FLN (National Liberation Front) regime in Algeria, support for the FIS (Islamic Salvation Front) rocketed and gave rise to a mass Islamic party which quickly reached the fringes of power. The new Islamic party, operating in France's

immediate environment, was rooted in an ideology of virulent opposition to all the values embodied in France, which the FIS orator Ali
Benhadj described as a 'poisonous milk' sucked greedily by the 'sons
of France' (that is, 'Westernized' Algerians).

These important changes in the internal and external context of
Islam in France at the start of the 1990s led the socialist government
to favour centralized management of the Muslim religion in order to
free the country from Algerian influence. This 'Jacobin' state-centred
approach, which had no equivalent elsewhere in the Western world,
did not succeed. However, as in the United States and Britain, 're-
Islamizing' movements in the underprivileged city areas have begun
to fill the gaps in public services (the fight against drug pushers, provision of educational support services and so on) and are seeking to
trade support for candidates in local elections for the satisfaction of
community demands. But it is difficult to see how religious identity
could be translated into a Muslim vote, because of the hostility
towards separate communities which forms the basis of the political
tradition of the French state (unlike its British or American counterpart) and the threats which hang over the Algerian situation in the
near future, given that the Algerian population in France (nationals
and people born in Algeria) numbers over one million. Nevertheless,
these institutional blocks should not obscure the novel modes of
social dislocation which the reference to communities reveals in
France as in other Western countries.

The *Weltgeist*, according to Hegel, is moving towards the West. In
following the same trajectory, the expansion of Islam in the postindustrial era faces a double challenge. Outside the intellectual protection afforded in the past by the boundaries of traditional Muslim
societies, Islam must now place itself on an equal footing with this
'spirit of the world', within the religion's strongholds in the West
which produce and transmit throughout the world the values,
images and wealth which form the basis of its power. Between conflict and compromise, the features of the Islam of the twenty-first
century are taking shape. But leaving aside the specifically Islamic
features of the phenomenon, we can observe in the communalist
demands expressed by some of the Muslim faithful settled in the
West, a certain number of new fault-lines which are appearing to
restructure the world of tomorrow.

PART I
'In the Wilderness of North America'

Hadley

Amidst the tumult and confusion following the Los Angeles riots of May 1992, one episode all but escaped public attention. The leaders of the two big rival gangs, the Crips and the Bloods, which had turned the ghetto streets into a battlefield, met in a local mosque. The imam of the mosque was 'Brother Aziz', the California representative of Louis Farrakhan, leader of the Nation of Islam. A few days earlier, these gang-leaders had been ready to kill each other, and indeed some of them still bore bullet wounds inflicted by their opponents. But in the mosque they signed a truce, thus for the first time entering into a process which was meant to bring peace to their deprived districts. The truce had just about as much real effect as the ceasefires being signed at around the same time in the former Yugoslavia. What it did show is that, in the midst of the chaos surrounding young Black Americans torn between anger and despair, 'the only national leader whom most Crips and Bloods seem to take seriously is Louis Farrakhan.'[1]

Meeting in another Los Angeles mosque to be interviewed for a radio programme, gang-leaders explained that they were in the mosque 'with the Muslims, because basically they believe in what we believe, what we want, what we're fighting for. They support us and advise us.' They concluded the interview with these words: 'The Muslims come and talk to you as a person. They respect you as you are. They don't look down on you, whether you wear blue or red, whether you're a Crip or a Blood.[2] They don't insult you, they don't call you a killer, they respect you as a man. And that's what we want, respect. To be treated like the others.'[3]

Chicago is another city where the spatial segregation of races and classes has parked young Blacks in 'hyperghettos', where killing and drug-dealing form part of the daily scenery and are the only really lucrative activities.[4] In 1992 one of the city's leading Black councillors, alderwoman D. Tillman, expressed the view that 'Not only could Minister Farrakhan get young people's attention, but he also can transform them from a criminal preying on their own neighborhood into hard workers who are an asset to the neighborhood.'[5]

However, the charismatic leader of the Nation of Islam, Minister Louis Farrakhan, as he styles himself, is one of the most intensely controversial figures of the United States in the 1990s. The main Jewish associations, headed by the Anti-Defamation League, accuse him of anti-Semitism[6] (a charge he denies) and insistently demand that Black politicians denounce him whenever he appears in public. These politicians may disagree with Farrakhan's views, but they do not usually take kindly to these demands. On the contrary, the lobbying seems to have the opposite effect on a considerable section of the Black population, and Farrakhan's popularity increases because he is the target of outside pressure groups. Thus, wherever he is invited to speak by students, local politicians and workers' associations, 'Farrakhan makes his speech, splits his audience down the middle' and scores points, as a liberal Jewish author notes.[7]

The figure of Farrakhan has crystallized community antagonisms between 'Jews' and 'Blacks', especially those among the latter who profess their worship of Allah (in their own way). In 1991, the controversy was revived by the publication by the Nation of Islam of a book[8] which describes the involvement and responsibility of Jews in the slave trade, presented by the authors as the genocide above all others, the major holocaust of human history.

But the demonization of Farrakhan by his opponents and the fierce criticism he receives in the American press in general cannot obscure his social and cultural impact on poor Black circles and on 'non-white' America. At the time of the Democrat convention before the presidential campaign of 1984, three candidates were competing for the primaries: Walter Mondale (who was to win the nomination), Gary Hart and Jesse Jackson, the famous Afro-American preacher and politician who was heading a 'rainbow coalition'. In response to pollsters' questions on their opinion of Farrakhan, 47 per cent of Black convention delegates stated that they had a favourable opinion of him, whilst 76 per cent of non-Black delegates were hostile.[9] Similarly, 65 per cent of Jackson supporters declared themselves sympathetic or very sympathetic to Farrakhan, as opposed to only 5 per cent of Mondale's and 3 per cent of Hart's supporters. The followers of the three candidates divided into distinct groups on all issues in the survey, whether on a heavy increase in the public health budget (respectively 63 per cent, 38 per cent and 31 per cent of Jackson, Mondale and Hart supporters in favour) or on the economic situation (59 per cent, 45 per cent and 35 per cent respectively thought it was bad).[10] The socio-cultural gap between the way Jackson supporters and those of the two white Democrat candidates viewed the world was considerable. These survey results revealed the existence of 'two Americas'. Mainstream society supports reformism within the existing system and refuses to identify with a leader rejected as anti-Semitic and originating from the ghetto world and the sects of the 'other America'. But in the 'other America', there is anger and dissatisfaction; for many of the young in this group, Farrakhan's words, however outrageous, make sense.

The 'other America' that produced Louis Farrakhan is the subject of our investigation here, or rather the social conditions in which the 'other America' lives: the 'wilderness of North America' which gave birth to the Nation of Islam. Since the 1930s, the Nation of Islam has campaigned for the economic self-sufficiency of Black people, a break with white society and community resocialization as a first step towards the construction of a separate Black state. Its ideology is based on its own version of Islam, largely reinvented for the purposes of the cause by its Messiah, W. D. Fard, and its Prophet and first propagandist, Elijah Muhammad (who died in 1975). Malcolm X then became its most effective and famous preacher before he was rejected and later assassinated. This was the movement that Farrakhan took over in 1977. Its world view goes right to the heart of the community fragmentation of the postmodern era; spread by the best-known groups and rap artists like Public Enemy, Ice-T, Ice Cube, Sister Souljah and others, it now forms part of the universal subculture of Walkmans, clubs and ghetto-blasters.

In 1992, Spike Lee's epic film *Malcolm X* brought the man and the environment which produced him to the young Black generation. In the process he helped to reactivate the Islamic dimension of Malcolm X which had until then been overshadowed by his role as opponent of the system. Lee's film took on cult status; whole classes of Black high school pupils went to see it; young Muslim groups organized showings all over the world, especially in France and Britain. In fact, it lent itself to appropriation by a variety of causes. Hollywood took hold of the life of a revolutionary and transformed it into merchandise, through a whole industry of products marked with X, from T-shirts to baseball caps. *The Wall Street Journal* even saw Malcolm X as 'a conservative hero'[11] who, beyond the subversive aspect of his political action, preached a discipline which took

young Blacks away from the disorder of the ghetto and prepared
them for the discipline of paid work once their youthful follies were
over. Even more extraordinary is the fact that, from the beginning,
the Nation of Islam has enjoyed a certain amount of support from
various white extremist groups like the Ku Klux Klan which are in
favour of racial segregation and see the idea of a separate Black state
as a step towards the fulfilment of their own desire for an ethnically
'pure' white state.[12] Despite determined attempts by liberal intellectuals and American Jewish groups to undermine it, and despite the
extremist discourse of some of its own leaders, there is no denying
that the movement has forged strong links with many components
of American society.

Some local authorities and other bodies in the United States,
unable to deal directly with the social problems of the ghettos and to
stem rising crime and drug-trafficking, have even turned to the paramilitary wing of the Nation of Islam, the Fruit of Islam (FOI), to
maintain order on the streets and the housing projects. Thus, in July
1992, in the traumatized and riot-torn city of Los Angeles, the state-
run housing office made a deal with a vigilante group belonging to
the Fruit of Islam for the group to patrol a project area which had
been overrun by crime and drugs.[13] The following month, on a
beach in Queens (New York), the Fruit of Islam stewarded a traditional student festival which in previous years had resulted in violence and killings. The movement's bi-monthly paper, *The Final
Call*, described the scene:

> The F.O.I. of Muhammad's Mosque #7 [based in Harlem] under the
> charge of Bro. Captain Dennis Muhammad stormed the beach wearing
> their warm weather patrol uniforms (crisp white shirts, bright red bow
> ties, dark slacks, sun glasses, straw hats and lace up leather shoes) to
> assume security post. Within a few hours the beach was packed with
> Black people and the ... Fest was well under way. Members of the city,
> state and park police were so impressed by the level of stamina and disci-
> pline of the Muslims that they surrendered their posts to the FOI and
> took up positions outside the perimeter. No incidents of violence were
> reported.[14]

The same publication also reported that the housing ministry in
Washington was considering 'making a deal with the Dopebusters,
the FOI's anti-drug patrol', in spite of pressure from Jewish organizations.[15] The chief of Washington's police similarly put out a joint
statement with the Nation of Islam's 'chief of staff' to mark their
collaboration in the rundown Clifton Terrace project in the fight to
chase out dealers and restore order.[16]

Leaving aside the polemics, we must try to analyse the emergence and formation of Farrakhan's movement as a symptom of American society's ills and as a response – even in its most outrageous forms – to a certain number of social, political and cultural challenges. It is also necessary to understand how Islam has come to take on such significance in the context of the United States, so far away from the traditional centres of operation usually associated with the Islamic world, such as Saudi Arabia or Iran. We need to examine the ways in which the 'Black Muslims' have developed their own version of Islam to suit their own situation, like an inverted myth or a negative print of the 'American way of life'.

There is continuity between the organization set up in Detroit in the early 1930s and the movement led by Farrakhan since the second half of the 1970s, but despite having kept the same name and some of the original institutions, the Nation of Islam has adapted its words and actions in line with the considerable changes undergone by American society in the course of the twentieth century. The Nation of Islam grew out of the radical separatist groups which sprang up in the first decades of the century and made considerable headway during the Great Depression of 1929. In the process it developed a double aspect, which is preserved in the main by Farrakhan and his friends.

On one hand, the movement is characterized by an extremist discourse advocating a radical break with outside society, with the ultimate goal of a separate Black state. This discourse glorifies Black supremacy and demonizes the white man, the 'blue-eyed devil'. In support of this break with white society, the movement has constructed a strange cosmogony and mythology which draw explicitly on Islam but also on the Messianism of the many Black churches and sects or the Jehovah's Witnesses. Within them, we find the exact reverse copy, rather like a negative print, of the racism which runs through American society. The choice of terms and the reasoning vilify the white man in order to demean him as Black people have been demeaned: first dehumanized by slavery, then defined by the first Constitution of the founding fathers of American democracy as equal to just three-fifths the worth of their white fellow-citizens.[17]

On the other hand, the Nation of Islam also fulfils a function of resocialization. Its followers are converted to a new 'virtuous' community which is the exact opposite of the world of the ghetto streets. The ghetto is condemned as the ultimate place of degradation and corruption of Black people by the 'blue-eyed devil'. The Black Muslims paint the ghetto as a world of alcoholism, prostitution, crime and drugs, rather than in the euphemistic terms habitually used in anti-racist rhetoric. The words and images used by the Black Muslims recall the most hostile stereotypes used by white racists against Blacks. But whereas white racists attribute the situation of Black people to an inherited racial inferiority, the Nation of Islam identifies one single cause: the evil hand of the white man, who corrupted the pure natives of Africa. The solution is to build a virtuous community of Black Muslims as the only way out of lawlessness and the jungle of the streets. The community is seen as the embryo of an idealized self-sufficient organization based on strict discipline of oneself and one's social relations. This second aspect of the movement has led some writers to describe it as something akin to an ethic of civilization, rather like the Protestant ethic which, in Weber's classic description, enabled the spirit of capitalism to flourish.[18]

I

The Birth of an American Religion

The Detroit Messiah

The Nation of Islam began in 'Paradise Valley' (the name given to
the Black ghetto of Detroit) in the most terrible period of the Great
Depression, in 1930. In this wretched place, unemployment plunged
the Black population, who had emigrated in the previous decades
from the south to supply cheap labour to the industrial factories,
into a much worse state of destitution than that of the southern
plantations and cotton fields they had fled. It was in this setting that,
according to the traditional historiography of the Nation of Islam, a
mysterious character made his appearance.[1] He was a silk pedlar,
and he told his Black customers that the fabrics he sold were their
native clothing, worn by their 'race' in Africa before the slave trade
brought them to America's shores. His gift of the gab allowed him
to go into his clients' homes and talk to them of the Africa he
claimed to know. He taught them how to cure physical and moral
sicknesses, which were prevalent in the northern American towns
during the freezing winters for which they were ill-equipped and
which were aggravated by the poverty of the Great Depression. At
that time, pedlars and street vendors in American cities were usually
Syrian or Lebanese; our man thus told his listeners that he came
from the East, and that his name was Fard (or Farrad, or Ford) and
his first name Wallace or, in Arabic, Wali.[2]

To cure sickness, Black people were first told to give up the 'poisoned food' the white man gave them, and eat according to Fard's
instructions, since he knew what kind of food was eaten 'at home'
and made Black people in Africa 'the healthiest in the world'. It is

true that soul food, the traditional food of poor Blacks, is rich in fat and stodge, and low in nutritional value, like other kinds of poor diet; together with the irregular pace of life, this diet contributes to the poor general health of ghetto-dwellers.[3]

One of Fard's first followers described his appearance on the scene:

> He told us that the silks he carried were the same kind that our people used in their home country and that he had come from there. So we all asked him to tell us about our own country. If we asked him to eat with us, he would eat whatever we had on the table, but after the meal he began to talk: Now don't eat this food. It is poison for you. The people in your own country do not eat it. ... So we all wanted him to tell us more about ourselves and about our home country and about how we could be free from rheumatism, aches and pains.[4]

Food restrictions seem to have been the first sign of a break with the customs and practices of the lawless society around them, and the first step on the road to the formation of a community and allegiance to Fard. In any case the many disciples attracted by his charismatic presence were more than happy to give up their supper to listen to him speak. Between 4 July 1930, when he first appeared, and 30 June 1934, when he went into hiding, Fard took on the mantle of prophet and organized a spiritual community of around 8000 Detroit Blacks.

The new cult saw its main function as restoring the true Black identity which whites, the 'Caucasian slavemasters', had robbed them of. An essential part of this was to change the names used to describe Black people. Disciples would no longer be 'so-called negroes', as their masters had called them, but claimed descent from the original Blacks of the Shabazz tribe. Their true religion was Islam and their true language Arabic. In the United States, they represented 'the lost found nation of Islam in the wilderness of North America'. It was Fard, the Messiah and incarnation of Allah, who had found the lost nation and given its members back their hidden identity. He began by stripping them of their 'slave name' and restoring their 'true' (Muslim) name: John became Karim, Richard Muhammad, and so on. In order to obtain their new name, each follower had to copy out by hand an application letter and pay Fard ten dollars – a considerable sum at that time. For the illiterate and destitute population, writing a letter meant a sizeable effort, proving depth of commitment, and it was a source of pride.[5] As for the money, it enabled Fard to live comfortably in a hotel in town, and to delegate the running of the cult to his assistants.

Thanks to his disciples' organizational skills, a Temple of Islam was set up in a rented hall, and his followers' children were put in the care of a 'University of Islam' – in fact a primary school – to be taught 'our own knowledge', as opposed to 'the Caucasian devils' civilisation'. This too meant a break with all universal values which were not first and foremost those of the community of the pure, and based on its own criteria. The movement also rejected American nationality and created its own flag, a white crescent and star on a red background, surrounded by the words 'Equality, Justice, Liberty, Islam'. The strict discipline of the movement's followers helped to take them out of the corrupting influence of the ghetto and make them into efficient and reliable workers, whose wages added to the movement's funds. Any potential threats to the internal equilibrium of the community were outlawed, and marital fidelity was monitored especially rigorously because ghetto morals were traditionally loose on this question. But as is often the case in sects, the charismatic leader did not have to abide by the rules and could have any woman he chose.

The activities of the Nation of Islam rapidly came to the attention of the authorities, particularly when its followers took their children out of municipal schools to study under the 'University of Islam''s own special programme. But the situation deteriorated in November 1932 when a member of the movement took literally one of Fard's prophecies that each member should sacrifice four 'Caucasian devils' in order to 'go home to Mecca', and stabbed a co-tenant during a voodoo-type ritual.[6] Police 'persecution' ensued, resulting in several splits within the movement, Fard's disappearance ('back in Mecca', his disciples believed) and the takeover of the organization by one of Fard's right-hand men, Elijah Muhammad.

The foundation years of the Nation of Islam are a key period for those wishing to understand why the model shaped then still operates sixty years later, in the era of rap and crack. At the end of the twentieth century, communalism flourishes in postindustrial society. We know that Christianity is in eternal debt to St Paul, without whom Christ's message could well have faded into insignificance, like the gnosticisms and the prophecies of the hundreds of miracle-workers up and down Tiberius' Palestine, condemned later as simony by a Church which wished to guarantee its monopoly on divinity. In the same way, by putting the finishing touches to the golden legend of Fard and systematizing the doctrine which Fard himself taught only in rudimentary form,[7] Elijah Muhammad ensured their longevity, whereas hundreds of Negro cults died as quickly as they had sprung up. Elijah Muhammad's work was all the more remarkable as already in the 1960s fairly precise and defamatory details about Fard's life were being publicized, although his disciples rejected them at the time as police disinformation.

According to FBI files[8] (made available to the public in accordance with the law on freedom of information), 'Fard' was really Wallace Ford, born in Hawaii on 25 February 1891. His father was a white Englishman who had emigrated to New Zealand, and his mother came from the native Maori people. Ford moved to California where he was arrested for various offences, first for distilling alcohol during Prohibition, then for heroin-dealing, which earned him a three-year stint in San Quentin penitentiary. Once released, he headed for Chicago, then Detroit, where among the Black people of the ghetto he adopted the name Fard and proclaimed himself Messiah and Allah made flesh. The FBI investigation was carried out mainly in 1957–8 and its findings were then passed on by J. Edgar Hoover to various 'friendly' newspapers, which published them in 1959 and later in 1963, with the aim of ridiculing the Nation of Islam by revealing that the movement which saw white people as 'Caucasian blue-eyed devils' had worshipped as a god an ex-convict whose father was white. Indeed, photographs taken of Fard in custody show a very un-African face.[9]

Elijah Muhammad's response was to deny that the FBI's Ford and Fard were one and the same person,[10] although echoes of Fard's mixed blood can be found in the Nation of Islam's belief that Fard was 'half Black, half white' to help him to accomplish his messianic mission, and it has not escaped attention that Ford's birthday coincided with 'Savior's Day', the day celebrated by the Nation of Islam as Fard's birthday (usually 26 February). Whatever the exact truth of Fard's past, there is no denying his remarkable ability to invent a religious product which satisfied the expectations of the target population. In particular, the 'Messiah' was skilful in recycling the pietistic materials to hand and blending them into a usable and coherent whole. In order to understand how the Nation of Islam not only won over but maintained its hold over its followers, however extraordinary its practices and its ideology may appear, it is first necessary to reconstruct the context in which it was formed and to examine the interaction between the exclusion of Blacks from the American political system and the political function of substitution fulfilled by the Black churches, sects and other religious movements.

The fight against exclusion

In 1866, at the end of the Civil War, Black Americans had won civil rights akin to those of their white compatriots, in the Civil Rights Act. For ten years, in the middle of the 'reconstruction' period, thousands of Black Americans put their names on the electoral list and elected, among others, coloured congressmen and senators.[11] But in 1877 the newly elected President of the United States Rutherford B. Hayes withdrew the federal troops policing the law in the defeated southern states. In so doing he hoped to win over the former ruling classes of the south, and especially the mass electorate of poor whites who competed with Blacks for manual jobs and access to social services. Hayes's action opened the way for a whole series of discriminatory measures ('Jim Crow' legislation)[12] legalizing racial segregation in public places, and thousands of Black people were lynched. Thus these new citizens of the United States were excluded from exercising their citizenship, and this situation lasted until 1965, when the Voting Rights Act came into force. The great abolitionist thinker W. E. Du Bois wrote of the reconstruction period: 'The slave went free; stood a brief moment in the sun; then moved back again into slavery.'

In this situation, the Black Methodist churches and to an even greater extent the thousands of independent Baptist congregations offered would-be Black political leaders a vast public forum: 'the Negro church ... provided the arena for the political struggles of a people shut out from the political life of the American community.'[13] As a result, spokesmen and political elites emerged out of the religious networks. It was to them that whites turned when they wanted someone to damp down social agitation, but at the same time these leaders expressed the revolt, frustration and expectations of the Black population. The exclusion of Blacks from the political domain allowed religion to take over many of its functions. Social promotion often coincided with the role of pastor, or even (for the most gifted) bishop or head of a congregation.[14] Thus, the language of religion served as the main vector for the expression of social conflict. The wretched situation of Blacks often gave rise to a millenarian theology: with nothing to hope for on earth, they lived in wait for a Messiah, a redeemer who would restore order to a world turned upside down by evil. Amid such tensions, and given the fragmentation of religious life among a multitude of sects, each interpreting the Holy Scriptures in its own way according to its leading preachers, there was room for an endless series of fantasmagorical doctrines of salvation. Each preacher, carried away by his own soothsaying, added his piece to the edifice.

At the same time, in the decades preceding the Great Depression, an elite of Black businessmen and journalists began to emerge. Excluded from participation in the white world, they 'subscribed to a philosophy of mutual aid and racial solidarity' aimed at constructing an autonomous 'Black metropolis', an institutionalized ghetto.[15]

The early decades of the century also saw the 'great migration' of Black people from the south. Many of them were sharecroppers in the huge plantations and lived in absolute poverty. During the First World War, the factories of the north sought unskilled labour, and their recruiting agents brought the poor southern Blacks up to the industrial belt of the United States stretching from Chicago and Detroit to New York and Pennsylvania. The rural exodus and the new living conditions it brought with it encouraged forms of religious behaviour far removed from the tradition of the mainstream Protestant churches, whilst retaining much of its vocabulary. In this complex mixture of loss of habitual framework of reference, reinforced pietism and a confused desire for autonomy, the first significant references to Islam began to appear among the Black American population.

It is generally estimated today that around 20 per cent of the slaves sold in Africa (usually by Muslim traders) to work on the American plantations were themselves Muslim, in that they came from the Islamized regions of the western African coast.[16] But there are no data available to suggest that Islam survived the destruction of African cultures during the centuries of slavery.[17]

In fact, when Islam grew among the Black American population in the first quarter of the twentieth century, its style was peculiarly American and far removed from what serves as Sunni orthodoxy in its various forms prevalent in the traditional Muslim world. In 1913, in Newark, New Jersey, a Black immigrant from the south named Timothy Drew founded a 'Moorish Holy Science Temple', whose name evokes the Christian Scientologist Church as much as the East. When Drew died in 1927, the 'Moorishes' ran temples in the Black ghettos of the east and the north, and had some 30,000 active members. Drew's syncretism tacked an Islamic vocabulary onto a millenarian syntax drawn from the southern Baptist sects. In this way it went along with the movement of destructuring, the loss of customary values, experienced by the Black immigrants from the south. To a familiar way of thinking and a traditional pietism, Drew's doctrine added new elements which suited the strong, urgent and desperate desire for a new identity felt as a result of the painful living conditions in the north and deep social frustation. It was Islam which instilled these new elements. Drew, who had the benefit of only a rudimentary education, had gained some knowledge of Muslim doctrine (it is unclear how),[18] and was sensitive to the fact that it did not contain any formal reference to distinction between races.[19] Drew saw Black Americans as 'Moors' or 'Moorish'. They were to wear a red Moroccan-style fez and a beard. As proof of their change of identity, followers received a new 'identity card' from Drew, who renamed himself 'Noble Drew Ali, the Prophet'. The card was decorated with the star and crescent of Islam as well as the magic number seven; it decreed that the bearer worshipped all the prophets (Jesus, Muhammad, Buddha and Confucius) and was 'a Moslem under the Divine Laws of the Holy Koran of Mecca, Love, Truth, Peace, Freedom, and Justice', concluding with the declaration: 'I am a citizen of the United States.'

The first thing to note about this surprising mixture is that it refers to everything that was denied to the disciples in their daily lives. American citizenship was proclaimed all the more insistently because in reality it had no meaning for most Black people in the 1910s – and it was the same with liberty and justice. The reference to love and the magic number, and the amazing melting-pot of prophets, are probably drawn from the many Baptist sects. But it was Islam that crowned this syncretism: the 'Moors' thought of themselves as Muslims and claimed to obey the 'Koran of Mecca', although we do not know whether they really read the Koran itself. Islam is the name Drew's followers gave to their break with their former identity, to the new communion of faith and to the feeling of regained pride and roots in the hallowed ground of Mecca, where the white man had no control.[20]

This pride led them into an escatalogical confidence that the white race would be annihilated and they would triumph. This is perfectly in keeping with pre-millenarian beliefs about the Messiah who would come to restore the world to its original order by turning the hierarchy of races, colours and classes upside down. But some 'Moors' did not want to wait for the end of the world: in Chicago in particular, they deliberately jostled white people they met in the street. Brandishing their 'identity card' like a talisman, they forced them to leave the pavement and walk around them in the road, thus reversing whites' traditional behaviour towards Black people, who in segregated America were forced to give way.[21]

The story of Noble Drew Ali ended mysteriously in 1927, three years before the 'advent' of Fard. It seems that the sect's leaders became involved in various lucrative activities, making their disciples buy potions, 'pure' foodstuffs and talismans. The disputes over the control of this business appear to have led to a settling of scores, in the process of which the prophet was murdered. Unless, that is, he died in police custody.

This, then, was the social and cultural context in which Islam made its appearance in the deprived Black neighbourhoods of the early part of this century. Islam served as a means of breaking with dominant society. Christianity was seen as a means of legitimating the oppression and injustice experienced by Blacks, as the blue-eyed Christ was appropriated for the use of white people only. Islam coexisted with other mass movements aiming to dissociate Black people's fate from that of the United States, the most famous of which was the Universal Negro Improvement Association. Founded by the Jamaican Marcus Garvey in 1914, the Association's objective was to take Blacks 'Back to Africa', in the words of its campaign slogan. Garvey attracted great enthusiasm among many poor Blacks, to whom he restored a sense of dignity. He was imprisoned in 1925 on embezzlement charges, and expelled from the United States two years later. One of Garvey's most devoted followers was a Black immigrant from Georgia living with his family in Detroit: Elijah Poole, who under the name Elijah Muhammad was later to become the main organizer of the Nation of Islam.[22]

Poole was born in 1897, one of thirteen children of a Georgia sharecropper who worked as a Baptist preacher for his community. In 1923 he fled from poverty and the racism of the south where, as a child, he had witnessed a lynching; he emigrated to Detroit in search of work. During the Great Depression, in 1929, he lost his job and survived on social assistance in miserable conditions. Then, worn down by unemployment and having lost all hope,[23] in 1931 he met Fard, who sold silks to his wife. Fard gave him a new strength: 'I recognized him to be God in person and that is what he said he was, but he forbade me to tell anyone else. I was a student of the Bible. I recognised in him the person the Bible predicted would come two thousand years after Jesus' death.'[24] Abandoning his 'slave name' Poole for Karim, then Muhammad, he soon became Fard's right-hand man. Fard appointed him 'Minister of the Nation of Islam' and delegated the major organizational jobs to him. When Fard mysteriously disappeared in June 1934 (having been under constant police surveillance), Elijah Muhammad took over the leadership of the Nation of Islam. But the new leader became entangled in disputes with other disciples who also claimed to be trustees of Fard's divine leadership powers, as well as internal problems within the movement caused by attempts by the American Communist Party, then by a Japanese sect linked with the Japanese secret services, to infiltrate the Nation. He was forced to flee across the United States. The Nation of Islam, which had some 8000 members at the time of Fard's disappearance, saw its membership decline. In May 1942, Elijah Muhammad was arrested for draft-dodging and remained in prison until 1946. His long spell in jail provided him with an opportunity to disseminate the movement among his fellow prisoners, many of whom were Black, and in fact prisons would remain one of the main recruiting grounds for the Black Muslims throughout the twentieth century.

Between 1934 and 1952, the influence of the Nation of Islam remained limited. But the social behaviour established by Fard was given a theoretical framework by Elijah Muhammad: a movement which represented both a radical break with dominant society and resocialization within an exclusive community. In order to achieve this, Elijah Muhammad had to develop a body of doctrine giving sacred legitimacy to the original aim of separatism.

Variations on Genesis

Elijah Muhammad – whom the *Reader's Digest* once called the 'most powerful Black man in America' – systematized Fard's doctrine in a book which is still today used in the temples of the Nation of Islam to give to people interested in learning about the movement. Entitled *Message to the Blackman in America*, it resembles the pietistic literature of the many American evangelist sects. It consists of a collection of short texts with flamboyant, apocalyptic or down-to-earth headings, such as 'Submit to Allah (God) and fear not!', 'Plan to destroy our race', 'America is falling: her doom is sealed', 'Prayer in Islam', or 'A programme for self development'. The texts are like articles from a campaigning newspaper or sermons, and seem very strange to anyone used to the Islamic rhetoric of the late twentieth century; but the stylistic and thematic connections with Black evangelical preaching in North America strike the reader straightaway. The book's main sections deal with religious themes ('Allah is God', 'original man', 'Islam', 'The Bible and Holy Qur-an') as well as escatological predictions of the Day of Judgement, but also social and economic action programmes and the plan for the construction of a separate Black state.

The style of the book is extremely spare and basic, and the rhetorical figures too resemble those of traditional preaching in the Black churches. Elijah Muhammad had not attended school beyond primary level, and his disciples liked to stress that every word in his writing – dictated 'until late at night . . . to his four highly competent secretaries' (on whom, more later) – 'is fashioned with loving care and a supreme regard for truth. What he writes is told in the language of the little fellow so there can be no mistake or confusion of purpose or shades of meaning.'[25] The sacred and unimpeachable nature of the document are underlined by Elijah Muhammad's status as 'Messenger of Allah', and the book's epigraph invites readers to 'seek the wisdom of Allah, the Best Knower and Guide in the person of Master Fard Muhammad (to Whom be praise forever). The reader will find that light in this book.'[26]

In the chapter headed 'Original man', Elijah Muhammad explains that Blacks are descendants of the 'tribe of Shabazz', who were 'the tribe that came with the earth (or this part) 66 trillion years ago when a great explosion on our planet divided it into two parts. One we call earth and the other moon.' He continues: 'We, the tribe of Shabazz, says Allah (God), were the first to discover the best part of our planet to live on. The rich Nile Valley of Egypt and the present seat of the Holy City, Mecca, Arabia.'[27] Everything went wonderfully for these original men with black skin, 'until the birth of another God, Yakub (Jacob)'. Jacob was extremely intelligent and came first at 'all of the colleges and universities of his nation', but he was bent on evil. He discovered

> by studying the germ of the black man, under the microscope, that there were two people in him, and that one was black, the other brown. He said if he could successfully separate the one from the other he could graft the brown germ until its last stage, which would be white. With his wisdom, he could make the white, which he discovered was the weaker of the black germ . . . rule the black nation for a time . . .[28]

According to Elijah Muhammad's account, Yakub won followers among the '30% of malcontents' living in Mecca at that time. But he was expelled from Mecca and exiled with his followers to the island of Patmos. There he devoted himself to the 'grafting' of successive generations, using the lightest-skinned individuals, in order to eliminate the Black race. Meanwhile, the darkest-skinned babies were systematically killed at birth by a nurse, who stuck a needle into their brain. Thus, within two centuries all the Blacks disappeared from Patmos; only 'Browns' remained. Then, by the same method of genetic selection, the 'Browns' became 'Reds' or 'Yellows' after another two centuries. Two hundred years after that, the grafting process finally ended with the creation of the Whites: 'The Yakub-made devils were really pale white, with really blue eyes; which we think are the ugliest of colors for a human eye. They were call [*sic*] Caucasian – which means, according to some of the Arab scholars: "One whose evil effect is not confined to one's self alone, but affects others".'

The white devils left Patmos and went back among the Black Nation, to Mecca. The king of Mecca then had them expelled, saying to his men:

> Gather every one of the devils up and strip them of our costume. Put an apron on them to hide their nakedness. Take all literature from them and take them by way of the desert. Send a caravan, armed with rifles, to keep the devils going westward. Don't allow any of them to turn back; and, if they are lucky enough to get across the Arabian desert, let them go into the hills of West Asia,

the place they now call Europe, as Elijah Muhammad has it.

For 2000 years, the Whites thus lived in the caves of Europe, walking on four legs and climbing in the trees. After various changes in fortune, they acquired 'the knowledge and power to bring every living thing, regardless of its kind of life, into subjection'. This was their main occupation for the 4000 years leading to the present day, during which they dominated the world: the slave trade represented one of the peaks of their ignominious activity. But worse was to come in the American plantations, where the white masters tried again to eliminate the race of the original men, the Black descendants of the tribe of Shabazz, just as Yakub had done on Patmos: by fornicating with their slave women, they created a bastard race, whom they named 'Negroes'. However, despite these diabolical plans, Elijah Muhammad notes, in the world in the twentieth century, 'The black nation, including its three other colors brown, red and yellow, outnumber the Caucasian race, eleven to one.'

Finally, in 1930, the original men, 'lost in the wilderness of North America', were refound by God incarnate in the person of Fard and identified by him as the 'Nation of Islam'. Fard announced that the persecution of the Black race in America, which had lasted 400 years, would end in 1955, and that the destruction of America was close at hand, accompanied by the annihilation of the white race and the end of its domination over the world.

Following Fard's pronouncements, liberation would take the path of a radical separation from the 'grafted devils' in all aspects of daily life and would take the concrete form of the construction of an independent Black state in North America, as a prelude to the universal triumph of Allah. Allah would then lead 'the great decisive battle in the sky' against the white race, 'for the sake of His people (the Black people), and especially for the American so-called Negroes.'[29]

This account of the creation of the world and the destiny of the human race reuses ideas, situations and characters from the three Abrahamic traditions, without reproducing any of them whole. The main source of inspiration appears to be apocalyptic language of the Bible. In this sense, the 'founding myth' of the Nation of Islam borrows from the millenarian doctrines present in the Protestantism of the American South, both in the white fundamentalist sects and the Black churches. The followers of these beliefs, who look forward to the millennium when the Messiah will lead the great decisive battle against the ungodly and restore the Righteous to their true place, are organized in two main groups. The 'pre-millenarians' do not feel it is worth carrying out any actions to change the order of things, since only the Redeemer will do this; the most important job is to build up a community of chosen people. The 'post-millenarians', on the other hand, think that political commitment and action as such are possible and can help to prepare the coming of the Redeemer and the final battle against the ungodly. The first position is frequently found in the most marginalized groups, for whom political activity would be doomed to failure; the second often occurs in movements which hope to transform their ability to mobilize religious support into votes at the time of elections. White American evangelism moved from the first to the second position in the 1970s.[30] The Nation of Islam, after taking up a pre-millenarian line, gradually chose to intervene in the political arena, without abandoning its own doctrine of the creation of the world or its wait for the final destruction of the white devils at the battle of Armageddon.

Elijah Muhammad's narrative of the world's creation in his *Message to the Blackman in America*, which we have summarized here in the order in which it is given, is punctuated by anachronistic comments which form a constant to-and-fro between the daily experience of poverty in the Black ghettos in the 1950s or the habits and attitudes he ascribes to whites, on one hand, and the events in his story which refer to them or are meant to provide the explanation for them. Thus, the apron worn by the 'white devils' to hide their nudity when they were expelled from Mecca is presented as the origin of the aprons worn by Freemasons in their ceremonies. For the Black Muslims, Freemasons embody the secret white societies which strive to annihilate the 'original man'.[31] The whites who walked on four legs and climbed in trees – at the time when the 'tribe of Shabazz' was at the high point of its civilization – are the mirror-image of the racist cliché that Blacks live in palm trees and are closely related to monkeys; indeed, Elijah Muhammad says that monkeys in fact descended from the white man living in the caves of Europe, who tried to recover his original colour by reversing the grafting process and ended up as a gorilla![32] Similarly, whites' immodesty and excessive drive for fornication are the negative image of the common prejudices in America concerning Blacks' sexual promiscuity. The whole of Fard's and Elijah Muhammad's cosmogony may thus be seen as an exact reversal of the depreciated self-image of Black people reflected by dominant American culture.

A particularly strong motif is the dread inspired by the adulteration of the pure Black race. In his autobiography, Malcolm X took up this theme very forcefully:

> In one generation, the black slave women in America were raped by the slavemaster white man, until there had begun to emerge a homemade, handmade, brainwashed race, that was no longer even of its true color, that no longer even knew its true family name. The slavemaster imposed his own family name on this rape-mixed race, which the slavemaster began to call the 'Negro.'[33]

This founding rape, which goes right to the heart of identity, is what 'integration' means to the Nation of Islam. Those 'so-called Negroes' who seek integration and the company of white people or even marry them are the supreme symbol of alienation and brainwashing. They have assimilated white values and become their agents and traitors to their race brothers. With the literal demonization of white people, the only future which Blacks can contemplate is total separation from them.

In this way, Elijah Muhammad's account of the creation and development of the world provides an ontological justification for the goal of separatism and the construction of a community which rebuilds 'in the wilderness of America' the original tribe of Shabazz, which knew happiness and enjoyed the highest level of civilization in the holy city of Mecca. The cosmogony of the Black Muslims elevates communalism and separatism into a holy truth. The first and most significant image is that of Moses leading the Hebrews in the exodus out of 'the wilderness of Egypt' into the Promised Land. Elijah Muhammad writes in this connection:

> Separation of the so-called Negroes from their slavemasters' children is a must. It is the only solution to our problem. It was the only solution, according to the Bible, for Israel and the Egyptians, and it will prove to be the only solution for America and her slaves, whom she mockingly calls her citizens without granting citizenship.[34]

Pushing this image further, Malcolm X preached in Harlem in 1955 that the then President Eisenhower was none other than an American Pharaoh who kept Blacks in slavery just as the Pharaoh of Egypt kept the Hebrews, and that Elijah Muhammad was the Moses who would lead Blacks out of servitude and guide them to a Promised Land, which would be an independent state.[35] The image of the Exodus is frequently used by religious movements which question the social order: thus, for example, the Mormon doctrine gave rise to a real exodus in the United States, when the persecuted disciples of Brigham Young moved to the banks of a great salt lake, which represented for them the Dead Sea of Palestine. There the Mormons laid down behavioural norms which differed from the American laws then in force, such as the practice of polygamy. In this way, they accomplished a form of separatism, but later came to an arrangement with the state, to which they did not really pose a threat.

However, it was Islam which allowed Fard and Elijah Muhammad to formalize, extend and make irreversible this founding separatism. Islam is the name given by the 'so-called Negroes' to the absolute otherness they wish to give to their identity, because of the long history of antagonism between the Christian universe and their own. It is at this level that the Black Muslims' discourse moves from the biblical register to the Islamic exemplar. The biblical vocabulary was necessary, because it was the only meaningful reference for Black Americans brought up in the Protestant tradition; preaching directly from the Koran would have meant nothing to them. But once the biblical vocabulary had been used to establish the account of Black suffering and the demonization of whites, reference to Islam allowed the Black Muslims to highlight the break with white society by introducing a field of reference completely outside white culture. Extending the account of the Exodus led by Moses, this separatism finds its definitive religious image in the break leading to the foundation of Islam, the Hegira. The Hegira, which forms the reference point for calculating the beginning of the Muslim era (AD 622 in the Christian calendar), marks the Prophet Muhammad's and his companions' break with idolatrous Mecca, when they were forced to flee for their lives to Medina, where they would eventually set up their own state.

When the Nation of Islam began, Fard and later Elijah Muhammad did not have to worry too much about whether their doctrine conformed to the 'orthodox' Islamic dogma.[36] Islamic scholarship was virtually absent from 1930s America, and there were no *ulema* in Detroit at that time to purge the Black Muslims' beliefs of their 'heresies'. In any case, Islam has always been characterized by great internal pluralism, to a much greater extent than the Roman Catholic Church.

Despite the ductile nature of Muslim doctrine and practice, however, outer limits exist, beyond which transgressors are condemned as 'ungodly' or 'hypocrites'. One of these limits is the belief that the Prophet Muhammad was 'the seal of prophecy', that is, that no other prophet could come after him. But in the history of Muslim societies, Shiite imams, marabouts and the sheiks of Islamic brotherhoods have occupied a position bearing many of the hallmarks of prophethood, even though they never identified with the Prophet Muhammad or declared themselves superior to him. Thus, Elijah Muhammad's status as prophet may seem 'heterodox' but can just about fit within the corpus of Muslim practice. Indeed, Islam in Black Africa abounds in sects whose founder enjoys a status close to divinity, such as Ahmadou Bamba, founder of the Mouride brotherhood which has spread from Senegal across the world through the network of travelling pedlars on the beaches and streets of Europe and America,[37] just as Fard travelled the streets of the Detroit ghettos selling his silks in 1930.

Infinitely harder for the 'traditional' Muslim to accept is the incarnation of Allah in the person of Fard. Movements claiming to follow Islam which have adopted this extreme form of Messianism have been subjected to violent rejection and persecution in Islamic countries. In the history of modern Islam, the Ahmadiyya sect is the movement which has paid for this belief most dearly. Its followers were persecuted in independent Pakistan after 1947, at the instigation of the militant Islamists of Abul A'la Mawdudi's Jama'at-i Islami, and had to transfer the centre of their activities to Britain.

How to eat to live

The founding separation desired by Fard and Elijah Muhammad was established in practical terms by a radical departure from the customs of the ungodly environment. This was achieved by applying the restrictions and requirements of Islam, although these were stretched considerably and in some cases modified.

First came the dietary restrictions: pork and alcohol were categorically outlawed, following Fard's preaching in Detroit. In one of his first pamphlets, *The Supreme Wisdom*, Elijah Muhammad wrote:

America . . . eats the dirty and filthy hog, to Allah's dislike, and almost forces the so-called Negro to eat it, or I would say everyone. Americans drink more alcohol – forbidden by Allah – than anyone else. . . . [America] teaches the so-called Negroes to eat CORNBREAD and the HOG, both of which are a slow death to my people in the southern parts of this country.[38]

Pork and alcohol are seen as the main instruments by which the white devils keep Blacks in dependence and servitude, but they are not the only ones. In fact, almost all the traditional diet of Blacks during the centuries of slavery in the southern states falls foul of the Nation of Islam's restrictions.

These restrictions, laid down by Elijah Muhammad in his booklet *How to Eat to Live*, are highlighted and discussed in a column in the bi-monthly magazine *The Final Call*, the mouthpiece of Louis Farrakhan and his disciples. One illustration,[39] under the heading 'Read what Allah revealed about this poisoned pig!', reminds readers that we are what we eat: 'Eating bad food: it forms your features, and your characteristics.' Pork, described as a hybrid of cat, rat and dog, transmits its defects to those who eat it – as is shown in the porcine appearance of a family portrayed sitting round the table feasting on 'this poison swine'. As well as reminding readers of the prohibitions in the Bible and the Koran, the arguments put forward use medical theories on the diseases caused by trichina ('pork worm'), but above all they refer to the Nation of Islam's own account of creation. Thus, they argue that pork was created by God to attract the diseases and germs which the white man traditionally carries and wants to transmit to Blacks with the aim of poisoning them, in order to weaken their race.

Besides pork and alcohol, a second illustration shows, under the heading 'The diet the devil prescribes for the Righteous', a tablecloth covered with virtually all the traditional dishes of southern soul food (catfish, peas, cornbread, nuts, pecans, crab, shrimps, cabbage) as well as a plucked chicken and a T-bone steak.[40] In fact, none of these foods is Islamically prohibited; the objective is to create a new Black individual, conscious of belonging to the Nation of Islam, and breaking in his daily existence with the traditional 'so-called Negro' of the south, as defined in his diet. Many regular pieces in *The Final Call* are similarly dedicated to combating the mediocre diet (junk food) of young ghetto Blacks, which has taken the place of the fatty, stodgy food of the plantation era.

From the very beginning, the Nation of Islam campaigned vigorously against obesity, and overweight followers were fined until their girth slimmed to a suitable size. In the summer of 1991,

Farrakhan followed this tradition by launching a 'war on obesity', held responsible for the degenerative diseases affecting poor Black Americans, and called disciples in his own movement to order: 'I will not have an obese (fat) Laborer standing as a representative of the Teachings of the Honorable Elijah Muhammad to an obese (fat) Nation of people. Every Laborer has six months to correct that condition. If, after six months, there is no significant progress, you will have to find a position elsewhere.'[41] Farrakhan went on to link female obesity with the breakdown of Black marriages: 'Our women are so frustrated with living with and relating to the opposite sex, they often find themselves sitting in front of the TV eating junk food, growing fatter by the minute and dying at an early age.'

The plan of the white devils is in fact to make Blacks die young. The secret of health and long life is to become vegetarian ('the best of menus for our health')[42] and to eat only one meal a day. Followers are kept to this strict discipline. They may go even further: 'A man 200 or 300 years old is not an old man, if he has eaten the right food and taken it once every two or three days. A man can live 1,000 years if he eats the right food twice a week.'[43]

Beyond this heroic but impracticable self-discipline, the strict codification of the Black Muslims' dietary regime has a triple significance. First, it is a diagnosis of the general problem of public health affecting an important number of American Blacks, especially in the ghettos. The diagnosis contains undeniable elements of truth, but more than that it claims to be the absolute, unbending and universal truth. This maximalist viewpoint therefore treads the same ground as the most derogatory racist clichés. The first of the illustrations discussed above, which shows a Black family engrossed in an orgy of pig-meat, fits in with such racist images. The message is clear: outside the Nation of Islam, in the world of the white devils, the destiny of the 'so-called Negroes' is bound for the most abject decline, fuelled by malnutrition and its effects.

Second, the type of food prohibited and the diet imposed by the movement on its followers reflect a break both with white society and with Blacks' own traditional identity – hence the prohibition of 'southern-style' dishes in the second illustration. The objective of the Nation of Islam is not solely the defence of Blacks as a racial group, defined by skin colour, but also the construction of a separate community of individuals with a new identity built around belief in the doctrine of Elijah Muhammad.

Third, in requiring a strict self-discipline in everyday life, the dietary regime reinforces the cohesion of the chosen group of followers and makes it difficult to express individual freedom, as the monitoring of followers' weight shows very clearly.

The Black Muslims' special diet gave rise to specific needs which the Nation of Islam set out to satisfy by opening shops, restaurants and a chain of supermarkets, by putting a range of products on the market (such as canned whiting, 'imported from the pure waters of Peru', under the name 'Muhammad's Fish') and even establishing a bank, the Guaranty Bank and Trust Company. The latter's advertising proclaims: 'Guided by the Honorable Elijah Muhammad, we are based on the economic growth and the productivity of the Nation of Islam.' Such undertakings also constitute a step towards self-development and the foundations of the future State of the Nation of Islam.

At the same time, they protect the followers from the competitive market of American society and keep them captive within a specific market which, at the time of Elijah Muhammad's death in 1975, constituted a 'commercial empire' worth around $46 million. A basic element of community restructuring may be seen at work here: by encouraging or obliging followers to consume only 'pure' products supervised by the movement, control by the group over individuals is reinforced, just as halal or kosher requirements form an important part of re-Islamizing or re-Judaizing movements as a measure of their support among followers.[44]

The inner fortress

The redefinition of a community of the pure by the application of rigorous dietary restrictions made particular sense in a social context where extreme deprivation stripped Blacks of their dignity and their moral values. Indeed, from its beginnings in Fard's preaching in 1930 to the death of Elijah Muhammad in 1975, the Nation of Islam recruited above all among the 'Black masses' of the ghetto, and very little among the 'Black bourgeoisie' who mocked the excessive nature of the restrictions.

The first disciples were, like Elijah Muhammad himself, recent migrants from the southern states, crushed by the effects of the 1929 crisis, which plunged Black proletarians into the depths of poverty. The Nation of Islam offered them a strong and clearly defined identity. According to most observers of the movement in its early days, many of its followers experienced significant upward social mobility and in particular found stable employment in the automobile industry after 1937.[45] In later years, it was prisons which furnished the major recruiting ground for the movement. Elijah Muhammad had been incarcerated for three years during the Second World War; and Malcolm X was also typical of the movement in that he was converted to Islam whilst in jail. For a Black convict experiencing the brutality of American prison life, the Nation of Islam world view would not have seemed unreasonable. In a letter written to Malcolm X in his prison cell, Elijah Muhammad explained that 'the Black prisoner symbolised white society's crime of keeping black man oppressed and deprived and ignorant, and unable to get decent jobs, turning them into criminals.'[46]

Throughout the history of the Black Muslim movement, a significant number of its leaders have started out in gangs and street culture, have been involved in drug-taking and dealing and pimping, and have spent time behind bars, before their lives were changed when they came into contact with the preaching of the Nation of Islam. The movement's strict leadership, the monitoring of individual behaviour and the wearing of a quasi-uniform all constitute a targeted response to the loose morality prevalent in the ghetto. Similarly, verbal violence and even the use of force serve to sublimate the physical violence and brutality of the environment. The career of Malcolm X is a perfect illustration of this process, which transformed the Nation of Islam from a tiny sect with little influence into a powerful mass movement. Malcolm X attracted hundreds of thousands of new recruits because he was not only a charismatic figure, but one with whom brutalized young Blacks could identify.

2

The Three Lives of Malcolm X

In the last decade of the twentieth century, Malcolm X has become a legendary, heroic figure. The generations that came after him and modern-day temple traders wrangle over his spiritual heritage. His aura is so brilliant that it has often eclipsed the organization which he rescued from decline, then later left for dead: the Nation of Islam.

In the space of forty years, Malcolm X's short life spanned three main phases before he fell under assassins' bullets: from criminal youth to star preacher of Elijah Muhammad's movement, then finally 'orthodox' Muslim and Third World activist. Born Malcolm Little in May 1925 in Omaha, he (like Elijah Muhammad) was the son of a Baptist preacher close to Marcus Garvey's movement. The family home was burned down in a racist attack, then when Malcolm was only six his father died in unexplained circumstances. His mother, 'who looked like a white woman', was born on the island of Grenada, the child of a white father and a Black mother. Malcolm inherited her very pale skin and almost red hair which later earned him the nickname 'Red'. Of his unknown white grandfather, he declared that he 'learned to hate every drop of that white rapist's blood that is in me'.[1] Despite a very unfavourable family and social environment, he did well at school, but when he told his teacher of his ambition to become a lawyer, he was advised he would be better off becoming a carpenter's apprentice, a trade this educationalist thought would be more suitable for a Black man. Looking back later on this experience, Malcolm saw the sign of Allah's inscrutable will: if his teacher had not discouraged him, 'I would probably be among some city's professional black bourgeoisie, sipping cocktails, and passing myself off as a community spokesman for and leader of the suffering black masses, while my primary concern would be to grab a few more crumbs from the groaning board of the two-faced whites with whom they're begging to "integrate".'[2]

Unlike Martin Luther King, who grew up sheltered from need in an educated, middle-class family, Malcolm X completed his education on the street.[3] He was sent to live with a relative in Boston, where he became fascinated by life in the Black ghetto of Roxbury. Here he quickly settled into a miscreant lifestyle, abandoning his Black fiancée for a white mistress: 'in any black ghetto in America, to have a white woman who was not a known whore was for the average black man at least, a status symbol of the first order.'[4] His alienation or 'brain-washing' led him ever deeper into the low-life of the ghetto, into pimping, racketeering and drug-trafficking, until his arrest and conviction for theft and receiving stolen property, in 1946, at the age of twenty. He was sent to prison, where he spent six years. This marked the end of the first phase of his life: 'I had sunk to the bottom of the American white man's society when . . . in prison I found Allah and the religion of Islam and it completely transformed my life.'[5]

In the eyes of many an Islamist leader in the twentieth century, the experience of prison, where the codes of social life are reduced to violence, has come to represent the gross injustice within society. It was in the Egyptian internment camps that Sayyid Qotb, a major figure of inspiration for Islamist activists today, gave the name *jahiliyya* (pre-Islam) to the society he wished to destroy and replace with an Islamic state.[6] It was also in prison that Malcolm Little became aware of the degraded state into which he had fallen, attributed the cause to white Christian society and discovered in the Nation of Islam the path to his own salvation and that of his race brothers.

From the moment Malcolm found out about the existence of Elijah Muhammad in a conversation with one of his brothers, the course of his life changed completely. The first open sign of a break with his former life was his refusal to eat pork in the prison canteen, followed by a new thirst for reading and learning. Learning the dictionary by heart and devouring all sorts of textbooks, he discovered, with the zeal and the unshakeable conviction of the neophyte, that the history of humankind had been 'whitewashed', that it had become a huge lie aimed at concealing the superiority of the Black people and of the Islamic religion preached by Mr Muhammad.

After his release for good conduct in 1952, he rapidly became a close friend of the Messenger. He sent him the letter written by all new followers to ask to abandon their 'slave name', and received an X to replace Little whilst waiting to be judged worthy of a Muslim name.[7] Malcolm made this X, denoting the anonymity of Blacks exploited by white society, but also carrying the sense of 'ex'(-slave), his own, and turned it into a potent universal symbol. By identifying X with himself, he incarnated the anonymous Black of the ghetto and gave him *his* voice, *his* face, *his* anger and *his* aspirations. With this, Malcolm X embarked on a dazzling career as a wandering preacher. His new calling used to good advantage the fiendish charm which had served him so well in his flamboyant previous life. Thanks to his oratory skills, charisma and organizational ability, the Nation of Islam grew rapidly, and news of the movement spread from limited Black circles to the mass media.

The press and especially television were fascinated by Malcolm X. By rejecting integration, advocating separatism and preaching a religion alien to the American public, he became the indispensable movie 'bad guy'. For the Blacks on the street, the man who defined himself as a 'field Negro' (as opposed to the 'domestic Negro' represented by Uncle Tom) became the supreme spokesman: whilst denouncing exclusion, poverty and racism, he also represented the possibility of getting out of the ghetto by joining the closed community organization of the Nation of Islam. For the Black Muslim movement, he represented an exceptional financial boon: the new members flocking into the movement and its sympathizers (between 100,000 and 250,000, according to reliable estimates)[8] were encouraged to contribute generously to collections and buy products from the shops and companies run by Elijah Muhammad and members of his 'royal family' (as they liked to call themselves), thus allowing the Messenger and his entourage to live like kings in Chicago. Malcolm X on the other hand led an ascetic life completely devoted to the cause.

Discipline was the subject of close attention. Followers who failed to sell their quota of *Mr. Muhammad Speaks*, the Nation of Islam's publication, were beaten – methods which echo the violent environment of prison life.[9] The organization of rallies and of the conventions held each year on 26 February, Fard's birthday (Savior's Day), also reflects the development under Malcolm X of the paramilitary group, the Fruit of Islam, whose members stewarded the meetings, and of the Muslim Girls' Training, whose slender,[10] white-veiled activists sat apart from the men.

In April 1957, Malcolm had the chance to demonstrate his ability to lead the movement and maintain discipline, and also to protect the community from outside aggression, when police smashed the skull of Hinton Johnson, a follower of the Nation of Islam, in Harlem and took him, still unconscious, to the police station, where he was given no medical attention. In response to taunts from a crowd of Blacks that the Black Muslims were all talk and no action, Malcolm and his followers laid siege to the police station until his 'brother' was released and treated. The police were impressed (and alarmed) by the military discipline with which he manoeuvred his troops.[11] Five years later, on 27 April 1972, when Los Angeles police killed another Nation of Islam activist during a street battle, Malcolm X made a vengeful speech in which he rejoiced that an Air France aircraft 'full of Whites' had crashed, killing all its occupants; this, he pronounced, was the vengeance of Allah.[12]

Such virulent outbursts, expressing the 'hate that hate produced'[13] characteristic of the Nation of Islam in Malcolm X's time, acted as an outlet for anger, in the absence of the kind of concrete activities carried out by the civil rights movement under the leadership of Martin Luther King. By its campaign of marches, sit-ins, strikes and civil disobedience, the civil rights movement forced schools, public transport and businesses to implement desegregation. This campaign followed the opposite logic of the Nation of Islam's goals: it laid claim to universalist ideals, whilst Elijah Muhammad and his disciples worked towards an extreme form of separatism and the construction of an autonomous community. Most observers in the 1960s thought that American society was moving towards individual equality and the absence of discrimination between races;[14] the civil rights movement was in tune with these perceived trends, whereas, despite Malcolm X's charisma, the views represented by the Nation of Islam were seen as doomed to marginalization. But the same observers were to discover fifteen years later that, by a quirk of history, American society had become not colour-blind but more colour-conscious than ever, to the extent that today the law lays down criteria for positive discrimination between citizens on the basis of self-proclaimed belonging to a community (ethnic, racial, sexual etc.). The existence of distinct communities, which tends to dilute the values shared by the whole of society and to highlight differences and peculiarities, is inspired by a philosophy which already informed the main demand of the Black Muslims several decades ago.

In a radio interview in May 1963,[15] Malcolm X distinguished 'segregation ... that which is forced upon inferiors by superiors' from 'separation [which] is done voluntarily by two equals'. As an example, he pointed to the 'Chinatown' in many American cities, whose residents had their own banks, schools and indeed their own internal economy. He contrasted Chinatown with the Black ghettos where 'even the mind of the Negro community is controlled by whites'. This ideal of a community enclave first bringing together an atavistic population, then rebuilding its identity around allegiance to self-proclaimed leaders, was intended to institutionalize the fragmentation and segmentation of society. For the Nation of Islam in the 1960s, it proved difficult to put this plan into action. But the communalist environment of the 1980s and 1990s provided more favourable conditions for Louis Farrakhan.

In 1964, the success of the civil rights movement in obtaining desegregation gave the impression that its actions were slowly but surely changing American law and attitudes on the question of race. The Black Muslims, faced with the threat of marginalization or even elimination from the scene, found themselves obliged to mark out their own position on civil rights. Malcolm X took up the challenge; he staked everything on the failure of Martin Luther King's campaign, ridiculed non-violence, attacked the integrationist leaders as Uncle Toms and 'wet blankets', and stepped up the violence of his own language. His aim was to portray integration as a middle-class demand mainly intended to open access to higher education, management or high-ranking civil service jobs. Malcolm, on the other hand, as a 'field Negro', represented those who could not care less about having the right to eat a 'desegregated' hamburger, because they did not even have a cent to put towards one.

Malcolm's extreme rhetoric culminated in his comments on the assassination of President Kennedy. Ignoring Elijah Muhammad's instructions to stick to moderate language, Malcolm X said in a press conference on the day following the shooting that he was 'happy when chickens come home to roost'. His remarks caused outrage, and Elijah Muhammad then banned him from speaking in public. The ban was at first meant to be temporary, but it was extended indefinitely. Malcolm put an end to the situation by leaving the Nation of Islam to form his own organization, Muslim Mosque Inc. Thus ended the second phase of his life, as Elijah Muhammad's protégé.

Divergent demands: radicalization or communalism?

Malcolm X's expulsion crystallized the internal contradictions of a communalist movement confronted with a wider social dynamic transcending the interests of its own followers. Faced with the upheaval in attitudes and the legislative reforms undertaken since the beginning of the 1960s as a result of the civil rights movement, the Nation of Islam was no longer able to combine the two divergent forces found in any community movement recruiting particularly among underprivileged groups of the population. On one hand, it led a militant campaign against the established order, using a strategy of separation and resocialization appealing to those with nothing to lose in the destruction of the social system. On the other, participation in an organized, disciplined structure brought concrete benefits in the daily life of its activists, giving them stability, the opportunity to learn and develop a network of contacts and mutual assistance, encouraging them to save, in short, upward social mobility and a form of embourgeoisement.

Within the Nation of Islam, the gulf widened between the establishment, which reaped the fruits of Malcolm X's preaching and managed the flows of money he produced, and Malcolm X himself, whose personal leadership qualities and lifestyle kept him close to the living conditions of the Black ghetto masses. For ten years, the division of labour between Elijah Muhammad and Malcolm had allowed the former to remain aloof from the movement (and thus guard his mystique), whilst the latter appeared on platform after platform, always invoking the name of 'the Messenger of Allah'. The Messenger's close entourage, especially his family, stirred up the tensions in this situation, fearing that Malcolm hoped to succeed the ailing Elijah Muhammad and dispossess them of their claims as members of the 'royal family'. Malcolm had also succeeded in earning the jealousy and resentment of preachers from other mosques, unable to compete with his fame. As early as 1959, some of the most senior leaders of the Nation of Islam feared that the violence of Malcolm's speeches threatened the future of the movement, since it could lead the police to take radical measures. In fact, although the Nation was under close surveillance by the FBI, it was never classed as a subversive organization by the Procurator General, since as a religious association it was protected by the Constitution.[16]

In 1963, the conflict between Malcolm X and the family of Elijah Muhammad came to a head when the Messenger was prevented by an asthma attack from appearing at the annual celebration of Fard's birthday, in Chicago. Malcolm did not allow members of the 'royal family' to speak; they for their part omitted all mention of Malcolm in the Nation of Islam's publication *Mr. Muhammad Speaks*, at a time when he was never off the front covers of the national press. Finally, the decisive break came when Malcolm discovered and revealed that the Messenger, who preached chastity and strict conjugal fidelity, did not merely dictate letters to his 'highly competent young secretaries' during their late night sessions. Nine of his secretaries had become pregnant by him and were then expelled from the Nation of Islam for adultery and threatened into silence. The two men had an 'exchange of words' during which Elijah Muhammad defended his behaviour by invoking biblical precedents such as King David. This did not stop Malcolm from encouraging two of the women to file a paternity suit for maintenance.

With Malcolm's departure, the Nation of Islam lost much of its radical discourse. It continued to carry out its function of resocializing followers snatched from the 'wilderness of North America' and to work towards a 're-Islamized' (in the sense of its own particular version of Islam) enclave and the creation of a separate Black identity, through education in the 'University of Islam', a diet of 'Muhammad's Fish', the control of financial services and so on. For the movement's leaders, the need to subordinate political action to the separate community had become an absolute priority. Control over activists was policed by the Fruit of Islam militia. The movement was in the process of creating a 'Nation within a Nation', to use Elijah Muhammad's expression, and opposed participation by its members in any activities alongside other social, ethnic or religious groups which could dilute the Black Muslims' identity or undermine their position as community leaders. The logic of communalism, here in its ultimate form of demands for autonomy, coincided with political conservatism in its opposition to any global movement, whether revolutionary, progressive or reformist.

Outside the Nation of Islam, Malcolm X embarked on the third phase of his life, which lasted only a year until his assassination on 21 February 1965. In the course of his many travels to Africa and the Middle East, he went on the pilgrimage to Mecca and in the process dissociated himself completely from the 'heresy' of Elijah Muhammad. He renounced the doctrines of racial separatism, having broken bread with white Muslims in the tents of Arabia during his pilgrimage. His former identity as a Black Muslim was replaced by a new 'orthodox' Islamic identity. He preceded his 'Muslim name' Malik al Shabazz with the honorary title 'Hadj' given to those who have accomplished the pilgrimage. Carried away by the Third Worldist euphoria of the 1960s, Malcolm X had little interest in the issues involved in the 'Arab Cold War' between Nasser's Egypt and Saudi Arabia, and professed an absolute admiration for the leaders of both countries. During his visits to the African capitals in the heady days of post-independence, he became familiar with the 'anti-imperialist' themes which he took up on his return to the United

States. As a result, the former Black Muslim, now reviled and harassed by Elijah Muhammad's men, became popular with the Trotskyites in the Socialist Workers' Party, who published his last speeches. He presented a new view of social conflicts in which he sang the praises of Fidel Castro's Cuban revolution and likened the situation in Harlem to that of the Algiers kasbah during the Algerian war.

During this last year of his life, he made many speeches explicitly rejecting the separatist thinking of Elijah Muhammad and his disciples, which he accused of conservatism and consensus-seeking. The US political leaders, he proclaimed, 'hope that Elijah Muhammad remains as he is for a long time because they know that any organization that he heads, it will not do anything in the struggle that the Black man is confronted with in this country.' But 'they do know that if something were to happen and all these brothers, their eyes were to come open, they would be right out here in every one of these civil rights organizations making these Uncle Tom Negro leaders stand up and fight like men instead of running around here nonviolently acting like women.'[17] Because of his untimely death it is difficult to say where his calls to Black people to defend themselves against racism and violence, by taking up arms if necessary, would have got him. He did not manage to organize a large number of activists behind him. His message was ambiguous enough for activists and observers later to interpret him as the ideological inspiration for the Black Power movement or as a revolutionary thinker on his way to becoming a socialist.[18]

Malcolm X was killed in the middle of a meeting in the Audubon dance-hall in Harlem. The only one of his killers to be caught in the act confessed to belonging to the Nation of Islam, which had constantly persecuted Malcolm since his defection; Malcolm had lived in fear of an attack by the movement, whose leaders had condemned him to death, he claimed. But Elijah Muhammad denied any responsibility in his murder. The people behind the killing have still not been identified with any degree of certainty. Several authors directly or indirectly claim that the American security services were at least partly involved.

After Malcolm

Ironically, the assassination of Malcolm X came only months before the achievement of the goal of the civil rights movement: in August

1965, President Johnson signed the Voting Rights Bill, with the aim of encouraging political participation by Blacks and closing the long parenthesis opened in 1877, when the failure of reconstruction had stripped the emancipation of slaves of any civic meaning. But a few days later, riots broke out in Watts, Los Angeles. The riots, which resulted in thirty-four deaths, some 4000 arrests, and the devastation of the neighbourhood by fire, ended when the national guard besieged the smoking ruins – thus foreshadowing the 1992 riots. Young Blacks ran through the street shouting 'Long live Malcolm X', and when Martin Luther King went to visit the area he was booed.

The Black Power movement brought to life the wishes Malcolm X expressed before his death: to see Black youth involved in a revolutionary challenging of the American social order, whilst extolling Black specificity and pride in Black identity. The disappearance of the term 'Negro' from American usage and its replacement by 'Black' date from this period, and it is a mark of Elijah Muhammad's influence that the terms he used passed into common parlance. As Jesse Jackson testified in 1975, on the Messenger's death: 'He was the father of Black consciousness. During our Negro and colored days, he was Black.'[19]

In this sense, the Black movement of the 1960s was the combined result of the civil rights activists' wish to situate their struggle squarely within the American political forum, and the separatist identity politics of the Nation of Islam, as reformulated by Malcolm X. It was no longer a question of working towards the creation of a separate Black state some time in the distant future, but of taking their claim to their own identity right to the heart of urban struggles in the rundown inner cities. Where the Fruit of Islam militia displayed its strength through its quasi-military discipline, the Black Power activists and especially its most radical version, the Black Panthers, organized themselves into armed detachments to protect their 'community' from police violence and keep watch on police activities. The various forms of Third Worldism which informed their discourse and provided a bridge between socialism and Black consciousness helped to shape their image – from the raised fist of the Black American athletes at the Mexico Olympic games in 1968 to the part played by Angela Davis. Through such symbols, the revolt of Blacks was integrated into the universal youth protest movement of the late 1960s, represented most notably in American counter-culture and in France's May 1968 events. But beneath the apparent universalism of the Black movement's activism and ways of thinking, as seen by the students in Europe who stuck pictures of the

Black Panthers on walls of their bedsits, the thread of community politics and the glorification of difference which the Nation of Islam had engendered continued to be central. Indeed, the concrete problems of racism and unemployment only grew with the transition to postindustrial society, starting in the mid-1970s, which threw sections of Black youth into 'hyperghettos' where social exclusion, drugs and crime are concentrated.

The legacy of Malcolm X as activist and political thinker contains all these ambiguities, thus providing many different ways of identifying with his message or appropriating his career. His trajectory has been compared with that of Benjamin Franklin, in that both exemplify the quintessential values of the American ideology exalting the self-made man and individual success.[20] In this sense, his life has a universal significance which transcends the experience of Blacks alone and makes it part of the sum of human struggle against social adversity. But it also functions at various levels within Black political culture: most of Malcolm X's speeches and sermons promoted the separate identity of Blacks gathered within an autonomous community guided by the values of the Nation of Islam, while during the last year of his life he preached a revolutionary universalism combining both Third Worldism and Muslim orthodoxy, Nasser and the Saudi kingdom. But whatever the ambiguities of this spiritual and political legacy, the career of Malcolm X retains a permanent exemplary value for the constitution of an indigenous form of Islam in the United States.

3
Farrakhan in the Looking-Glass of America

The battle for succession

In the period between Malcolm X's defection and the death of Elijah Muhammad on 25 February 1975 (Fard's birthday and the day before Savior's Day), the Nation of Islam no longer attracted press attention, but the movement continued to manage the various community resources it had created. Among other things, it bought 15,000 acres of farmland, farms, apartments and an aeroplane. As the Messenger of Allah's health gradually worsened, two key figures got ready to play an important role in his succession. One of these, Wallace D. Muhammad, was the seventh son of Elijah, conceived during Fard's time and named after him. Fard himself was supposed to have prophesied that the child, born in Detroit on 30 October 1933, would be a boy and would contribute to the spread of Islam. However, in the first half of the 1960s relations between father and son deteriorated when, under the influence of his brother Akbar who had gone to Cairo to study at the Islamic University of Al-Azhar, Wallace questioned Fard's divinity. He was excommunicated from the movement from late 1964 until 1970, and had to earn his living as a carpet-cleaner, then as a welder.[1]

Once he was accepted back into the Nation, Wallace continued to preach a form of Islam which put Fard's role into perspective, but his father, weakened by illness, did not take offence; he himself had stopped describing white people as devils in *Mr. Muhammad Speaks*, and seemed concerned above all to avoid any major conflict with the US institutions, after the confusion surrounding Malcolm X's death, and to manage his financial empire. Elijah Muhammad's caution appeared justified, given the inner turmoil of the organization: after all, Malcolm X had been assassinated after launching a campaign against the Messenger of Allah, articles were appearing depicting the Fruit of Islam as an extortion gang and uncertainties hung over the viability of a good many of the Nation's commercial ventures. Press revelations about a $5 billion interest-free loan from Colonel Gaddafi's Libya and substantial gifts from oil-producing Arab states (linked by several newspapers to the movement's anti-Israeli stance) further helped to muddy the Nation of Islam's image.[2]

The second influential figure within the Nation from the mid-1960s was none other than Louis Farrakhan. Born in 1933 (like Wallace) of a West Indian mixed-race mother (like Malcolm X) who gave him a very pale skin, Louis Wolcott (as he was baptized)[3] was much more highly educated than most of the movement's leading figures. He was a brilliant student at one of Boston's best high schools, but dropped out after three years of teacher-training college at Winston-Salem (North Carolina) to devote himself to music. A renowned pianist and violinist and singer of calypso and country music, he played in Boston's clubs until Malcolm X met and converted him in 1955. He placed his musical gifts at the service of the movement, writing a song which would become the unofficial anthem, 'A white man's heaven is a Black man's hell', and a play, *Orgena* ('A Negro' backwards). The play, in which a white man is tried for all humanity's evil-doing and condemned to death by an all-Black jury,[4] made a strong impression in the 1960s with its reversal of the stereotypes associated with the lynchings which took place at the turn of the century. Making his way in the shadow of Malcolm X, Louis X (who later received the 'Muslim name' of Abdul Haleem Farrakhan, although he used only the last part) became imam of the Boston Temple of the Nation of Islam. Malcolm X considered him a close friend and ally, and in 1964 he confided in him his doubts about Elijah Muhammad's morals, in relation to the secretaries made pregnant by the Messenger then expelled from the movement. Farrakhan's reaction was to distance himself very sharply from Malcolm, and he took part in the movement's indictment of Malcolm's activities. When Malcolm started to accuse Elijah Muhammad publicly on white television talk-shows,

we felt that Malcolm had become a traitor to that man. Malcolm's own work made every one of us a potential killer.... I am not a killer, but when you mess with that man [Elijah Muhammad] I become that, because that man gave me life. If you want to live, you leave that man alone where we are concerned. When Malcolm stepped across that line death was inevitable.[5]

Following Malcolm X's expulsion, Farrakhan took over most of his functions, as imam of Harlem and National Representative of Elijah Muhammad. He became the second most powerful figure in the movement after the Messenger, especially after the latter's repudiation of his son between 1964 and 1970. In 1974, he published a collection of his own speeches (7 *Speeches*), an honour given to none of the Nation's other preachers.

Nonetheless, it was Wallace whom the movement chose as successor on his father's death and who became Supreme Minister of the Nation of Islam. In spite of his quarrels with his father, his brothers and sisters and other members of the 'royal family' saw Wallace as the best hope of maintaining cohesion after the loss of the charismatic leader. Wallace organized his father's funeral, where he received the oath of allegiance of all the movement's preachers, and where various leading personalities, including the future candidate for the Democratic Party nomination for the presidential election, Jesse Jackson, came to pay their respects to Elijah Muhammad. 'I sat at the Messenger's feet, and was taught', Jackson declared, describing Elijah Muhammad as 'the father of Black consciousness'.[6]

In his first interview in *Mr. Muhammad Speaks*, Wallace referred to Fard, but introduced all sorts of terms and code belonging to orthodox Islam and representing a break with customary terminology: no reference is made to the cosmogony exemplified in the Yakub myth, and the movement's 'policy of racial separation' is subtly modified.[7] On 18 June 1975, just a few months after Elijah Muhammad's death, Wallace announced that there was no such thing as Black Muslims or white Muslims, just 'Muslims', whatever the colour of their skin.[8] Then, throughout 1976, a whole series of major upheavals in the movement's organizational structure and doctrine followed.[9] All these changes were aimed at bringing the movement into line with Islamic orthodoxy and making Arabic the main language of prayer. Thus, the Nation of Islam had always fasted for Ramadan in December, so as to accentuate its break with Christian culture at a time when the Christian churches were preparing to celebrate Christmas. From 1976, Wallace timed Ramadan to coincide with its celebration by other Muslims throughout the world; based on the lunar calender, Ramadan takes place at a different date each year. He even changed the name of the movement, which became the 'World Community of Islam in the West', later to be known as the 'American Muslim Mission'. The 'Temples of Islam' took the more standard name of 'mosques', with 'imams' replacing 'preachers'. Wallace himself Arabized his name completely to Warith Deen Muhammad[10] and claimed the Arabic title of

'Mujeddid' or renewer of the faith (within strictly defined traditional limits). In 1978, he rejected the figure of Fard, whom he portrayed as a mystic who took advantage of the naivety of the Detroit ghetto Blacks, but who at least paved the way (albeit idiosyncratically) for the later expansion of Islam across the American continent.[11]

Organizationally, the Mujeddid rapidly applied himself to the liquidation of the paramilitary Fruit of Islam and the Muslim Girls' Training (MGT), both well-disciplined factions with the potential to resist his reforms. The Fruit of Islam came in for particularly harsh criticism; he portrayed it as a gang of thugs who harassed and even assaulted rank-and-file activists who failed to sell their weekly quota of 300 copies of *Mr. Muhammad Speaks* or who annoyed them in some way or other. Finally, Wallace liquidated the financial empire, reckoned to be worth $46 million in 1975, but many of whose companies were struggling in the high inflation of that time.[12] His aim was to dissociate the religious message from financial practices he saw as unhealthy. In the process, he undermined the foundations of the economic enclave laid down by his father and thus abandoned the demand for an independent Black nation. The American flag replaced the star and crescent as a backdrop for the movement's meetings. The movement itself became a confederation of mosques spread across the United States.

Although as Muslim chaplains they maintain a presence in prisons and the number of convicts converting to Islam increases steadily, W. D. Muhammad's disciples have nonetheless moved away from the world of the ghetto where the Nation of Islam was born. Many of the followers have climbed the social ranks, thanks in particular to the discipline and asceticism of the movement, and now belong to a petite bourgeoisie which finds extreme forms of communalism and the politics of difference repugnant.

In a sense, W. D. Muhammad continued on the path laid out by Malcolm X, by 'purging' the movement of all its 'heresies' (as defined by Middle Eastern Sunni Islam). Unlike Malcolm, however, he stayed well away from any revolutionary involvement. On the contrary, he cultivated links with the most socially conservative forms of world Islam, embodied in the Saudi rulers. During the Gulf War in 1990–1, he supported the war against Iraq, and in 1992 he became the first Muslim to say grace at the opening of the new session of the American Senate.

W. D. Muhammad's takeover and dismantling of the Nation of Islam threw many of the movement's followers into turmoil. The main pretender to the leadership, Louis Farrakhan, kept his distance; he travelled to Africa, where he met among others the

Ugandan leader Idi Amin Dada, with whom he was on especially good terms.[13] Then he remained silent for two years. It was not until 1977 that he publicly stated his disagreement with the direction in which W. D. Muhammad was leading the movement. That year, several of the movement's preachers split off and formed their own group which claimed loyalty to Fard's original teachings. But the only group to survive was Farrakhan's.

Resurrection

Farrakhan chose Savior's Day, celebrated on 21 and 22 February 1981 in Chicago, to announce the resurrection of the Nation of Islam under his leadership. Before an audience of several thousand followers dressed in the traditional uniforms – which W. D. Muhammad had banned – of a white veil for the 'sisters' and shaved head, tailored black suit and bow tie for the Fruit of Islam, Farrakhan delivered an extremely lengthy speech.[14] According to him, Elijah Muhammad's death was in reality murder, the result of a plot involving the American government, the Christians and the Jews, but also the Arabs, whom he called racists and hypocrites and who, he said, had tried to offer the Messenger millions of dollars to bring his teaching in line with their version of Islam. In reality, the Messenger was not dead; his tomb, like that of Christ, was empty; and his voice would restore life to the Nation through Farrakhan.

At the time of this speech, Farrakhan's group was still in embryonic form, and his main concern was to justify his breakaway from the group led by W. D. Muhammad – hence the virulence of his attacks on the Arabs. He asked his disciples to renounce the Muslim names they had spontaneously adopted since Elijah's death, and to go back to using X until he himself provided them with their Islamic name.[15] The return to the strictest precepts of the Nation of Islam also entailed the readoption of the demand for a separate Black state.

However, the exact use of the old terminology did not mean a failure to recognize the changes that had taken place within American society. On the contrary, Farrakhan adapted his organization's strategy to the new social realities of 1980s and 1990s America, whilst making use of his dogmatic intransigence in order to enhance his image as an implacable opponent of compromise with the existing social order. In this sense, his approach resembles that of the re-Islamization, re-Judaization or re-Christianization movements of the late 1970s onwards, which interpreted the holy texts literally in order to induce a fundamental break with the customs and practices of the surrounding society.[16]

The issue which most explicitly contains this idea of separation is radical opposition to integration. In highlighting this theme, Farrakhan aligned himself with the campaign waged with great verbal violence by Malcolm X against the civil rights movement under the figurehead of Martin Luther King. But American society had undergone structural change since the 1960s: legal desegregation has allowed a sizeable educated Black elite to reach important posts – in the top ranks of the civil service, in business and to a lesser extent in academic life – as well as to gain elected office: many American cities had Black mayors in the 1980s and 1990s. However, the successful outcome – for some – of the integrationist struggles begun twenty years earlier contrasted with the rather different fate of others. Two separate trends may be identified which darken the rosy picture: first, the success of the elites in breaking through social barriers did not spill over into the dispossessed masses, who have been plunged into new forms of poverty; second, multiculturalism sharpened competition between ethnic and racial communities for access to jobs and resources, thus exacerbating separate identity at the expense of integration. The rhetoric and militancy of the re-formed Nation of Islam chimed exactly with the conditions resulting from these twin phenomena.

From gang warfare to the army of Allah

From the mid-1970s onwards, new forms of exclusion have been appearing in the United States. An ever-increasing number of poor Blacks have been dumped in 'hyperghettos' from which there is no escape. In these 'hyperghettos' live the people some American sociologists term the 'underclass', a group of individuals who have dropped down to the bottom of the social ladder and become increasingly marginalized in relation to average America.[17]

The complex phenomenon of 'hyperghettos' – a term which all too often serves as a pretext to stigmatize the victims – arises from changes in work and employment in the postindustrial era. The effects of these changes first became visible in the mid-1970s, with the transition from an industrial economy, providing numerous 'blue-collar' jobs open to relatively uneducated workers and access to efficient systems of social protection and union organization, to a service economy. The service economy has substituted automation or robots for many blue-collar jobs, and demands a level of education unattainable for the young Blacks leaving rundown ghetto schools, thus effectively barring them from decently paid jobs with social benefits. For many of these young people, their choice is restricted in most cases to insecure and unprotected jobs (known as MacJobs in reference to the famous fast-food chain) or the various forms of unemployment or welfare benefits.

The exclusion of unemployed, marginalized youth is aggravated by their spatial concentration in the rundown inner cities. Any families with the means to get out of the inner city move away, whereas the Black 'ghettos' created by segregation up until the middle of the century constituted a socially mixed counter-society where different social groups mingled and where institutions like schools and churches remained important. To make matters worse, job opportunities in the postindustrial era are increasingly situated in out-of-town sites accessible only by car (as is customary in the United States), when the new poor cannot afford cars.

For these reasons, and to highlight structural differences between the current situation and the ghettos of the old days, these places of absolute exclusion and virtual imprisonment are called 'hyperghettos'. The institutions which used to structure ghetto life have disappeared. Schools are now places of violence where children learn little of use to them in seeking to enter the labour market. Churches are scattered in a multitude of storefront sects, and have lost any real leadership function. Family structures are often destabilized by the absence of fathers. These zones form a fertile seed-bed for many forms of delinquency and crime. The primary impulse is the need to find means of support, and the most lucrative means are drug-dealing and prostitution. Gangs represent a highly efficient way of both controlling trafficking and racketeering and of creating a minimal structure of community order, by defending of residents of a particular 'turf' against attacks or threats from the neighbouring gang. We must certainly take care not to exaggerate the pathological features of the hyperghetto, as some have done; indeed, many have seized the chance to demonize Black and Hispanic youth and write sensationalized reports in which the hyperghetto's inhabitants are reduced to bestial figures. Nevertheless, the hyperghetto is an emblematic space, which demonstrates the failure of the welfare policies set up by President Johnson under the slogan 'War on poverty' and used by successive Reagan administrations as a justification for cutting social expenditure or 'welfare dependency'.

It is also an emblematic space for the Nation of Islam, as was

demonstrated by the huge meeting called on 25 June 1989 in the
Maryam mosque in Chicago (the organization's headquarters),
where Louis Farrakhan addressed thousands of young hyperghetto-
dwellers from all the major cities of the United States. In his lengthy
speech,[18] Farrakhan gave a dramatic description of the situation in
the ghettos, analysed the forces behind it and attributed the cause to
a conspiracy by the enemy – the US government. He also prescribed
the solutions: it was necessary to put an end to fratricidal wars and
to unite the gangs' forces in an 'army of Allah'.

Before Farrakhan came on stage to speak, three of his lieutenants
'warmed up' the audience by reciting the *shahada* (the Muslim profession of faith): 'I bear witness that there is no God but Allah and
that Muhammad is the Messenger of Allah.' There was no direct
allusion to Fard or Elijah Muhammad. The speakers invited the
crowd to chant Farrakhan's name, presenting him as a 'miraculous
father':

> Young black men and women, today that you have found that your
> mother has turned her back on you, and has given up on you, today that
> you have found that your father was not home ... today that your par-
> ents, the government, the educational system, everything has turned its
> back on you, who you gonna call, black men, what's his name? Say it
> loud!'

In response, the crowd chanted: 'Farrakhan, Farrakhan, Farrakhan!'

Taking the microphone amid thunderous applause, Farrakhan in
turn recited the *shahada*, then welcomed everyone with an *as salam
aleikum*. He continued:

> Today I asked to speak to the youth leadership, that is called by our ene-
> mies gang-leaders. I don't like the term: it doesn't properly describe you.
> And so I will call you youth leaders, but I want to tell you today why the
> enemy refers to you as gangs and gang-leaders. ... Our community, and
> black youth in particular, are about to become the victim of a conspiracy
> emanating from the government of the United States that is designed to
> bring about the destruction of our youth.'

Three weeks earlier, Farrakhan reported, he had watched on television the events of Tiananmen Square, the brutal suppression of the
Chinese youth by Deng Xiaoping's tanks; at the same time, he had
lamented the death of Imam Khomeini. In these televised scenes, he
had seen the prefiguration of what could happen in the United
States: the deployment of troops to massacre ghetto youths, and his
own assassination. Fearful of the growing birth rate of Blacks, the
white American government was, according to Farrakhan, rapidly

drawing up plans to exterminate them in order to preserve its own power, just as Herod had ordered the massacre of Hebrew babies. To support his argument, Farrakhan pointed to the high infant mortality rate of Black neighbourhoods and cited cases where Black women had allegedly been forcibly sterilized. There was, however, one way to stop this murderous conspiracy, and the gangs could help.

But, Farrakhan continued, how does a youth become a gang member? Using psycho-sociological jargon, he explained to his audience that it was perfectly normal for an adolescent (since 'the Qur'an teaches us that we are social beings') to want to be recognized by his peers, to defend his neighbourhood and to fight: this was a 'rite of passage into maturity'. Similarly, it was natural for leaders to emerge and to distinguish themselves by their bravery, their will to conquer and survive. Among whites and rich people in general, these impulses were channelled into team sports. But in the deprived social conditions of the ghetto, these natural tendencies degenerated into violent conflicts between gangs and even into murder. Black youths were killing one another just because they wore the visor of their baseball cap on the right or the left, or had their hair cut in a particular way. But, Farrakhan urged, all the young Blacks of the ghetto were 'one people, not tribes': their allegiance should be to the nation and not to their turf.

Farrakhan then addressed the issue of drugs: who had brought them into the ghetto? Who had armed the gangs? Only by dealing could young Blacks buy the clothes and shoes and the gold chains they dreamed of, and drive sports cars – certainly not by drawing welfare or unemployment benefit. White people were responsible for the situation: it was they who had armed the gangs so that they would kill one another and so that the public would accept the use of the National Guard to massacre the youth of the ghettos.

What could they do? There was no longer any institutional leadership to show young Blacks the way. At school, no one was interested in what the teachers talked about, in George Washington or Abraham Lincoln or other white heroes who 'don't give a damn about Blacks'. So why stay at school? The only remaining authority in the construction of young people's character and personality was the street. The family had broken down, fathers had disappeared from the scene: according to Farrakhan's figures, 62 per cent of Black children were born to single mothers. Farrakhan turned his sights on young Black mothers, who left their children in nurseries instead of taking care of them, and lost their bond with them: 'But now it's too late! The street's got them now! You're a frustrated woman, no man in your life at all, plenty of babies in your life, but no man! You ain't looking out for the children, you're looking out for some happiness, in the disco ...' But then, when the mother brought home her companion for the night, 'How do you think a young boy feels when he sees another man on top of his mother every night?' At this point, the audience, which had been responding noisily, fell silent.

All this, Farrakhan went on, was the responsibility of white power. For the Black youth were good; they belonged to the line of descent from the original man beloved of God. But they did not realize it. The first step therefore was for them to recognize who they really were, to which nation they belonged, and to identify other Blacks as brothers. Then they could not kill their brother. 'If you gotta kill anybody,' Farrakhan cried, 'kill those who harm your brothers!' This cry provoked thunderous applause, cheers and four collective chants of '*Allah Akbar*'.

> Brothers, we applaud your courage, your bravery, and your willingness to fight, that is why you are the generation that will bring liberation to our people ... God wants to establish you and show the government and the armed forces the very thing that they fear, it is written that you're going to stand up as an exceedingly great army, except there's a commander that will call you to the order of battle! They know it, brothers, they fear! Public Enemy, a wonderful strong group of brothers, fearless, first-time entertainers, put a strong message in their rap: 'You're gonna fight the power, you're gonna fight the powers that be!' So they wanna break up Public Enemy, destroy Public Enemy, so that the other rappers will not try to put the right message in their rap! But it's too late, white folks! ... But let us unite, pull out the forces, and own our own community, and determine how that community will run! If we want to take out brothers away from selling drugs, we got to give them a better way. Not just tell them: 'Say no to drugs!' So let us protect our members, our men, our women, our children, from anything that threatens to destroy us, let us unite, like one strong community ranging in ranks, then our courage, our bravery and our willingness to fight shall not have been in vain! Mothers, bring us your sons, we will teach them that which God has directed from the Honorable Elijah Muhammad that will make beautiful men out of these potential giants! Bring them to us! and you come yourself! Join the army of Allah! If you gotta join an army, join the army of Allah, and let us fight to deliver our people from the enemy! As salam aleikum! Allah Akbar, Allah Akbar, Allah Akbar!

Throughout his speech, Farrakhan expresses himself in quite formal and very clear language. The strong pedagogical intention evident in the speech even led him to use psycho-sociological discourse in order to describe to his young audience what had led them into gangs, without ever criminalizing them, but rather placing the blame on white power, the family and school. As is customary in the Nation of Islam's discourse since its inception, the situation in the ghetto is not portrayed in soothing terms – quite the reverse. Farrakhan's credibility rests on the impression that he is aware of the scale of the problems and can confront them openly, and that he can provide an alternative. Thus, the speech does not shy away from laying the blame at the door of young mothers – to the extent that one of them in the audience tried to leave the hall and was called back by the speaker – and accuses them of being unable to look after their children. The alternative proposed by Farrakhan was that, instead of leaving them in the nursery or in school where at best they would be brain-washed, or leaving them to roam the streets, they should entrust them to the Nation of Islam ...

But the main thrust of the message lay in the transformation of gangs into the 'army of Allah'. Beyond the association of ideas made at that time with Khomeini's Iran and the jihad, we can see in this speech the quintessence of the separatist community project. Farrakhan's plan takes shape: to channel the energies caused by social frustration and wasted on self-destructive crime into a plan for a separate community, to unite the ghetto youth behind a 'commander who gives the battle order', and to form a new identity around Islam, interpreted in this speech as an element separating Blacks from the existing social order. But instead of presenting himself, the 'miraculous father of fatherless youth', as the commander, Farrakhan mentioned the group Public Enemy.

The Islam rap

Farrakhan had been a musician and calypso singer before being converted by Malcolm X, but gave up his musical career, which the Nation of Islam considered dishonourable. His musical background was in evidence when he composed and arranged the movement's 'hymn', 'A White man's heaven is a Black man's hell', and when he wrote the play *Orgena*. It was not through calypso, but thanks to the movement's contacts and work with rap groups that the Nation managed to spread its message well beyond the circles of Black separatist activism.

From the beginning of the 1980s, when the movement was resurrected under Farrakhan's leadership, Mosque no. 7 in Harlem was frequented by a young man, Richard X, and his friend Chuck,[19] who were later to become famous as Professor Griff and Chuck D, founders of the most famous rap group in the world, Public Enemy. The album that shot them to fame in 1988, 'It takes a nation of millions to hold us back', pays homage to Allah in its acknowledgements, but also pays tribute to the Nation of Islam, to Farrakhan and his leading lieutenants. The first song, 'Bring back the noise', portrays one of the group members in prison, singing: 'They've put me in jail/ because of my records, because they're selling/ because a brother like me said:/ "Farrakhan's a prophet, and I think you should listen/ to what he's got to say to you, to what he's telling you to do."' Another track, 'Party for your right to fight', recounts the history of Black struggles, using the Nation of Islam's very specific vocabulary. The movement of rebellion which began in 1966 was broken 'at the midnight hour' by a force from hell: the 'so-called government' of the 'grafted devils' (a reference to the story of Yakub). The former head of the FBI, J. Edgar Hoover, is said to have killed Malcolm X, Martin Luther King and the Black Panther leaders Newton, Cleaver and Seale. But it is time for the movement to get back on course: 'It's the Honorable Elijah Muhammad who said it:/ know who you are to be Black.' Original man was the Black man from Asia; he is the 'cream of humanity/ he was here the first/ even if the devils hid it/ but check in their books/ even the Freemasons know/ but refuse to say it – Yo/ but it is proven/ and it will take millions of people to hold us back!'

In the spring of 1992, another famous rapper, Ice-T, a native of Los Angeles and a former gang member, hit the headlines with his song 'Cop killer'. The chorus – 'Die, die, die, pig, die. Fuck the police' – provoked an outcry from the police unions, and Time Warner was put under pressure to withdraw the record. President Bush himself publicly expressed indignation. In his defence, the singer explained that the feeling he was describing in his record was very common among young people, who were rising up against the police violence aimed at them, as symbolized in the attack on Rodney King. 'They are killing us out there and when they kill us they do not go to jail. Why?' said Ice-T. 'It's a rap that says: "Listen to me". The record goes: "I got my ski mask on, I got my black shirt on, I got my black gloves on, this shit has been too long. I got my twelve-gauge sawed off, my headlights turned off." And then the chorus is: "Cop killers, better you than me; Cop killers, fuck police brutality".'[20]

The Nation of Islam's paper, *The Final Call*, published a long article written by Farrakhan in defence of the singer, who was influenced by the Nation's leader to the point of calling his production company 'Afrika Islam'. The article was accompanied by a photograph showing Farrakhan with Chuck D, Sister Souljah, Ice Cube and Ice-T, their hands linked together in a sign of unity. President Bush had never condemned police brutality, wrote Farrakhan, but he criticized Ice-T because he was afraid 'that these lyrics, which describe the feelings of a growing number of people in the United States, might spark off a reaction. But it won't be because of Ice-T, but because of the actions of the police and the federal government's inability to defend the victims of police violence.' Farrakhan continued:

> The Holy Qur'an demands that when a life is taken a life must be given: A life for a life. Oppression will only cease when the oppressor loses his life for unjustly taking the lives of the oppressed ... But what should the people do if it is agents of government who take human life unjustly or without due process? Who can the people turn to if the lives of their loved ones are taken while in police custody in jails of America and police chiefs look the other way, and coroners back up the lies of the police? ... All of these unjustified murders produce the spirit of anarchy in the people and one day the people will revolt and take justice into their own hands and many innocent people will suffer with the guilty.[21]

Farrakhan himself does not call for insurrection or violence. In the article cited, he reminds readers that his disciples are law-abiding and that the Fruit of Islam militia helps to chase drug dealers from the areas it patrols. But, as the speech given on 25 June 1989 makes clear, his objective is to do away with violence within the community in order to channel it into strengthening the community, uniting it and mobilizing it behind the instructions or 'battle orders' given by the rappers associated with the movement. The aim is to build what he calls an 'army of Allah' which can defend the community and back up the demands made of the United States government.

The Nation of Islam's intervention in various aspects of daily life, hopes and cultural references of the inhabitants of today's American 'hyperghettos' is often overlooked by those who observe the movement. However, as we have seen, it is fundamental. It gives rise to an ideology and practice which dovetails neatly with the straightforward demands of those who live in such terrible conditions and have lost all hope of getting out by any legal means; they cannot identify with the values of average America.

Who are the chosen people?

Although Farrakhan used the ghetto as the basis for many of the themes developed in his preaching, he also reached outside to the wider political world. Under his leadership, the reconstituted Nation of Islam entered the field of institutional politics as early as 1983, when it came down in support of Jesse Jackson's campaign for the Democratic nomination in the 1984 presidential election. This represented a significant departure from the doctrine and practice of Elijah Muhammad, who had forbidden the Nation of Islam from entering the political fray and had always refused to support electoral candidates, with the exception of a few Harlem politicians such as Adam Clayton Powell, a charismatic leader who had won the support of Malcolm X.

From Farrakhan's viewpoint, the new strategy fulfilled several objectives. First, it allowed him to publicize the reformed Nation of Islam (and the angry exchanges with various Jewish groups helped to keep the movement in the public eye) after a seven-year media blackout during which he had not given any interviews, devoting his attention instead to building up the organization. Second, Farrakhan saw that the social background of the movement's followers had changed since the time of Elijah Muhammad: the proportion of young, educated Blacks had grown, and these new recruits wanted the Nation to reflect their interests in the ideological battle sparked off in the 1980s to define the identity of 'multicultural' America.

But above all, the growing segmentation of American society along 'ethnic' or 'minority' lines, encouraged by various mechanisms of 'affirmative action' or positive discrimination, boosted the position of elites drawing their legitimacy from their self-proclaimed status as exclusive representatives of their 'community'. This legitimacy was reinforced by constant reference to the community representatives in the media. Even if coverage was hostile, their presence on talk-shows and frequent reference to their name ensured their leading status. Legitimacy was also achieved by virulent attacks on the elites of other communities which made use of values establishing a hierarchy of rights and obligations. Thus, the Nation of Islam embarked on a kind of victims' 'one-upmanship', illustrated particularly in the arguments about the relative scale of extermination involved in the Holocaust and the slave trade.

This set of motives led Farrakhan to adopt Jesse Jackson's campaign for Democratic nomination in 1983. Jackson himself was no stranger to the Nation of Islam. After his funeral oration for Elijah

Muhammad in February 1975, he gave a long interview to *Mr. Muhammad Speaks* several months later. In this interview, he spoke admiringly of the example set by the Messenger of Allah. Jackson stated that he had used the social programmes of the Black Muslims as inspiration for the charitable organization he had himself set up, PUSH (People United to Save Humanity). Drawing on 'cultural pluralism' rather than 'integration', Jackson and his organization were at that time working to lay the economic foundations for Black autonomy in order to raise the community's living standards; they spent 'substantial time fighting to build Black banks and to build Black insurance companies'.[22] In 1983, when Jackson decided to go for the Democratic nomination, Farrakhan supported him because he felt that 'more than any other Black leader at that time, [he] could inspire the masses of Black people with hope.' Moreover, he placed the Fruit of Islam at Jackson's disposal to protect him, raised funds to finance the campaign and arranged to have the Nation's followers enrol on the electoral list so that they could vote for Jackson.[23]

From Jackson's viewpoint, Farrakhan's support was invaluable not only because of the infrastructure supplied by the Nation of Islam but also because of the Black Muslim leader's reputation in the ghettos. Jackson saw the opportunity to attract votes from the substantial proportion of the electorate who normally never voted because they could not identify with the invariably white, middle-class presidential candidates selected by the Democratic or Republican party machinery. However, this strategy was risky because it frightened 'moderate' supporters and brought to a head conflicts between the Jackson camp and a large section of the Democrat-leaning Jewish electorate.

From the outset, a number of pro-Israeli groups were firmly opposed to Jackson's candidacy. As soon as his decision to run for nomination was announced on television, it became apparent that Jackson stood apart from the other candidates on foreign policy. His feeling that he had been born 'in occupied territory' and had grown up 'under apartheid' gave him a natural empathy, he said, with other peoples suffering similar conditions across the world, in particular with Palestinians and South African Blacks.[24] In January 1984, accompanied by Farrakhan, he visited Damascus to obtain the liberation of a Black American pilot who had been captured by the Syrian army, at a time when the US government considered President Assad a terrorist and refused to have any dealings with him. Then, on 13 February 1984, the *Washington Post* reported remarks made by Jackson during a conversation with one of its journalists, describing Jews as 'hymies'. Responding to attacks made on him by Jewish groups because of his pro-Arab sympathies in the Middle East conflict, Jackson had said: 'All hymie wants to talk about is Israel; every time you go to Hymietown [i.e. New York], that's all they want to talk about.'[25] Jackson only succeeded in fanning the flames of the ensuing outcry when he first denied, then admitted making these remarks and apologized for them.

Meanwhile, on 25 February, the Nation of Islam invited Jackson as star guest to its celebration of Savior's Day. In his presentation speech, Farrakhan addressed 'the Jews who do not like our brother' and beseeched them in Allah's name not to attack him. His appeal made matters worse. Nathan Perlmutter, leader of the Anti-Defamation League of the B'nai B'rith, likened Farrakhan to Hitler.[26] Farrakhan responded in a radio interview in March:

> Here, the Jews don't like Farrakhan, so they call him Hitler. Well, that's a good name. Hitler was a very great man. He wasn't great for me as a Black man, but he was a great German, and he rose Germany up from the ashes of her defeat ... Now, I'm not proud of Hitler's evils against Jewish people. But it's a matter of record: He rose Germany up from nothing. Well, in a sense, you could say there's a similarity in that we're rising our people up from nothing.[27]

Farrakhan's remarks forced Jackson to distance himself from the Nation of Islam leader, but he avoided breaking off relations with an ally who appeared to control a significant section of the popular Black electorate. But Farrakhan went too far in a speech broadcast on the radio on 24 June, in which he declared that the creation of the state of Israel was an 'outlaw act' and that the Israeli state did not represent the will of God but was the product of a conspiracy: 'Now you have taken the land and you called it Israel and you pushed out the original inhabitants, making them vagabonds in the earth. You have lied and said this was a promise made by God to you.' Thus, Farrakhan accused Israel of 'using the name of God to shield your gutter religion under His holy and righteous name'.

The next day, Farrakhan's description of Judaism as a gutter religion hit the headlines. There was immediate uproar. Jackson dissociated himself publicly from Farrakhan and announced that the Black Muslim leader no longer belonged to his campaign. Farrakhan might have brought him substantial support from the Black ghettos, but he now alienated a large part of the centre-left electorate Jackson wanted to win over and threatened to reduce his project of a 'rainbow coalition' to the supporters and sympathizers of the Nation of Islam. Moderate Black organizations as well as the leaders of the Democrat Party were outspoken in their condemnation of Farrakhan, and the American Senate unanimously passed a resolution declaring that 'There is no place in our society, nor in our electoral process, for hateful, bigoted expressions of anti-Jewish and racist sentiments such as those reportedly made by Louis Farrakhan, and all such vicious expressions must be condemned.'[28]

Despite this rejection from American institutional politics, Farrakhan had nonetheless benefited substantially from his temporary alliance with Jackson. The controversial image which brought him to the centre of the nation's attention did not displease him, nor did it particularly repel potential supporters who were looking for someone on whom to place the blame for their poverty and degradation.

Nevertheless, Farrakhan felt the need to go back over this incident several times. In another speech in 1985 (recorded on a cassette which is still available in the Nation of Islam's bookshops, under the title 'A Warning to the Jews'), Farrakhan referred to Jackson's remarks about 'hymies' and 'Hymietown' and his subsequent apologies.

> You don't have to worry, brothers and sisters, I'm not gonna apologize! Rvd Jackson gave one of the most brilliant speeches a Black man has ever given in a political arena, or any man has ever given! It took him less than forty seconds to apologize in a fifty-minute speech, and the next day, all you could hear was: Jesse Jackson said 'Please forgive me!' Why do you think they put that out there? It is because Jesse Jackson is a symbol of strength to Black people, and they wanted to show that his strength was compromised, and that his knees had bent under their pressure, this is why they put that on their headlines!

Explaining why he had threatened those who 'conspired' against Jackson, Farrakhan shouted in defiance: 'So, now I'm public enemy number one among the Jews! [The crowd shouted out: 'Fuck the Jews!'] ... Black leaders, you listen. If you allow Jewish leadership to press upon you to repel me on the basis of lies, you will never lead Black people ever again, you can be sure of that!'

Taking up his expression 'gutter religion', Farrakhan accused his detractors of taking his words out of context and replaced them within his world view:

> I would never condemn a revealed religion of almighty God! That is so far away from me that you can wake me up three o'clock in the morning out of a dead sleep, give me sodium penthotal, talk to my subconscious mind, and nothing in my subconscious mind will allow me to speak against a revealed religion of almighty God! Brothers and sisters, here's

what I said: I said that that nation called Israel had not had any peace in forty years and she will never have any peace because there can be no peace structured on injustice, thievery, lie and deceit. You think God's name could shield your gutter religion under His holy and righteous name! That is what I said ... When the men and women use God's name to sanctify evil doings, cover their wickedness with a pious, hypocritical righteousness: that is a gutter religion, using God's name as a tool! Christians have practised a gutter religion bringing our fathers to America in the name of Jesus, ... raping and robbing Africa of its substance, giving the people the Bible and taking the mineral resources of Africa for Europe and America ... And to them: to claim to be the chosen people of God, and you do lie! Claiming to be the chosen people of God, and having a right to somebody else's land, and taking it in the name of God, using the Bible and the Torah and the revealed word of God to steal, rob, lie and deceive, that is a gutter religion and I'll maintain what I said! How dare you run around calling yourselves the chosen of God when you know you are not the chosen – of what God? Surely not the God of righteousness: the Scripture tells us that when God chooses, He will choose the despised, the rejected, the disinherited, the lost people. He said: I will be their God and they will be My people. You Jewish people who claim to be Jewish and are not, the Scripture says you are members of the synagogue of Satan, you're wax of the works of Satan, your wickedness is seen everywhere on the earth. How could you be the chosen of almighty God? ... *You* are the people of almighty God, Black brothers and sisters, you are the people that the Bible is talking about from one cover to another, you are the people the Holy Qur'an is talking about, there is no other people but you that God is after! ... You are the bottom that God intends to bring to the top! ... You are the lost sheep of the Bible and the prodigal son of the Scripture![29]

These remarks carry elements of the traditional anti-Jewish polemics which have persisted throughout the centuries, but it would be wrong to reduce the Nation of Islam's rhetoric to anti-Semitism, without analysing the specific forms it adopted in the context of the United States of the 1980s and 1990s. In the parts of Farrakhan's 'Warning to the Jews', quoted above, we can see several levels of meaning and different shades of emphasis. The starting point is the Middle East situation. Like Jackson, but more aggressively, Farrakhan questions the legitimacy of the state of Israel, based on 'lies, thievery' and the plunder of Palestinian lands. The feelings of solidarity many Black Americans have with the Arab world and their sympathy with the Palestinian cause are well known, and by themselves would not spark off controversies about ethics or values.

Links between the Nation of Islam and the Muslim world have always been important, although as we have seen there have been ups and downs. When W. D. Muhammad was steering the movement 'back on course' towards Muslim orthodoxy, Farrakhan had very severely criticized the Arab states which generously supported his rival, even calling them racist.[30] Later, in 1985, having previously turned down arms and access to Libyan training camps, Farrakhan received an 'interest-free loan' of $5 million from Colonel Gaddafi to 'overthrow our oppressor'.[31] The Nation of Islam leader made several trips to Muslim countries and in 1985 was able to boast that he had made the pilgrimage to Mecca at the invitation of the general secretary of the Muslim World League, an organization aligned with Saudi Arabia, thus playing down his clashes over dogma with the leading Islamic authorities in the Middle East.[32] In the months between the Iraqi invasion of Kuwait and the Gulf War, Farrakhan took part in a series of meetings organized by Abdullah Umar Nassif, none other than the general secretary of the Muslim World League, whose mission it was to mobilize support among the Muslim world against Saddam Hussein.[33] By expressing the hostile views shared by many Arabs and Muslims towards the state of Israel, Farrakhan automatically aroused the wrath of pro-Israeli pressure groups in the United States, who equate any expression of anti-Zionism with anti-Semitism.

In order to dissociate anti-Zionism from anti-Semitism, Farrakhan takes up again the expression 'gutter religion', used earlier in relation to Judaism, and puts it into context by applying it also to the Christianity which was used to justify colonial conquest, the slave trade and the dispossession of native Americans. According to Farrakhan, it would be ridiculous to accuse him of anti-Semitism, because he is more Semitic than the Jews of Europe:

> The word itself, Semitic, deals with Afro-Asian people. If I am anti-Semitic, I am against myself. You have Arabs, and they are called Semitic people. Semi means half. They are in-between. There is a mixture of the blood of Africa and Asia and Europe in there, and you have what you call a Semitic people ... Now, most of those who call me anti-Semitic are not Semites themselves. These are Jews that adopted the faith of Judaism up in Europe: they're called Ashkenazi Jews. They have nothing to do with the Middle East – they're Europeans.[34]

This argument, which uses a rather surprising etymology in order to deprive Ashkenazi Jews of their 'Semitism', parallels the section of the speech where Farrakhan uses the Scriptures to deny Jews their Jewishness and reduces them to the 'wax of Satan's work', following the thread of anti-Semitic attacks in classical Christian preaching.

Farrakhan's arguments culminate in his denial of the Jews' claim to be the 'chosen people'. According to him, they could not be chosen by God, because they are too sinful, but more importantly because the position of 'chosen people' is already filled: the true chosen people, and the 'true Israel' in the biblical sense of the term, are the poor, the rejected, the last, the Blacks of America gathered under the leadership of the Nation of Islam.

This attempt to substitute one 'chosen people' for another provides us with the key to decode the particular form of anti-Jewish rhetoric championed by Farrakhan: it is the transposition and amplification into religious terms of the community fragmentation of postmodern society, of which the United States is the prototype. For the proponents of community organization, there is no longer one society sharing identical values, but one community claiming its right to the title of 'chosen people' to the exclusion of all others, and another community trying to take the title for itself.

In order to understand this phenomenon, we need to trace the development of relations between Blacks and Jews since the 1960s. At that time, both were waging a common campaign for integration, against an American establishment where racism combined with anti-Semitism. Since the inter-war years, discriminatory rules and practices had established ethnic quotas limiting the number of Jewish students at Harvard and other prestigious universities, and barring Jews from various private establishments open to the public, such as some hotels, which in their advertisements stipulated that 'Hebrews', consumptives and dogs were unwelcome.[35] These practices helped to spread the feeling among many Jews that they shared a common destiny and a common struggle with other unfairly treated or persecuted groups, especially Blacks. Admittedly, the denial of rights and oppression suffered by Blacks were much more intensive and systematic than those affecting Jews, but according to a liberal Jewish author the latter 'recognized in the black struggle for rights elements that could benefit them and conditions with which they could sympathize.'[36] However, as the famous Black writer James Baldwin wrote in an essay evoking his childhood in Harlem, when shopkeepers, landlords and money-lenders – all Jewish – were the instrument of Black people's misery, 'it is not acceptable for an American Jew to tell us that he is suffering as much as an American Black. It is not true, and you can tell it is not true by the way he claims it to be true.'[37] Nevertheless, a significant number of Jews became involved in the major anti-racist organizations, primarily the National Association for the Advancement of Colored People (NAACP), and wealthy Jews or Jewish-run institutions contributed heavily to anti-racist groups.

Until the end of the 1950s, writes Nathan Glazer,

> most sympathetic analysts of the ethnic and racial scene [saw] assimila-
> tion [as] a desirable consequence of the reduction of prejudice and dis-
> crimination, while acculturation, that is, becoming more like the
> majority, would contribute to the reduction of discrimination and preju-
> dice. Such was the dominant liberal view ... Although it was clear that
> blacks could never because of race be indistinguishable from whites, it
> was desirable that they become culturally, socially, economically and
> politically assimilated, that they be simply Americans with dark skins.[38]

Neither Black separatists like Elijah Muhammad nor militant
Zionists ever accepted this 'integrationist' vision, and from the mid-
1960s it came increasingly under fire as the more militant groups
saw their following grow rapidly. On one hand, uprisings in the
ghettos, the Black Panther movement and the glorification of Black
identity, on the other the Six-Day War and the glorification of an
identity based on the state of Israel weakened the doctrinal under-
pinnings of integration and assimilation, in both their 'bourgeois'
and Marxist versions.[39] The young elites of both the Black and
Jewish populations had an interest in radicalizing community discourse, which would also allow them to take over leadership from
the integrationists of the previous generation. The Black Power
activists, in the tradition of Malcolm X, saw that by excluding Jews
from their movement they could take back exclusive control of their
own struggles and their own destiny. In an interview published in a
far-left multiculturalist review, Farrakhan recalled the history of
relations between Blacks and Jews after the creation of the NAACP:

> It is an organization that has helped to advance every one of us. But if it
> is manipulative of the Black experience so that it is detrimental to us, we
> ought to be able to speak about that. If, for instance, we are always the
> tenants and Jews are always the landlords ..., this always puts us on the
> weak side of the relationship. We are always in the inferior position. We
> don't want that anymore. If Black folk are to be free, we have to break
> all these kinds of inferior relationships and re-establish them along the
> lines of mutual benefit, equity, and justice.[40]

In 1967–8, a nationwide controversy broke out in Ocean Hill-
Brownsville, a poor district of New York once inhabited by poor
Jewish immigrants but later home to a majority of Blacks. A Black
teacher, Rhody McCoy, was appointed head of the educational district. McCoy, from a disadvantaged background and the first member of his family to obtain a university degree, had attracted
attention because of the remarkable progress he had achieved with

difficult classes. Until the assassination of Malcolm X, he was one of the most faithful and diligent disciples of the Temple of the Nation of Islam in Harlem, and took an active part in the discussions going on around him about plans to set up an autonomous Black community. He represented the young elites who had managed to get out of poverty, and who would later flock in much greater numbers to Farrakhan. For these young Blacks, the relationship with Jews was no longer that of tenant to landlord or borrower to lender – to go back to James Baldwin's image – but one of competition in the workplace, where power and resources were to be had through a subtle mixture of promotion by merit and cooptation.

McCoy, appointed to a post which gave him the power to reorganize education in his district, as well as to hire and fire teachers, wanted to put into practice the ideas concerning 'community control' of education which he had developed in the company of Malcolm X. His first goal was to bring schools and the community closer together, and to fight against academic failure and the alienation felt by pupils in their daily lives, by recruiting teachers able to understand their problems, who lived locally and shared their culture and their suffering, in other words, Black teachers. Clashes over the content of teaching and the selection of teachers by parents' committees led McCoy to dismiss ten teachers, most of them Jewish. The New York teachers' union, many of whose members also happened to be Jewish, went on strike demanding the reinstatement of the teachers. The incident hit the headlines, although at the time it was not known that the man behind ideas on 'community control' had been exposed to the ideology of the Nation of Islam. When a tribunal ordered the teachers' reinstatement, McCoy handed in his resignation.

Some of the pupils and parents reacted angrily to this decision, seeing it as a racist act engineered by the Jewish leader of the teachers' union. Their reaction culminated in the reading on a local radio programme of a poem written by one of the pupils. It began with the words: 'Hey, Jew boy, with that yarmulke on your head/ You pale-faced Jew boy – I wish you were dead', and went on to say that the author was sick of hearing about the Holocaust when Hitler had been in power for only fifteen years, whereas the suffering of Black people in America had lasted four centuries. The pupil also mentioned that the 'original Hebrews' had been Black and that the Jews had stolen their religion. The targets of the poem made sure that it was widely circulated, and this created a huge scandal which played a major part in building up Blacks' and Jews' perceptions of the antagonism between their two communities.[41]

It is noteworthy that in this case the antagonism between Blacks and Jews emerged in the area of intellectual formation and the transmission of values. As in Farrakhan's speech entitled 'A Warning to the Jews', analysed above, the dispute concerns two main questions of identity. Who are the true chosen people, who are the 'Hebrews', what is the original 'Israel'? Which genocide is the one which forces us to rethink the history of humanity? Which genocide elevates which community to the status of supreme victim because of the unparalleled enormity of its suffering, and thus gives it a specific identity and an unsurpassable moral legitimacy?

This debate is not exclusive to relations between Farrakhan and his Jewish adversaries in the United States. During the trial of Klaus Barbie in Lyons, France, in 1987, defence lawyers put forward a similar line of argument, emphasizing that the Nazi extermination of the Jews in Europe was exceptional only in that it was carried out by whites, whereas Africans and Asians had suffered such treatment throughout the history of colonialism. But the quarrel between competing claims to special status has found particularly violent expression in the context of heightened community identities in postindustrial societies, and in the pursuit of wholly contemporary interests.

Indeed, once community elites emerge with the aim of mobilizing specific populations, and redefine the identity of these populations in opposition to the national identity (which is accused of seeking cultural genocide under the cover of 'assimilation'), it is vital for their credibility that the number of factors differentiating their community from the national population grows. At the most basic level, dietary restrictions serve as a watertight boundary defining identity, because they reduce the common ground with other individuals in wider society; all community movements need to stress the importance of such restrictions and impose strict obedience of them. They also allow the best organized groups to take their followers out of the national market and oblige them to consume products sold by the group's traders, as in the case of Elijah Muhammad's 'royal family' or businesses approved by a religious authority to sell 'pure' foodstuffs. But the most efficient marker of exclusive community identity remains the invocation of a dramatic event, a 'founding myth' which stays constant throughout history regardless of the vagaries of the lives of the populations concerned. The Exodus, the Crucifixion, the Hegira all constitute archetypes of the founding myth in so-called 'Abrahamic' cultures. The Holocaust and the slave trade have been interpreted in a similar way as events creating a specific community identity, particularly after the 1970s in the context of postindustrial community fragmentation.

Gorée Island versus Auschwitz

Communalism is based on strong personal attachment to a reconstructed identity and necessarily resists the reflexive process of comparison between diverse human experiences. Outside the community of the self-proclaimed 'pure', there can be only barbarism. No other communities can claim ethical justification for their status. In today's multicultural American society, elites wishing to organize community allegiances and set themselves up as the sole legitimate mouthpieces of the community need to reject as barbarous and nonsensical the claims made by the elites of other communities that their truth is the supreme Truth. This gives rise to a new hierarchy of values and access to political, cultural and economic power.

Thus, the Nation of Islam has attempted to reinterpret the slave trade not only as the major event determining the fate of the Black populations of the United States and bringing them behind Elijah Muhammad's and Louis Farrakhan's movement, but also as the ultimate genocide in the history of humanity. Naturally, this attitude has brought it into conflict with those who consider the Nazi extermination of European Jews to be the major event in world history, after which nothing could ever be the same again. In this macabre competition between Gorée Island[42] and Auschwitz, it was important for Farrakhan's disciples to show that Jews could not be portrayed uniformly as victims of Nazism; they needed to depict the Jews in turn as participants in the slave trade and therefore as perpetrators of genocide.

This is the thrust of a book published in 1991 by the Nation of Islam's 'Historical Research Department' under the title *The Secret Relationship between Blacks and Jews, Volume One*. A prefatory note on source material used in the publication indicates that it is mainly 'Jewish' and that 'sources considered anti-Semitic and/or anti-Jewish' were discarded. Such careful use of source material reveals a surprising code of ethics, with the aim of strengthening the book's main message, which is that 'Jews have undeniably been linked to the biggest criminal operation ever undertaken against an entire race: the holocaust of the Blacks of Africa. They took part in the capture and forced export of millions of citizens of Black Africa into a life of inhuman and degrading servitude, all for the financial benefit of Jews.' The authors accuse Jews of using slaves 'infinitely more than any other ethnic or religious group in the history of the New World and [taking] part in all the international aspects of the trade.'[43]

The book's introductory chapter, in the form of a history of Judaism before the discovery of America, reduces the history of the Jews in Spain to their participation in the purchase and resale of slaves for the Moors. The Jews' expulsion from Spain is explained as punishment for their part in the slave trade. It continues: 'Though scattered throughout the globe by political, economic and religious circumstances, they would reunite later in an unholy coalition of kidnappers and slave makers.'[44] In its 334 pages, the book identifies 358 Jewish slave-owners and where relevant describes the atrocities committed against the slaves. More generally, the book seeks to show that Jews played a primary role in the slave trade. Estimating the number of dead at 100 million, it claims that 'as key operatives in the enterprise, Jews have carved out for themselves a monumental culpability in slavery – and the holocaust.'[45] In a similar vein, the authors continue: 'Much like the Nazis at the concentration camps of Auschwitz, Treblinka or Buchenwald, Jews served as constables, jailers and sheriffs, part of whose duties were to issue warrants against and track down Black freedom seekers.'[46]

By reiterating these contentions *ad nauseam*, the authors aimed to persuade readers of their truthfulness simply by piling up a series of individually separate facts. This approach is often adopted by authors writing non-academic, ideologically biased accounts of history. It is used to similar effect in old or contemporary uses of the *Protocols of the Elders of Zion* (which can be obtained by mail order through *The Final Call*).[47] In fact, many of the facts recounted in *The Secret Relationship between Blacks and Jews* are based on reality: Jews did take part in the slave trade. Some were virulent defenders of slavery and published articles in support of it in American newspapers during the plantation era. But the leading role attributed to the Jews is not borne out historically. Muslim slavers and African tribal chiefs also played a leading role in the slave trade. In a 1992 article in the *New York Times* on 'the new Black American anti-Semitism', Henry Louis Gates, who heads the Department of Afro-American Studies at Harvard University, described *The Secret Relationship* as 'the bible of the new anti-Semitism' and observed that it 'may well be one of the most influential books published in the black community in the last 12 months. It is available in black-oriented shops in cities across the nation, even those that specialize in Kente cloth and beads rather than books ... Meanwhile, the book's conclusions are, in many circles, increasingly treated as damning historical fact.' According to Professor Gates, 'the book massively misrepresents the historical record, largely through a process of cunningly selective quotation of often reputable sources.' For historians of the slave trade, 'the repeated insistence that the Jews dominated the slave trade depends on an unscrupulous distortion of the historic record.'

For Gates, the most troubling aspect of the book was 'the tacit conviction that culpability is heritable', which suggests 'a doctrine of racial continuity, in which the racial evil of a people is merely manifest (rather than constituted) by their historical misdeeds. The reported misdeeds are thus the signs of an essential nature that is evil.' Gates asked: 'How does this theology of guilt surface in our everyday moral discourse?'[48] No doubt part of the answer to the question lies in the decontextualized identity which any group needs in order to build itself into a community. This identity, unchanging throughout history, homogeneous and unadulterated, stands as the yardstick for what is pure. The rest of the world is therefore tainted, impure, barbarous, composed of enemies and persecutors. But the real question is how such a logic can operate in contemporary American society. Why have national solidarities within civil society weakened to such an extent that community organization, with the barriers and antagonisms it creates, has emerged as a credible way of defining identity and resocialization?

One of Farrakhan's lieutenants, the Nation of Islam's 'Minister for Youth', Conrad Muhammad (who has organized several meetings in American universities to promote *The Secret Relationship*), explains that in the United States today Jews have developed an extreme form of 'this notion of community that bonds them together, whether they live next door to each other or not'. 'They don't say: I'm a lawyer first, I'm a doctor first, but I'm a Jew first'; they drive miles if necessary to have their clothes cleaned by a Jew, send their children to Jewish schools and so on. But, he bemoans, Black people say they are first and foremost a Democrat, a judge, a policeman, an actor: consciousness of belonging to a community is insufficiently developed. Conrad Muhammad goes on to inveigh against the integrated Black elites who have 'given up their Blackness, like H. L. Gates.' Beyond the polemical nature of these remarks, Conrad Muhammad is using the example of Jews, 'who exercise an enormous amount of power because they are organized and unified in the oneness of their Judaism, [which is] more significant than their nationality', to show his view of what Blacks should do.[49] Since Jews are felt to be the perfect example of community organization, Blacks need to copy their example in order to build their own united community in the Nation of Islam, but in so doing they must turn the example on its head. Thus, just as the Hebrews withdrew from Egypt in order to settle in the Promised Land, the

Black community will fulfil the ideal of separatism here and now, through self-organization of the ghettos, whilst waiting for the state which will give them independence from the 'wilderness of America'.

In this respect, the virulence of the anti-Jewish outbursts made by many Nation of Islam leaders between the announcement of Jesse Jackson's candidacy in 1983 and the publication of *The Secret Relationship* in 1992 appears to stem from a process of community-building rather than from any atavistic or cultural anti-Semitism specific to Blacks or Muslims. In order to legitimize their role, the community elites must both erect the highest possible barriers separating the community from others, and also compete with the other communities which want to deprive it of the privileges they think it enjoys. This is the context which helps to explain the Nation of Islam's transition from demonizing whites, during the time of Elijah Muhammad's leadership, to Farrakhan's indictment of Jews. During this time, American society has changed: whereas formerly it operated (in the eyes of the Nation of Islam) in a racist and segregationist way, excluding all Blacks, today it favours communities organized into well-structured, homogeneous pressure groups. Within this view of society, Jews appear as both enemy, on the Arab–Israeli question as well as in domestic politics, and model to imitate and surpass, by transforming the Black population of the United States into a community gathered together under the leadership of the Nation of Islam.

Organizing the community

In its dealings with gangs – as in Farrakhan's speech to gang-leaders, or in the truce signed between the Crips and the Bloods following the Los Angeles riots of 1992 – the Nation of Islam has played an important role as the ideologue of community unity, against the internal conflicts which bring bloodshed to the ghettos. But the movement also fulfils a crucial unifying function in the daily lives of the populations concerned, in its policing activities and its fight against Aids. In both cases, the movement is to a large extent compensating for the lack of institutional help from the US state, thereby proving that 'in the wilderness of North America' it is the only agency within the community to which Blacks can turn when faced with their many daily problems.

Washington, the capital of the greatest power on earth, is one of the most dangerous cities in the world, with the record number of

490 murders in 1991.[50] It has a majority Black population. Living conditions in the sprawling ghetto districts of the northeast are particularly tough because of the criminal activities linked with the drug trade. In several of the housing projects, the Nation of Islam has put into place a policy of community control, which has succeeded in getting rid of dealers and drug-related crime. At the northern extremity of the Black area of the city, close to the Maryland border, the formerly crime-ridden neighbourhoods of Paradise Manor and Mayfair Mansions have now been completely 'cleaned up'. The contrast is striking for anyone arriving by car from the inner city, having travelled for over half an hour through ghetto avenues which recall the bombed-out streets of war-time Europe and where groups of young dealers do their business on almost every corner, to find an unassuming but perfectly clean and quiet neighbourhood with no dealers, no graffiti on the walls, no boarded-up windows. There are lawns, and young trees, which no one has uprooted. In the town centre, Dr Abdul Alim Muhammad, the Nation of Islam pastor for Washington and the movement's 'Minister for Health' and national spokesperson, has his medical practice, the Abundant Life Clinic.

In an interview with the author at his clinic, Dr Muhammad explained how he set about 'cleaning up' an area which in 1987 was classed among the ten worst drug-trafficking zones in the United States. When the Black Muslims came to the area in 1987–8 to sell *The Final Call* door-to-door, their presence disturbed the traffickers, who left the area and returned when the activists had gone. Some residents noticed this manoeuvre, and asked members of the Fruit of Islam to stay in the area in order to discourage trafficking and the murders, rapes and robberies which accompanied it. The local residents' association and the owner of the flats agreed to try the experiment: 'We set up patrols where our brothers, who are unarmed, no weapons of any sort, just began to circulate through the neighborhood. We were authorized to identify anyone that was on the property, who didn't seem to belong there, to ask them who they were, and what they were doing, and if they didn't live there we would ask them if they would move on. And so, the very first day, we were able to clean out all of the open-air drug markets in Mayfair ... At that time, there were hundreds of people peddling dope on the breezeways and the parking lots, and every day there was shooting and stabbing.'[51] Dr Muhammad denied that the Fruit of Islam militia used the slightest intimidation against the dealers, and explained that 'We believe that the teachings of the Honorable Elijah Muhammad and the discipline of those teachings produces in human beings a compelling moral force and power that not only corrects that person who has submitted to the teachings of Islam, but it also has the power to compel us, in a very non-violent, non-threatening way, to do whatever is right.' Whatever the methods used, the results of these actions made the Nation of Islam and its spokesperson renowned throughout Washington. Referring to a study carried out by a local university, Dr Muhammad said that 89 per cent of Washington residents are apparently in favour of the Fruit of Islam patrols.

In 1992, the Mayor of Washington, Mrs Sharon Pratt Kelly, decided to honour these charitable actions by celebrating 'Abdul Alim Muhammad Day' on 11 July each year, in line with the city's policy of acknowledging distinguished service to its inhabitants in this way. The decision sparked heated reactions from various Jewish organizations, primarily the Anti-Defamation League. Mrs Kelly had to issue a Solomon-like judgement which attempted to placate each of the different sections of her electorate. Whilst praising Dr Muhammad's charitable works, she 'unequivocally condemned any and all of his anti-Semitic statements in his official and/or personal capacity or otherwise.'[52]

Speaking about the incident in 1993, Dr Muhammad himself considered that such antagonism belonged in the past, and that through its social activities the Nation of Islam was now too firmly established in the Black community to be criticized in this way. To illustrate his point, he recounted a conversation he had in the Saudi embassy just before the Gulf War. Having asked his Saudi interlocutors why they found it so difficult to criticize Jews or the Catholic church in the United States, he received the following reply: because the Zionists control the press. But he retorted that the real reason was that

> In each community in this country, there is a Catholic church that runs a school, they have a hospital, in larger cities you would have a Jewish hospital, a Mount Sinai hospital, and so when you have that kind of grassroots service in a community, then how dare you say anything critical about the group that is providing the service, so you can't criticize the Pope, you can't criticize the Catholics, you can't criticize the Jews because someone's mother is in their facility, or their children are attending their school ... So this is something that the Islamic community has to understand: it is through services that we win the respect and the honor of the people. They would never listen to our religious ideas until we first show them that we care about them.'[53]

Here too, this 'bottom-up' work of Islamization, through social and charitable services, is perfectly in tune with the community fragmentation of American society and the general inefficiencies of public social infrastructures. In a country where state education is in crisis and the public health system works badly, community elites emerge to assume responsibility for these services, in order to reinforce their own ideological stance and to increase their authority among the segments of the population in whose name they claim to speak.

The same is true of an equally dramatic issue which severely affects the downwardly mobile Black population of the United States: Aids. Besides his involvement in the anti-drug activities of the Nation of Islam, Dr Muhammad has become well known through his work against Aids. However, here too his campaign provides an opportunity to highlight community solutions to the problem, with reference to Africa and Islam, and to lay the blame for the outbreak of the disease on the white authorities. According to Dr Muhammad, the Aids pandemic, which when it first appeared was associated with male homosexuality, is in fact a disease which mainly affects the Black population. It is therefore up to the self-aware community, incarnated by the Nation of Islam, to take its destiny into its own hands, for 'we obviously have more to lose than any other population group around the world.' He estimates that at least 5 per cent of Blacks in Washington are contaminated by the Aids virus, with high concentrations of people affected in the prison population (25 per cent) and among the homeless (40 per cent). He gives little credence to theories which attribute a natural origin to Aids, believing instead that 'there are several unique characteristics of HIV that would lead one to conclude that perhaps this might be a man-made organism.' He links the appearance of Aids to research carried out by not only the American but also the Israeli and Soviet armies into the production of biological weapons, and suggests that there might be a causal connection, although he is careful not to make any precise accusations in the presence of people outside the movement.

Louis Farrakhan is a little more explicit, although he too takes care not to accuse anyone by name. Referring to American research into germ warfare, he has declared: 'This means we have to work even harder because if the government is responsible for producing the Aids virus, then they do not plan to allow for any cure or medication ultimately that may be successful in fighting this dreaded disease.'[54] In line with the Nation's view that the community should stand on its own feet, the movement has opted for an African drug developed in Kenya – known originally as Kemron, then Immunex – for which it has acquired the import and distribution franchise in the United States. Dr Muhammad came across the drug during a trip to Kenya in 1991 and has since then prescribed it exclusively in treating his many Aids-affected patients. In his view, AZT is costly and ineffective, whereas Immunex develops natural immunities and thereby helps the body to defend itself against the opportunistic diseases generated by immune deficiency. It is therefore the best available therapy, while the search goes on for a drug which will eliminate the virus.[55] According to *The Final Call*, although the National Institute of Health at first dismissed Immunex as a worthless treatment, it is now testing the drug, thanks to pressure from the Nation of Islam.[56]

But according to Dr Muhammad, the best antidote to Aids is Islam: 'If we look at the Islamic countries throughout the world, we would see that the greatest preventive to the spread of this virus is the practice of Islam in the society. The moral rules of Islam don't allow for the spread of this epidemic ... We have to go into action ... but the praise belongs to God. And I think that this could be a way of demonstrating in a very contemporary fashion the power of Islam to affect public health and public well-being.' His reasoning may be disconcerting to some; nevertheless, it has great persuasive power among groups excluded from society, who feel the full force of the unequal spread of the disease. This feeling is reinforced by the mainstream treatments available, which merely seek to limit the patient's suffering in the absence of any hope of recovery.

Moreover, the religious message accompanying the Nation of Islam's treatment of the HIV virus echoes the response of the wealthier groups in American society, where a new climate of moral disapproval and abstinence has replaced the permissiveness of the 1970s. However, the Black Muslims put forward Islam as the only solution, since they see it as an opportunity to encourage the transformation of anomic Black populations into a re-organized, disciplined Muslim community based on moral rules. Just as Aids is indicative of the disorder within the Black populations, the destruction of the family unit and the social fabric, so the organization of the community around Islam represents the only way of halting the spread of the disease. Otherwise, 'Aids could accomplish what over four hundred-fifty years of slavery, miscegenation, brutality, psychosocioeconomic slavery, poverty and covert racism has failed to accomplish – the mass elimination of Black people from the planet earth.'[57]

The quest for social recognition

Whereas, in the public's view of the Nation of Islam, 1992 appeared to be dominated by the controversy surrounding *The Secret Relationship between Blacks and Jews*, the following year saw Farrakhan devoting considerable energy to getting his message across to middle-class audiences, not only Black, but also Hispanic, Native American and even white. He played down the anti-Jewish polemics and emphasized his organization's social work in the community, putting it forward as a model for the reconstruction of US society.

The most spectacular event took place in April 1993, when Farrakhan, who was taking part in a conference at the University of Winston-Salem where he had been a student, took up his violin to give a public performance of a Mendelssohn piece. When asked what his rendition of a concerto written by a Jewish composer meant, Farrakhan replied that he wanted 'to try to do with music what couldn't be done with words, and try to undo with music what words had done.'[58]

The following month, at a time when Bill Clinton's first hundred days in office were being very negatively evaluated in the press, Farrakhan surprised everyone by speaking up for the President. Traditionally, the Nation of Islam had shown indifference or hostility to the White House, as its relationship with the US state generally remained antagonistic. Farrakhan's support for Clinton coincided with the publication of his latest book, *A Torchlight for America*. The book was greeted by one of the most respected Black academics, Cornel West (a professor at Princeton, later at Harvard), as a 'call for dialogue'.[59] Leaving behind the rhetorical violence associated with his public image, Farrakhan deliberately targets a wider, more sophisticated audience in this book. In it, he reflects on all the social problems of the United States today, not just those affecting Blacks. There is no reference to the creation of a separate Black state.

The book begins with thoughts on America's external trade deficit and goes on to extol Bill Clinton's moral and intellectual qualities. Farrakhan presents the President with solutions to the many crises afflicting 'America on her deathbed': the collapse of state education, poverty, the crisis of moral values and the public health system in ruins. The answer is to apply to all communities the model implemented by the Nation of Islam to regenerate the Black community. Thus, the 'universities of Islam' (which are actually primary and

secondary schools) begin by teaching the omnipotence of God, separate girls and boys and impose a school uniform and strict discipline. This approach, according to Farrakhan, produces good
results. Similarly, the Black Muslims save money by abstaining from
tobacco and alcohol and over-eating, and use their savings to invest
in Black businesses and shop at Black establishments, which sets off
a process which will eventually do away with the need for costly
social aid programmes. As regards moral values, Farrakhan sees the
Nation of Islam as highly successful: its behaviour code guarantees
harmonious family life, outlaws promiscuity and premarital sex
(which have been responsible for millions of illegitimate, fatherless
children) and discourages homosexuality. In the fight against drugs,
the successes of the Fruit of Islam, notably in Washington, speak for
themselves; and in the jails, conversion of Black prisoners helps their
future rehabilitation (the latest celebrity convert being the boxer
Mike Tyson). As for public health problems, most of these could be
solved by following the example of the Nation's disciples and applying the rules laid down by Elijah Muhammad in his book *How to
Eat to Live*, thus helping to reduce considerably state spending on
health.

By setting himself up as a model and leaving aside the more controversial aspects of his teaching, Farrakhan has thus embarked on a
route similar to that of Elijah Muhammad in the latter half of the
1960s. In contrast with the revolutionary radicalism of Malcolm X,
Elijah Muhammad had moved towards a strategy of 'community
management', aimed at creating a community of followers all eating
'Muhammad's Fish' and depositing their savings in the movement's
bank. As his financial empire expanded, Elijah Muhammad aspired
to more respectability and social recognition, so that his little
Nation could prosper within the greater American nation. Thirty
years later, Farrakhan's approach not only has the aim of advancing
his organization within the American nation, but is also an attempt
to get the state to recognize the legitimacy of his objective of organizing the Black populations under his leadership into a community
guided by the rules of the Nation of Islam. To this end, he presents
himself as a model not only for Blacks but for Americans as a
whole. It is up to the other communities to follow this example, as
the Jews have already done, according to the Black Muslims.

Thus, the 'appeasement' approach laid out in *A Torchlight for
America* does not contradict the violence of Farrakhan's earlier
speeches; rather, it complements the earlier discourse and extends
the community logic. In the first phase of organization, community
feeling was galvanized by the demonization of the enemy, the mobi-

lization of the faithful, the glorification of revolt against oppression and the multiplication of rituals which distinguish the community of the pure from surrounding society. In the next phase, violent anti-Jewish polemics in *The Secret Relationship* expressed the desire to strip a rival community of its moral legitimacy by downgrading it from its victim status to that of a perpetrator of genocide, in order to acquire for the Black community the highest moral status. In the process, the movement reinforced a world view based on the community fragmentation of the United States, by placing itself inside that system. On Savior's Day in 1993, Farrakhan for the first time invited onto the platform representatives of other 'minorities', particularly Hispanics and Native Americans, presenting them with a model on which they could build their own communities in order to further their own sets of demands.

At the same time, the movement attempted to play down its differences of opinion with 'orthodox' Islam by making constant reference to Saudi Arabia, the ally of the United States in the Middle East, and laying emphasis on the visits made there by Nation leaders. In December 1993, for example, Dr Muhammad explained that W. D. Fard, the founding father of the Nation of Islam, was simply a Messianic figure and that Muhammad bin Abdallah (Islam's Muhammad) remained in his eyes the last prophet, the Prophet of Islam for all the world's Muslims. This marks a significant departure from Elijah Muhammad's declarations elevating Fard to the status of 'Allah incarnate'. But these remarks may be interpreted in a figurative sense: at grassroots level, activists maintain a radical stance which is hostile to the American establishment, and this antagonism finds expression in Fard's discourse of separation and difference, including his 'heresies' which mark off the Nation of Islam from traditional Islamic doctrine. In December 1993, *The Final Call* reprinted an article by Elijah Muhammad entitled 'Why and how we fast in December', although such practice is unacceptable to most Muslims who consider that fasting should take place during the lunar month of Ramadan.[60]

In January 1994, the Nation of Islam leaders' desire to reorient the movement and integrate it more closely into mainstream American politics was put to the test with the publication in the *New York Times* of a full-page advertisement taken out by the Anti-Defamation League of the B'nai B'rith. The advertisement reproduced extracts of a speech by Khalid Abdul Muhammad, one of the 'hard-line' leaders of the Nation of Islam, in which he criticized the new leadership approach and violently attacked Jews. Farrakhan found himself in an awkward position within the organization and, under pressure from a number of Black politicians and from those Black Muslims who sought to cultivate links with the public author-ities, had to distance himself from Khalid Muhammad, although he did not dissociate himself completely for fear of alienating the more radical grassroots elements. The cycle of provocation–repression–solidarity was set in motion, just as at the time of the Jesse Jackson campaign in 1983–5. As a result, in a survey published in April 1994, 62 per cent of the Black Americans polled felt that Farrakhan represented a 'positive' viewpoint within the Black community (whereas 28 per cent described him as a 'dangerous extremist').[61]

Thus, the Nation of Islam finds itself at the heart of the dilemma facing a community movement which tries to negotiate its place with regard to the state and wider society, without itself being able to take power: how to reconcile the leadership's aspirations to recogni-tion with grassroots radicalism. In many ways, the movement founded by Fard and Elijah Muhammad, made famous by Malcolm X and brought into the thick of public controversy by Farrakhan operates as an ideal type reflecting the conflict-laden reorganization of the social system in the crisis of the postindustrial world.

PART II
The Britannic Verses

On 14 January 1989, in Bradford, West Yorkshire, a small crowd led by the town's Council of Mosques performed a public burning of Salman Rushdie's book *The Satanic Verses*. They were protesting against the content of the book, which they held to be blasphemous in its treatment of the Prophet of Islam. The Bradford imams and their flock proved themselves to be not only ardent supporters of Muhammad but also children of Marshall MacLuhan: they made sure the events were recorded on video and dispatched to the television stations, which had not managed to send any reporters to the scene.

Just as the Los Angeles riots were sparked off by the television broadcast of an amateur video showing the Black motorist Rodney King being beaten by local police officers, so too it was a 'rough' video recording which set the tone for the Rushdie affair. Broadcast over and over again across the whole world, the televised images of a burning book nailed to a pole became the ultimate symbol of the affair and went on to represent the assertion of Islamic identity in Britain. But the authors of the image could not control the way it was interpreted by television audiences. In filming their 'act of faith', they were using shock tactics to attract the public's attention to the outrage that they felt the book perpetrated against their beliefs and their identity as Muslims. However, television viewers saw the scenes differently: they recalled engravings of Inquisition bonfires or black-and-white images of Nazis burning books. The Muslims of Bradford, who had not foreseen these reactions, became identified in the public's view with the most extreme form of religious fanaticism. Ironically, though, whilst commentators in the Western press used these images to wax indignant about the *auto-da-fé*, international royalties from the video cassette brought in thousands of pounds to finance the Bradford Council of Mosques' campaign against *The Satanic Verses*.[1]

The screen image of the burning book also represented the demonization of a certain type of literary fiction created by the European intelligentsia. The cultural codes of this written form, which had given such offence to some Muslims, or which had been completely misunderstood by them, were suddenly transposed through a different medium onto another system of meanings. As Umberto Eco wrote in relation to the Rushdie affair, 'One of the side effects of the mass media is that they bring fiction to people who've never read a novel before, and who don't share in the fictional agreement, the suspension of disbelief.'[2] It is unlikely that many of those who burned *The Satanic Verses*, members of the Indian–Pakistani immigrant working class, were regular readers of English–language novels. For most of them, whether illiterate or readers of English, Urdu or Arabic, any printed text would belong to a register which had at its peak the Sacred Book and would be evaluated according to the criteria of the revealed Truth, especially if dealing directly with themes related to Islam.

Thus, the authors of an anti-Rushdie book argued that, for Muslims,

> by working in fiction with that which is fact, and debatable fact at that, the only conceivable result is to publish a confusion. By virtue of Rushdie's reputation and the support of his publishing agents, this confusion will become widespread among those without the means to judge or to evaluate the facts contained within the fiction. Knowingly to spread confusion, especially to such an audience, is a blasphemy and a fitna (strife), since it defies one of the most central tenets of Islamic consciousness.[3]

The Rushdie affair represented a chance for them to incriminate an abhorrent, secularized intelligentsia whose writing does not correspond to the criteria of the Truth revealed by Muhammad, and to dispute their leading position in the contemporary market of the printed word.

Rushdie's novel was caught between oral culture and the media culture of the video clip and the fax. Before it went up in flames, the 547 pages of the novel had been reduced by its detractors to a few quoted passages, translated into Urdu and faxed around the world. The Islamic associations, which had made it the subject of their Friday sermons, used those passages of the novel which in their view attacked the Prophet and his companions, in order to mobilize the faithful, unite the community and reinforce cohesion. The novel as such was rarely read by its opponents, who were not afraid to proclaim: 'Yes, I have not read it, nor do I intend to. I do not have to wade through a filthy drain to know what filth is.'[4] It was on the basis of a montage of photocopied extracts that the book and its author were denounced from the pulpit in many mosques in Britain, India and Pakistan, even before word reached Ayatollah Khomeini, who issued the famous fatwa condemning Rushdie and his publishers to death on 14 February 1989, exactly a month after the Bradford *auto-da-fé*.

Since then, as is well known, the 'Rushdie affair' has become one of the most notorious *causes célèbres* of the late twentieth century. Salman Rushdie remains in hiding, in fear of an assassin carrying out Tehran's death sentence. The affair has led many different people to take up various positions on the issue and has played a significant part in many people's minds in hardening the cultural antagonism between the 'ungodly' West and Islam, the new 'evil Empire' after the collapse of Eastern bloc communism.

In the pages which follow, we will attempt to understand how the political dimension of communalism in the United Kingdom made the Rushdie affair possible, and how the Rushdie affair in turn serves to reveal the political dimension of communalism, which we can trace from the British Empire in India to the disadvantaged British cities of today.

Islam in Britain operates in a different context from the Islamization of Black Americans led by the Nation of Islam, but there are a number of common features. Whereas in the United States Islam concerns an African population whose ancestors arrived in America under forcible confinement in the early days of slavery and were uprooted from their culture in the process, in Britain it relates to a primarily Indian–Pakistani population, the first generations of whom chose to emigrate and are still alive, thus forming a continuum with the original culture. American Islam is a 'native' religion, with its own distinctive features and forms, as championed by Elijah Muhammad, Malcolm X (for most of his career) and Louis Farrakhan, although towards the end of his life Malcolm X, and later W. D. Muhammad, steered the movement towards a more 'orthodox' line. This Islam was created from new, without the benefit of a pre-existing Islamic tradition before slavery, which the slaves could have preserved and handed down. Islam in Britain is a different matter.

In Britain, assertion of an Islamic identity forms part of a traditional expression of identity through religion in the Indian subcontinent under British colonial rule. Most of the immigrants of Muslim
origin in Britain come from these ex-colonial territories. However,
living conditions in Britain and the political, economic and cultural
aspects of the social system have created a favourable environment
for the assertion of a distinctive Islamic identity which has not been
seen in other European countries. There are strong echoes of the
American case, where the history of racial segregation, and more
recently the structural changes taking place in the postindustrial era
such as the unemployment of disadvantaged young Blacks, have created a favourable environment for the Islamization led by Farrakhan
in the Black ghettos.

Differences between the Nation of Islam and the Bradford Council
of Mosques – over the relationship with Islam, dogma and even the
definition of the religious sphere – abound. In Bradford, Farrakhan's
disciples' claim to Islam would no doubt be regarded with considerable suspicion. Nonetheless, despite the different meanings given to
Islam, reference to the Muslim faith has in both cases helped to
define the contours of a community identity based on a culture of
separateness from wider American or British society. Moreover,
both populations consist mainly of individuals who have taken the
full force of postindustrial economic restructuring from the late
1970s onwards. Whereas previously these populations had access to
numerous unskilled or semi-skilled jobs, many of them now find
themselves condemned to long-term unemployment, and the future
for their children of working age looks bleak. Apart from a few elite
groups, they have rarely acquired the cultural capital needed in
'postmodern' societies to gain access to relatively stable jobs. Many
of them feel themselves to be victims of racist discrimination.

In both countries, the reconstruction of Islam-based communities
has been able to respond to a social demand characterized by a
strong sense of exclusion, whether real or imagined. But it has not
stopped there. In the United States, the patient construction of the
Black Muslim movement from the Detroit ghetto in the 1930s to the
present day has made this specific Islamic identity possible. It
includes the defence of the 'community' against drug dealers, care of
Aids patients and a redefinition of culture which involves 'conscious'
rap and the incrimination of Jews for their supposedly crucial role in
the slave trade. In the United Kingdom, the context in which the
Islamic community has been constructed, and which gave rise to the
Rushdie affair, may be analysed in the campaigns for Islamic
instruction to be given to Muslim schoolchildren, for the creation of

Islamic pressure groups to lobby parliamentary candidates and for a redefinition of the personal status of Muslims in line with the sharia. These campaigns highlight the specific character of the established immigrant Muslim population within British society, where the idea of 'race' has juridical status and a distinction is made between citizenship and nationality, unlike the situation in France where no distinction is made and the concept of 'integration' of immigrants has its own history quite different from that in Britain or the United States.

In 1986, the populations of Muslim origin resident in the United Kingdom numbered an estimated 936,000. More than a third of these (357,000) came from Pakistan, 84,000 from India and 64,000 from Bangladesh, as well as some 99,000 from East Africa (mainly Indians and Pakistanis expelled as a result of nationalist pressure, such as that of Idi Amin Dada in Uganda).[5] Thus, two-thirds of the people of Muslim origin belong to families originally from the Indian subcontinent and have been brought up in the religious tradition belonging to that part of the world. In order to understand the forms that Islamic community identity takes in Britain, it is first necessary to look closely at the most noteworthy elements of the history which the immigrants brought with them in the decades following the Second World War: the end of the Raj and the coming to independence of the states of the subcontinent, marked by the bloody religious partition of India and Pakistan in 1947.

I

Return to the Empire

India was the 'jewel in the crown' of the British colonial empire. The size of the territory and India's strategic position at the centre of Asia made the viceregal residence in Calcutta the counterpart of London in the rest of the world. But for England India also represented the incarnation of absolute otherness. It was in India, at the centre of the empire, that British civilization in the industrial era developed the paradigm of its attitude towards the Other – an Other subjugated to its authority. This attitude reflected above all the pragmatism of capitalist economy which sought to maximize the profits accruing from colonization whilst minimizing human costs. The geographical and cultural distance between Britain and India pushed capitalist pragmatism to the extreme, for administering the subcontinent represented something of a challenge. In 1881, the empire in India relied on a few thousand English and Scottish civil servants to administer 256 million inhabitants (74 per cent of whom were Hindus and 19.7 per cent Muslims). The Raj managed to hold on to power with a remarkable economy of means (in comparison with the dense French colonial presence in a sparsely populated North Africa, moreover so much closer to the French mainland) by leaning on local divisions and cultivating allies in each caste, each religious group, each sociocultural class in turn.

'Thus below an apparently autocratic system guided by a British bureaucracy and guarded by British redcoats [soldiers] there lay another system of Indian support and consent. This system mediated between the commands of Government House and the obedience of the men in the fields. It preserved an Indian role in the governance of the country.'[1] The system of indirect administration in the early days of the Raj involved keeping the old pre-colonial power structures in place as much as possible, whilst making them subservient or removing many of their real powers.

Before British paramountcy prevailed on the Indian subcontinent, power had belonged to Muslim dynasties. The soldiers of Islam were present in India as early as 711 and later reappeared in various raids and incursions. In 1211, they founded the sultanate of Delhi, the first real expression of Muslim political power; but the bulk of the population remained Hindu. The great Moghul dynasty of Delhi came to power in 1526 and remained there until 1857, when the last Moghul emperor was deposed by the British. Moghul rule distinguished itself particularly with the contrasting reigns of Akbar (1556–1605), famous for the important space he made for Hindus in his empire, and Aurangzeb (1658–1707), who initiated a strong Islamic offensive against them. After 1707 the Moghul empire gradually lost its substance to its various vassals – princes, maharajas, sultans and nawabs – whilst the British colonial presence took over.

Islam and the challenge of minority status

The concrete experience of Islam's establishment on the Indian subcontinent had straightaway forced the religion to reach a compromise with one of its most ancient doctrinal commandments concerning the precise ways of 'opening-up', or conquering, new territories to Islam (*fath*). Traditional Islamic law makes a distinction between the status of two classes of people in a conquered country. On one hand, *ahl al kitab* or 'people of the book' are monotheists who obey the injunctions of a Book revealed by God (such as the Old Testament and the Gospels), which the Koran considers to be a forerunner of its own ultimate revealed truth. These people may keep their religion but do not have the right to proselytize. On the other hand, polytheists must convert immediately to Islam, on pain of death. This juridical distinction is modelled on the Muslim act of faith ('There is no God but Allah and Muhammad is the messenger of God'): Muslims profess the whole of this creed, monotheists believe in the first part, whilst it is completely alien to polytheists.

According to this law, Hindus should have converted to Islam under Islamic conquest, or been killed. But the balance of forces between the sparse armies of the conqueror and the massive defeated population made it impossible to enforce dogma, even though as far as Islamic doctrine is concerned Hinduism represents the essence of loathed polytheism. The massacre or forced conversion of Hindus would have rapidly undermined the conquerors' power. Necessity made the law, and the polytheistic Hindus were broadly assimilated into 'people of the Book', whilst Islam spread among some sections of the population.[2] Uniquely in history, Islam remained confined to a small minority, but kept control of supreme political power. The dispersion of Muslims across the immense territory of the subcontinent and the internal linguistic and social differences – on the model of the Hindu caste system – prevented them from developing over time into a coherent 'Muslim' group, which could have defined itself in opposition to a coherent 'Hindu' group. In this sense, as the historian Peter Hardy notes, nostalgia for a homogeneous 'Islamic nation' which is supposed to have held sway in India in the past is the product of an ideological reappropriation of the past by modern Islamic elites.[3]

British domination gradually eroded the political power of Islam. Then in 1857 an event occurred which was to be highly traumatic for Islamic consciousness in India, an enormous challenge for the most deeply rooted groups of religious thought and a leap into the unknown: the deposition of the Muslim emperor of Delhi. The Sepoys, a regiment of native soldiers, had discovered that their cartridges were lubricated with fat from impure animals, and they had to tear open the cartridge wrappings with their teeth. The soldiers mutinied. The last Moghul emperor, Bahadur Shah, seeing the opportunity to loosen London's heavy grip, took over the leadership of the mutiny, which quickly turned into an anti-British revolt. The British set the seal on their suppression of the revolt by deposing the monarch. The events confronted Muslim Indians with the dilemma shared by all their fellow believers subjected to European colonial rule: how could they remain Muslim under a non-Muslim ruler? But unlike the colonized Muslims of the Middle East or North Africa, where the inertia of a mainly Muslim society protected Islamic power from 'ungodly' authorities, the Indian 'Muhammadans' not only lost political power, but also represented a minority whose past privileges were contested by the Hindu majority.

It was this double loss which made the situation so acute and so exceptional for the Muslims, and also exemplary in the way in which it foreshadowed the situation of Islam in the West a century later and the challenges which Islam would have to face, this time too in a non-Muslim environment. The lessons it offered would prove useful later.

First, how could believers remain faithful in a state whose ruler was non-Muslim and did not intend to apply the sharia, where their customs and rites and their world vision would not form the legal basis of the social system? How should they behave when the majority of their fellow citizens had complete freedom to use public space to practise their own rites, even if they contravened Islam – such as when the Hindus drowned out the muezzin's call to prayer with the music of their own festivals, or when the Muslim butchers were persecuted as 'sacrificers of sacred cows'? These unprecedented difficulties after 1857 led Indian Muslims to come up with original solutions which were later to reappear, across the oceans and the decades, in the context of immigration in the United Kingdom. The solutions which Muslims tried in nineteenth-century India in order to rebuild and defend a community identity in the face of a Hindu majority and non-Muslim rule would re-emerge as a response to British society in the late 1950s.

During the ninety years from the deposition of the Moghul emperor to Indian independence and the bloody partition of India and Pakistan, Islamic thought in the Indian subcontinent concentrated mainly on the resolution of the double crisis which the events of 1857 had pinpointed. In this period, two main paths – religious and political – were mapped out. The first reinforced the religious singularity of Islam and its radical separation from the non-Muslim world; the second reasserted Islam through the elaboration of a political strategy of communalism, involving the establishment of separate electoral colleges for Muslims and Hindus and leading eventually to the secession of Pakistan. These two levels of thought and action were sometimes, but not always, interwoven: the first defined an *Islamic* identity by emphasizing the establishment of rules and doctrine which would engender and intensify belief in the new political context. The second embraced a sociological definition of the whole population of Muslim origin, whatever the intensity or the boundaries of their belief, in order to lay claim in their name to a particular space which would find its ultimate incarnation in the creation of Pakistan, the state of the Muslims.

The internal hegira

Heightening the singular nature of Islam meant a completely new approach to a situation which Islamic tradition had hardly contemplated: non-Islamic rule over a territory containing a Muslim minority.[4] Would the country remain within the 'land of Islam' (*dar al islam*) or would it become a 'land of war' (*dar al harb*), that part of

the world where Islam does not rule? In the latter case, good
Muslims should leave the country, and embark on an 'hegira' (*hijra*)
just as the Prophet fled ungodly Mecca; then they should wage holy
war (*jihad*) to regain the territory.[5] The main Indian Muslim movements were unable to carry out these doctrinal injunctions and
instead worked out a strategy to reclaim their identity within the
existing territory, based on their faith and their specific beliefs – a
sort of internal hegira.

The field of Islam in the subcontinent was reconstructed around
two major axes which we find unchanged in contemporary Britain:
the 'Deobandi' movement, which advocates a strict Sunni orthodoxy,
and 'Barelvi' Sufism, characterized by the intensity of its devotion to
the Prophet.[6] In addition to these, two other major movements
appeared later, in the first decades of the twentieth century, both
making use of Deobandi orthodox conservatism but steering their
activities in different directions: the Tabligh movement, which places
Islamic teaching at the heart of daily life, and the Jama'at-i Islami,
which campaigns for the construction of an Islamic state. These two
newer movements have spread all over the world and exert great
influence in the international re-Islamization networks.

The Deobandi movement grew out of the seminary of Deoband
(*Dar al'Ulum*), founded in 1867, which aimed to give its pupils
intellectual resources to strengthen their assertion of their Islamic
identity, regardless of the position of the state.[7] The teaching, carried out in Urdu and delivered to young men from traditional arti-
sanal and commercial family backgrounds, created a non-Anglicized
elite who saw the strict application of the holy texts of Islam as the
only solution to the problems of daily life. To this end, the *ulema* of
Deoband played a significant role in codifying religious law. They
wrote several thousand fatwas, legal judgments based on the Koran
and the Sunna. These lay down rules for conduct conforming to the
sharia, in circumstances where a believer might not know how to
behave without violating the rules but cannot follow the dominant
social norm or state laws, which are considered 'ungodly'. At its
centenary in 1967, the Deoband seminary had 8934 schools
throughout the world which spread its teaching.[8] According to historian Francis Robinson, the Deobandis adapted well to the non-
Muslim Indian state, in which they 'hoped that some form of
jurisprudential apartheid would be achieved between the Hindus
and themselves.'[9] Their autonomy *vis-à-vis* the state prepared them
especially well for the task of decreeing the rules on which to base a
closed community identity, when the question of emigration to
Europe arose later.

The Sufism of the Barelvis has created a mental and cultural separation from the surrounding world which is at least as intense as the closed identity built by the Deobandis, but they have used other criteria for defining community boundaries. This mystic 'path' (*tariqa*) appeared towards the end of the nineteenth century, under the influence of Ahmad Riza Khan (1856–1921). Khan's writings and teachings are an impassioned defence of the superhuman nature of the Prophet of Islam, whom he portrayed as capable of penetrating the realm of occult realities and interceding on behalf of believers. This quasi-divinization of the Prophet is peculiar to Sufism and has throughout the history of Islam aroused the implacable opposition of the Deobandis and of the *ulema*, whose concern is scriptural orthodoxy. It is also characterized by worship of all kinds of saints and holy men, attributed with powers of protection and patronage. The Barelvis' popular pietism is not far removed from Hinduism, from which it borrows some rites. However, they have constructed a strictly defined Islamic identity: the intercession of saints and the Prophet allows the faithful to live according to Islam in its traditional form, without thinking about the attitude of the state or dominant social norms. Any lack of respect for the person of the Prophet is seen as a major attack on the identity of the group and triggers harsh reactions. Thus, since *The Satanic Verses* was received by Barelvis as a particularly insulting satire upon the person of the Prophet, the book was bound to provoke a deep and passionate hostility among them.

The other two main movements active in the Islam of the subcontinent were formed in the first half of the twentieth century. The Tablighi Jama'at ('association for the propagation of Islam', often referred to as Tabligh) movement pushes the desire for autonomy to an extreme by defining the community on the basis of strict religious observance, given the absence of an Islamic state; the Jama'at-i Islami starts from the same premise, but campaigns instead for the immediate construction of this ideal Islamic state.

The Tabligh came into being in 1927, under the influence of a Muslim scholar, Mawlana Muhammad Ilyas. He wanted to propagate as widely as possible, but especially among the uneducated, a simple, rigorous Islam shorn of the pedantry of the *ulema* and purged of Sufi deviations. His missionary work began in the region of Mewat, near Delhi, whose inhabitants were superficially Islamized. Ilyas went there to preach, following the Prophet's teaching to the letter, modelling his behaviour precisely on Muhammad's account of his words and deeds compiled in the Islamic tradition (*Sunna*). This behaviour constituted a radical break with the

customs and practice of Hindu society and also combated the adulteration of Islam represented by the population of Mewat. Ilyas had
retained Sufism's mode of action – presence among the ordinary
people – but rejected the 'suspect' elements like the worship of
saints.

Through the strength of its proselytism, the Tabligh has become
one of the most important re-Islamizing movements in the world.[10]
Its break with surrounding society and resocialization of followers
within an Islamic community, characterized by strong pietism, made
it the prototype of the most hermetic forms of Islamic communalism. By isolating its followers culturally from the ungodly environment, it offered a form of organization which could later be adapted
to the new conditions of immigration, in which followers needed to
be isolated from the potential attractions of Western societies.

Finally, the Jama'at-i Islami is the only re-Islamizing movement
originating in the subcontinent with explicitly political objectives. Its
followers see the restoration of an Islamic state, on all or part of the
territory occupied by Muslims, as a priority. The organization was
founded in 1941 by Abul A'la Mawdudi, an Urdu-speaking journalist who had taught himself English and Arabic. It became one of the
constituent parts of the Islamist movement worldwide, comparable
for instance to the Muslim Brotherhood founded in Egypt in 1928
by Hassan el Banna. Unlike the other Indian Islamic movements,
whose proselytism was shaped by a perspective which acknowledged
the absence of an 'authentically Islamic' state, Mawdudi and his disciples set themselves the immediate objective of restoring a state
which would apply the sharia.

In their view, sovereignty (*hakimiyya*) does not belong to the people, but to Allah alone. A power is only legitimate if it governs
according to the injunctions of God (*bima anzala Allah*), expressed
in the Holy Scriptures of Islam. By adopting this position, Mawdudi
went well beyond the goals of the existing religious movements.
According to him, the only legitimate state is an Islamic state which
brings together the Muslim population in one territory, with the sole
aim of applying the sharia. In the context of Muslim emigration to
Europe, the Jama'at-i Islami's demands would result in the conflict-
ual politicization of community organization, as the role of
Mawdudi's disciples at the start of the Rushdie affair was to show.

The invention of communalism

As we have seen, the upsurge in religious associational life had reorganized Islam in India, in response to the traumatic ending of Moghul rule in 1857 and its effects on the identity of the Muslims, who constituted a minority of the population. But at the same time, another process began to emerge, which identified itself as modernist and thus developed along radically different lines. This new movement wanted Muslims to participate fully in the political life of the British Empire, but within a specific community distinct from the non-Muslim world. As Louis Dumont observes, 'The religious element which came into its make-up appears to be merely the shadow of religion, religion seen not as the foundation and guiding principle of all aspects of life, but only as a sign of the distinctiveness of a human group, and at least virtually a political group, in relation to others.'[11]

The founders of this movement wished to appear, in the eyes of the British authorities, as the spokespeople of the community of their fellow worshippers, on the basis of a 'sociological' analysis of confessional groupings. Their first step was to establish a 'modernist' education system to train Anglophone elites. Then when the Empire gave voting rights (based on a tax qualification) to 'natives' at the beginning of the twentieth century, these elites demanded separate electoral representation for Muslims. Later, these demands would result in the 1947 partition of India and Pakistan on religious grounds.

In analysing this process of communalism,[12] we need to examine the actors and the underlying motivating forces on both the Indian and British sides. We also need to explore the extent to which communalism was able to survive and help forge a political feeling of specific Muslim identity capable of resisting the pressures created by decolonization and migration to Europe in the second half of the twentieth century, and which forms it took.

The promoter of this 'modernist' movement, Sir Sayyid Ahmad Khan (1817–98), came from a highly placed family in the Moghul court. After the deposition of the Moghul emperor in 1857, he wanted to show that the principles of Islam were not incompatible with Western modernity, contrary to the conclusions drawn by the Islamist movements which reacted by an 'internal hegira'. Allah had created all living things and had therefore also laid down the laws of nature, science and technology. Muslims should excel in their studies if they wanted to fulfil themselves in their faith. Over-insistence

on points of dogma and a refusal to move beyond a medieval conception of the world and oneself could, on the other hand, only lead
to a growing marginalization of the followers of Islam and the
diminution of their ability to shape their own destiny and that of the
world.

In Sir Sayyid Ahmad Khan's view, mastery of the intellectual
instruments of modernity would allow the Muslims of the British
Raj to participate fully in indirect rule (whereby an Indian administration managed a great part of the country's affairs) and prevent
the modernized Hindu elites from acquiring an overwhelmingly
dominant position. According to historian Peter Hardy, 'Sir Sayyid
Ahmad Khan was calling on his fellow Muslims to look at themselves in a new light and to take part in a new form of social
activity. . . . He called them to a life of joint endeavour rather than
to a life of individual obedience.'[13] To this end, Sir Sayyid set up the
'Anglo-Oriental Muhammadan college' in the town of Aligarh in
1875, with the backing of the colonial power. The aim was to create
a body of graduates who could function comfortably in both the
Urdu and Anglophone cultures and act as intermediaries between
the occupier and the indigenous population, thus reproducing under
British domination a Muslim state nobility to succeed the dynasty
which had prospered during the Moghul era.

Through the Aligarh college and other similar initiatives elsewhere
in India, an intellectual elite of secularized Muslims emerged, shak-
ing the hegemony of the traditional notables. In order to assume this
role fully, they needed to convince the colonial power that Indians
of Muslim culture should possess a specific political status, and there
also had to be in exchange a perceived advantage for the British, in
helping them to maintain their domination.

This convergence of interests between the emergent Muslim elites
and the colonial power produced the first manifestation of political
communalism in the history of the modern world. This early form of
communalism was able to transcend allegiances to groups of primary solidarity (known as *jati* or *biradari*), which include the
extended family and the village, to construct a wider sense of
belonging bounded by religious identity.[14] It was promoted by political leaders who wished to attain power by presenting themselves as
the exclusive representatives of a 'community' reduced to a single
will, by unifying heterogeneous populations on the basis of a sociological definition of their 'Muslimness'.

In the Empire, the communalist project took effect in 1909 with
the Indian Councils Act, which established separate electoral colleges for Muslims and Hindus. Faced with great political instability,

the colonial power wished to demonstrate their goodwill to the Muslim communalist elites, whom they saw as a useful counter-weight to the nationalists of the Congress Party.[15] These circumstances gave rise to the creation of the Muslim League, which aimed to represent Muslims as a specific group.

Throughout the half-century which ended with British withdrawal, Indian independence and the creation of Pakistan in 1947, communalism grew in importance through elections and the attempts of Muslim and Hindu politicians to boost their popularity by pitting communities against each other, particularly at the time of religious festivals. From the 1920s onwards, 'communalist' riots proliferated, causing a number of deaths. The climate of fear widened the gulf between Hindus and Muslims and reinforced the sense of confessional identity, since this could now mean life or death.

The British had not been directly involved in the origins of communalism, but they played a significant role in its development. The historian David Page writes: 'By treating the Muslims as a separate group, [the colonial government] divided them from other Indians. By granting them separate electorates, it institutionalized that division. This was one of the most crucial factors in the development of communal politics. Muslim politicians did not have to appeal to non-Muslims; non-Muslims did not have to appeal to Muslims. This made it difficult for a genuine Indian nationalism to emerge.'[16]

As we shall see, the electoral participation of Muslim immigrants from the subcontinent settled in Britain would in the 1970s follow a communal structure largely inherited from the communalism created in the Raj. Encouraged by the British political parties, which wished to rally the 'ethnic vote' behind them, this phenomenon was to culminate in 1992 with the controversial establishment of a self-proclaimed 'Muslim parliament' claiming to represent a fictional 'separate electorate' of British Muslims.

On the Indian subcontinent, the culmination of the communal process was the secession of Pakistan in 1947, at the instigation of the Muslim League. The creation of the Pakistani state transmuted the sociological community of Indian Muslims into a nation with its own state, indissoluble in the non-confessional state of the Indian Union.

In the beginning, Pakistan was governed by Anglophile elites whose reference to Islam was mainly instrumental. But later they saw their power and influence diminish, whilst demands for greater Islamization of society increased. Mawdudi and his disciples, as well as the *ulema* who had chosen to live in Pakistan, exerted very strong pressure in this direction. Although at first he had shown considerable reticence about the creation of a state which he judged too 'secular', Mawdudi worked to push Pakistan towards an Islamic state, where the sovereignty of God instead of the sovereignty of the people would be proclaimed.[17] His wishes were fulfilled to some extent when General Zia ul Haqq, who was sympathetic to the ideas of Mawdudi, came to power in 1977. Since 1947, the three decades of Pakistan's existence as an independent state had seen secular nationalism gradually lose its force, as in most parts of the Muslim world, whilst demands for the re-Islamization of society and the state have grown in importance. Political communalism has linked up with the re-Islamizing movement arising out of Mawdudi's vision.

In summary, two major guiding lines had reorganized Islam in the Indian subcontinent of the British Empire: on one hand, the 'internal hegira', and on the other, political communalism. In the unprecedented situation where Muslims found themselves in a minority, in response to the deposition of the Muslim ruler and the establishment of an 'ungodly' power, the movements we have observed above adapted their strategies, whilst the British rulers also made use of them to maintain their control. These strategies formed the mixed legacy which both sides, the immigrants from the subcontinent and the British authorities, later drew upon in the context of postwar Britain.

2

'Britishness' and Identity

In the context of a worldwide empire, British identity was defined by subjection to the Crown. Following decolonization and the creation of independent states, it shrank back to the geographical limits of Great Britain. But this process did not happen smoothly: for several decades after the end of the empire, British citizenship remained defined by imperial ties, based on the Commonwealth and not on membership of individual countries. People from the Indian Union and Pakistan who settled in Birmingham or Bradford in the 1950s enjoyed the same legal status as resident Britons, once they had gone through a few formalities. They had full political rights, including voting rights, even if they knew no English and their political behaviour remained essentially determined by allegiances formed in the Indian subcontinent. This juridical situation, unique in the world, meant that citizenship had no meaning as a criterion of national identity, since membership of the Commonwealth conferred automatic rights through nationality. But because of subsequent migratory movements, met with xenophobic and racist reactions, and later tensions in the labour market and unemployment, the very notion of British citizenship became a political issue. Since there was no possibility of identifying citizenship with nationality by law, the British system made use of the concepts of 'race' and 'ethnicity', which acquired a legal meaning.

The terms 'race' and 'ethnicity' were placed within a 'multicultural' vision of society, in which 'minorities' and 'communities' live side by side. According to this view, 'minorities/communities' represent the political identity of their members and act as recognized intermediaries in the relationship between their members and the state. Multiculturalism has thus encouraged the development of many forms of community organization – racial, ethnic and religious. In the case of Muslim immigrants from the Indian subcontinent, its impact has been all the greater because of the cultural legacy of the 'internal hegira' and 'community politics' inherited from the Raj. Working-class populations of Muslim origin looked to community organization for protection, then found it was an effective means of social advancement in a country in which they had political rights but little chance of individual integration into society.

It did not take long for the immigrant populations to assert their Islamic identity: mosques started to appear in Britain in the 1950s, whereas in other European countries with significant Muslim immigration mosques did not spread until after 1973. Let us now examine the relationship between the cultural legacy of the empire and the multiculturalism of the host society, which will throw light on the unique way in which Islamic community organization has developed in Britain.

From the Raj to multicultural society

Within the United Kingdom, British nationality is not a homogeneous concept, but the sum of various different nationalities: English, Scottish, Welsh and Irish. The British state is a 'multinational' state. In a 1968 survey about national identity, 67 per cent of Glaswegians declared themselves 'Scottish' and only 29 per cent 'British'; 69 per cent of Welsh respondents defined themselves as 'Welsh', 15 per cent as 'British' and 13 per cent as 'English'.[1] However in this case feelings of national identity do not coincide with the nation-state; the Welsh or Scottish nations are not states with the ability to confer citizenship on their members, although a certain amount of power is delegated to them.

This conception of British citizenship, where political identity is expressed by various national identities existing side by side, created the conditions in which the immigrant populations coming into Britain after the independence of former colonial territories were received within the political system. The response was not to assimilate the immigrants into the dominant society but rather to grant them a parallel status to that of the Welsh and Scottish nations which already existed. Thus was created a kind of 'potential nation' under the aegis of British citizenship, which included all the new arrivals – West Indians, Indians and Pakistanis, Chinese, even Cypriots and Italians – in the racial category 'Black'.[2]

The legal definitions of 'subject of the Crown' and later 'citizen of the Commonwealth' were too wide to control immigration to Britain from the former colonies. As sociologist Harry Goulbourne observes, according to the British Nationality and Aliens Act passed in 1914 at the height of the empire, 'the central principle or definition of "British" was perceived to be allegiance to the Crown, and the importance that a specific territory – the British Isles – was later to assume in nationality legislation was conspicuously absent.'[3]

In 1914, the number of colonial 'subjects' settling in Britain was negligible.[4] In 1948, the legislation was amended in response to the independence of the former colonies, not only India but especially the 'white' dominions of Canada, Australia and New Zealand. In order to try to retain its world power status, Britain needed organic ties with the fifty or so states which emerged from colonialism, through the structure of the Commonwealth. In this new legal framework, the former subjects of the British Empire became 'citizens of the Commonwealth'. Their new status guaranteed them considerable freedom of movement and gave them full rights to take up residence in Britain.

The legislators of 1948 did not however foresee the mass migration of Indian and Pakistani nationals and West Indians which then took place, as these migrants came to Britain to supply cheap unskilled labour to the industries which were helping to rebuild a Europe devastated by the Second World War. These immigrants were not 'foreigners' but citizens of the Commonwealth. They were allowed to enter the former 'mainland' freely and enjoyed full civil rights including the right to vote, once they had registered. Until 1958, 'immigration' was not a significant political issue in Britain. But that year, riots broke out in Nottingham and Notting Hill against the 'coloured' populations, leading to the arrest of several young English hooligans. The judge who sentenced them was categorical in his condemnation: 'Everyone, irrespective of the colour of their skin, is entitled to walk our streets erect and free from fear. This is a right which these courts will always unfailingly uphold.' But George Rogers, the Labour MP for Notting Hill, in whose constituency the families of the young rioters lived, wrote in a newspaper that 'The government must introduce legislation quickly to end the influx of coloured people from the Commonwealth ... overcrowding has fostered vice, drugs, and the use of knives. For years the white people have been tolerant. Now their tempers are up.'[5]

As this outburst bluntly showed, the debate on immigration was focused on skin colour or 'race'. In 1962, the Commonwealth Immigrants Bill was passed, restricting the entry of Commonwealth nationals born outside the United Kingdom and not possessing a British passport issued by the UK authorities,[6] by making them obtain a voucher from the Department of Employment. However, the law proved to be ineffective in controlling immigration, and indeed had the opposite effect, since the lone males comprising the majority of Commonwealth citizens already settled in Britain quickly sent for their families, in anticipation of a more rigorous immigration policy.[7]

Race or nation?

A more stringent immigration policy was not long in coming. The Commonwealth Immigrants Act of 1968, followed by the Immigration Act of 1971, 'racialized' the legal framework, without acknowledging it explicitly. The new laws stipulated that anyone carrying a British passport, including UK-issued passports, would be subject to entry restrictions, except in the case of people born within the then frontiers of the United Kingdom (or those with at least one parent or grandparent born in the United Kingdom). The 'true citizens' were described as 'patrials', a little-used term denoting 'native-born' British: English, Welsh, Scottish or Northern Irish, and their descendants. Thus, an Australian whose grandfather was born in Edinburgh could travel to Scotland as a 'patrial'. But an Indian or Jamaican would be very unlikely to have a grandparent born in Edinburgh and therefore be classed as a 'patrial'. This was a handy way of distinguishing the citizens of the 'white Commonwealth', classed as 'native-born', from citizens of the 'coloured Commonwealth'. The 'native-born' classification disguised the effective use of race as a criterion for determining entry into the United Kingdom.

The 1968 law was passed by a Labour government, the 1971 law by the Conservatives. Both were adopted in a climate of social tension: in 1967, thousands of Indians holding British passports arrived in the United Kingdom. They had settled in Kenya and other East African lands at the time of the empire, only to be chased out by xenophobic 'Africanization' policies carried out after these countries acquired their independence.[8] Their natural response was to turn to Britain, since they were British citizens. But Enoch Powell led a virulent campaign opposing their entry into Britain. Neither the

Conservative government nor the Labour opposition could afford to ignore the impact of this campaign on their electorates.

As well as laying down racial criteria (dressed up as patriality) to restrict the entry of coloured Commonwealth immigrants, the new laws criminalized various racially discriminatory practices. This made it necessary to establish legal definitions of 'race', 'ethnicity' and 'minority'. Since minorities suffered from 'negative' discrimination, they were now entitled to compensatory 'positive' discrimination, along the lines of developments in the United States, where a 'new anti-racism' based on the assertion of different racial identities ('color consciousness') had replaced the 'old anti-racism' which did not recognize colour differences ('color blindness'). The Race Relations Acts of 1968 and 1976 (with the creation of the Commission for Racial Equality) marked the trend towards an institutionalization of minority identities by granting sizeable sums of money and legal recognition to the representation of 'minorities' and by encouraging leaders who would give a concrete status to minority identities and thereby develop a process of community organization.

Thus, institutionalized anti-racism followed two tracks: legal proceedings against employers, estate agents, landlords and businesses which practised 'negative' discrimination; and also official recognition and encouragement of the autonomous expression of 'non-white British' identity. Accordingly, any behaviour which went against this glorification of cultural difference, seen as the legitimate expression of minority identity within 'multicultural' society, was stigmatized as 'racist'. In his comparison of the French and British responses to immigration, French sociologist Didier Lapeyronnie notes that 'French policies treat the question as one of ordinary law, within which specific initiatives may be taken, whereas British policies do not combine but simply juxtapose ordinary law, civil rights and specific initiatives.'[9]

This juxtaposition of policies targeted at minorities required the creation of a statistical apparatus which would allow the authorities to identify the minorities, that is, count the number of British citizens belonging to each racial or ethnic group, in order to measure discrimination in quantitative terms and to bring in the Commission for Racial Equality (CRE).[10] Thus, a series of official surveys included questions asking people to classify themselves by race or ethnic group, and the 1991 census included this information for the first time. Rather like a Russian doll, the racial/ethnic subdivisions fit into wider categories: for example, the subcategories 'West Indian' and 'African' fit into the broad group 'Black', and the 'Asian' category subdivides into 'Pakistani', 'Bengali' and so on.

The British system therefore has room for the representatives of all the various racial groups, who use the census figures to demand a proportionate quota of public resources and civil service jobs. This encourages community fragmentation. Moreover, as different pressure groups protest against under-representation of 'their' ethnic group, or demand further subdivision of categories, new boundaries are drawn up and the fragmentation continues. Most of the Islamic associations which have pronounced judgement on the statistical definition of minorities have contested the validity of racial/ethnic criteria and have demanded the inclusion in the census of religious affiliation.

For different reasons, Enoch Powell and the various 'minority' leaders arrived at the same conclusion: the 'majority community' and the 'minority communities' did not share a common national identity. As Harry Goulbourne has remarked, 'Enoch Powell's view of the problem from the perspective of a white Briton was clearly expressed when he argued that a person of either West Indian or Asian background cannot become an English person', whilst on the other hand 'the strong emphasis being placed on ethnic differences amongst minorities would suggest that for them too it is not simply a question of being accepted as English, or even as British.'[11] Goulbourne argues that community links are continually strengthening in 1990s Britain, thanks to the politics of 'difference' which makes it difficult to pursue integrative policies, favouring instead the 'communal option'.[12]

The workers' mosques

As the first Indian and Pakistani populations of Muslim origin settled in Britain, the mutually reinforcing influence of the cultural heritage of empire and the political structure of the host country strengthened the pull of communalism. For almost a century, Islam had learnt to live with minority status and exclusion from political power on the Indian subcontinent; postwar British society made room for parallel national identities. This explains why a network of mosques was built as early as the 1950s, whereas in France it was not until the late 1970s that places of worship and Islamic associations flourished. In France, the demand for an Islamic identity was put forward at a time when North African immigrant workers, many of whom had been living in France since the 1950s and 1960s, began to feel the effects of mass unemployment, just as the policy of 'family settlement' was allowing them to bring their wives and children to join them. Their 'precarious settlement' eroded the transitory identities which they had developed until then: they lost their 'immigrant' identity the longer they stayed, they lost their 'worker' status as jobs became scarcer and they grew increasingly distant from the North African homelands, but did not yet feel French. This uncertain situation prompted some of them at that time to develop an Islamic identity in France, in a political context of secularity and cultural assimilation which was not conducive to the social expression of religious identity.[13]

In Britain, on the other hand, the expression of Islamic identity was already present in social and political life before the effects of the economic crisis of the 1970s took hold.[14] Mosques had been founded in some Welsh ports in the 1930s, with the support of the colonial authorities, by Yemeni sailors who had settled there after their posting during the First World War.[15] With the arrival of Muslims from the subcontinent in the postwar period, the first network of mosques was established in most of Britain's industrial cities. By 1975, there were a hundred or so 'registered' mosques in Britain,[16] whereas France, with more than double the number of Muslims, had nowhere near the same number of mosques.

In Birmingham, whose Muslim population, concentrated in a few inner-city areas, was estimated at 80,000 in 1985 (8 per cent of the total population), 40 per cent of the fifty-five mosques registered in 1985 were founded before 1970. The oldest mosque dates back to 1947.[17] In Coventry, the first mosque was built in the late 1950s, when the city housed barely four to five thousand Muslims from the subcontinent, mainly single men.[18] In Preston in Lancashire, as early as 1960, the local Islamic association hired a dance-hall to carry out Friday worship. In 1962, a small house was used as a permanent place of worship, and in 1967 a renovated former presbytery became the first official mosque, with room for 500 worshippers.[19] In Manchester, the local Muslim association bought a house in 1954 which was converted into a mosque.[20] In Keighley, West Yorkshire, a house was similarly converted into a mosque in 1965.

Between the immediate postwar years and the early 1970s, the same process can be seen all over Britain: first, single prayer-rooms were set up to serve the whole Muslim population, then, as this population grew, unity gave way to a series of smaller, rival mosques. The mosques' founders represented the different currents of Islamic identity which had grown up under the British Raj, and also the regional and linguistic groupings of their followers. The two main movements supplying imams, associations and places of worship were the Barelvis and the Deobandis, although neither possessed a truly unified organizational structure.

In Birmingham, where immigrants of Muslim origin constituted a large part of the low-skilled industrial workforce, the rapid growth of mosques in the 1950s and 1960s had three causes. First, the concentration of immigrants in a few rundown blocks of houses in each inner-city area made it more convenient for Muslims to go to pray within that area rather than the neighbouring district. Second, before gathering as Muslims, people wanted to meet up with others from their own ethnic group and from their own region, who spoke their own language or dialect. Thus, a Punjabi mosque, a Mirpuri mosque and a Pathan mosque (all Pakistani) appeared; Bengali, Gujerati and Yemeni mosques were created.[21] Third, the diverse interpretations to which Islam is open is another cause of fragmentation. Each Barelvi *pir* founded his own mosque, as did each Deobandi group, to which the more recent movements must be added: the followers of the Tabligh, Mawdudi's disciples, various Saudi-inspired groups (the most important of which is the Ahl-e Hadith association, whose UK headquarters is in Birmingham, in a disused Victorian swimming-bath) and the non-Sunni Muslim groups (Shiites, Ismaili and others).[22]

Faced with these divisions, a committee was set up in 1965 to obtain a purpose-built central mosque in Birmingham in accordance with the rules of Islamic architecture, rather than the makeshift mosques housed in garages or residential buildings. The committee included several English-speaking professionals (a doctor, a dentist, a lawyer, a university lecturer) at a time when the members of the Muslim elite did not devote their energies to Islam, which was seen as a working-class concern. These professionals felt themselves to be better equipped to lead and unite the community than the various local associations representing sects, denominations and ethnic groups, whose leaders were largely unfamiliar with British cultural codes. The plans for the mosque did not receive universal support, especially among the leaders of these associations, but funds were collected among local Muslims and rich donors in the Middle East.

In 1969, the foundations were laid on a plot of land not far from the city centre, on a major road adjoining busy shopping centres (Belgrave Road in Balsall Heath). But construction then came to a halt, reflecting the difficulties the project met even within the Muslim community. The plan to unite the city's Muslims came at a time when the balance of forces within the community was still unstable. Construction was not resumed until 1971, and carried on slowly. The inauguration of the mosque took place in 1975. However, competition between the various Islamic groups continued, each wanting to supply the imam who would lead prayers and recite the ritual lesson with which evenings begin during Ramadan.

The mosque committee decided that there would be three imams, each working ten days in turn. They drew lots to decide the order of office, but the Barelvi imam who went first performed his job so well in the eyes of his followers that they refused to allow his Deobandi colleague to replace him after the tenth day. The dispute escalated; blows were exchanged, and then both sets of followers resorted to knives, before the police intervened to separate them and close the mosque. It did not reopen until after the end of Ramadan.[23] Thus the first attempt to unite the community on a city-wide basis did not succeed in transcending the power conflicts between the different Islamic factions. The Birmingham case was not an isolated one. In 1991, an Islamic activist, looking back on the proliferation of mosques across Britain, strongly criticized the entrenched sectarianism and vested interests which had marked their creation and which he saw as detrimental to Islam as a whole: 'The building of so many mosques in Britain does not reflect the fact that Islam is on the increase in Britain ... The mosque has become an instrument of sectarianism. This sectarianism is vented against other Muslim sects ... It also offers a platform for those aspiring to become leaders rather than to be of service to Islam.'[24]

It was in Bradford that this fragmentation was overcome for the first time, after a period of in-fighting similar to that seen in other cities. In the postwar years the Yorkshire city, capital of the British textile industry until the 1970s, had attracted a low-cost immigrant workforce to its local industries, where working and living conditions had not moved far beyond those of the nineteenth century. The first mosque appeared in 1959 in a house in a rundown working-class area in the inner city (Howard Street).[25] Prior to this, an informal prayer-room, established in 1955 by a Pakistani textile worker who set himself up as imam and who founded the Muslim Association of Bradford in 1957, had served as the main religious centre. In the 1960s, when unemployment was unknown and Muslim workers worked at least five days a week, the mosque was mainly used on Sunday afternoons: it functioned as a cultural centre, where the two sole English-speakers acted as translators for their fellow countrymen and addressed envelopes for them to send letters home to their wives and children.

Cinemas, dance-halls, pubs and the other distractions of British or Irish working-class life meant nothing to the Muslim immigrants;

prayer gatherings or discussions about Pakistan occupied most of their free time. A small grocery shop cum café set up business nearby, selling halal meat (from animals ritually killed on a local farm) which was kept in cold water in the cellar. Hygiene was poor, but nothing could have induced those who gathered in the mosque in the late 1950s and early 1960s to eat meat bought from a non-Muslim butcher.[26] This rigorous and exclusive insistence on halal meat is characteristic of practising Indian and Pakistani populations, both on the subcontinent and in the country of immigration. Strict observance of dietary requirements constitutes a key element marking the boundary between the community and others, for Muslims of the subcontinent as for Hindus. In Britain, the campaign for halal food in public catering (in particular in school canteens) was later to become one of the major issues on which the assertion of community identity entered the public arena.

In the early 1960s, this community identity remained fragmented and inward-looking. The expansion of the Muslim population gave rise to the proliferation of little 'ghettos', encouraged by the xenophobic reactions of landlords who refused to rent to 'Pakis'. In order to find accommodation, workers from the subcontinent had no choice but to club together to buy cheap, shabby houses in rundown working-class areas. Since at that time none of them owned a car, and the surrounding English society seemed a closed world to them, they recreated little villages, each with its own prayer-room. 'We were afraid to go out of our neighbourhood, to cross the street, to be attacked', remembers one worker who arrived in 1961, whose friends 'just wanted to remain with themselves.' If they did not go to the Howard Street mosque, it was because it was too far away, and because in order to get there to pray they would have had to venture out at night after a day at the factory, into the dark cold streets of a town they felt to be hostile. But as well as the reasons of proximity cited first of all, 'there were differences between us: they didn't want us to have *durud* and *salaam* after prayer': the Barelvis chanted these invocations to the Prophet, whereas the Deobandis held them to be an unacceptable form of idolatry.[27]

In the 1960s, five mosques appeared in Bradford. As in Birmingham, the growth of mosques reflected the local origins of the worshippers and the concentration of migrants from specific regions in blocks of houses, often far removed from other areas, but also disputes between different Islamic movements.[28] It was in the Barelvi population that the Jama'at-i Tabligh ul-Islam (Association for the Propagation of Islam) was created in 1963. Its members originated from the Mirpur district in Kashmir. Its founder is the *pir* Sayed

Mahroof Hussein Shah Arif Naushahi, descended from a prestigious lineage in the religious brotherhood (evident in his name) but known simply as 'Pir Mahroof'. He comes from a family of mystics and *ulema* which claims to go back to the Prophet Muhammad. But as the youngest son in his family he landed in England in 1961 as a humble worker to try his luck on the job market, like thousands of his compatriots. After six fruitless weeks in Birmingham, he arrived in Bradford with a cousin of his, and through family connections found a job in a factory, where he worked for twenty-five years. Thanks to his extraordinary determination and charisma, he was able to get together enough capital in 1962 to move into a house in Southfield Square, in order to organize prayers in accordance with Barelvi teaching. Half of the price was paid in cash, and the rest in monthly instalments but 'without contravening the Islamic prohibition of interest loans'. He called on people from 'back home' to pool their resources so as to buy another house in the same street, which was converted into a mosque.

Southfield Square, a nineteenth-century working-class district, has gradually been taken over by Pir Mahroof and his disciples over the years. It is a cul-de-sac, with two-storey houses arranged in a horse-shoe-shape around abandoned workers' gardens. Where English or Irish working-class wives used to tend lettuces and potatoes at the beginning of the century, there is now nothing but untended land where various kinds of underground activities – drugs and prostitution – take place under the cover of darkness (the square opens out onto Lumb Lane, Bradford's notorious red-light area). The entanglement of the recreated Barelvi village and the seedier aspects of post-modern society – of mosques, streetwalkers, junkies and illegal gambling dens – heightens the clash of cultures to which the re-Islamization activists point in order to stigmatize corrupt Western society and extol the virtues of Islam, a moral citadel under siege.[29]

Throughout the years, the Islamic association set up by Pir Mahroof has established thirteen mosques in Bradford, and several others in towns where immigrants from Mahroof's own region of Pakistan have settled. The movement he founded in 1973 in order to propagate a Barelvi view of Islam, the World Islamic Mission, has carried out proselytizing missions in Sheffield, Coventry and even in Amsterdam and the Paris textile quarter of Le Sentier.[30] This Barelvi Islam is based on a very strict definition of Muslim identity which rejects any adulteration of doctrine by Western societies, but also combats rival Islamic currents, whether inspired by Saudi Wahhabism, Mawdudi's political Islamism or the Deobandi movement.[31]

In religious zeal the Deobandis are not to be outdone. One of their main representatives, Sher Azam, arrived in Bradford in 1960, having interrupted his studies to emigrate, and began work in a textile factory. He attended the Howard Street mosque, and as he had learned English at night school became one of the first to be able to deal with the local authorities and to communicate various demands specific to the Muslim community. He soon became a key intermediary between the Muslim community and the local authorities, both as a religious and a business leader. He later became one of the leading figures on the Council of Mosques, which he chaired during the Rushdie affair in 1988–9. In early 1988, his standing as a community leader was reflected in the award of an MBE (Member of the Order of the British Empire). His business activities culminated in the establishment of a supermarket aimed specifically at a Muslim clientele, Al Halal Supermarket.

This large supermarket, whose assistants and cashiers wear a uniform with a veil, was set up as an Islamic cooperative in 1985. According to Sher Azam, it fulfils three objectives. First, its capital is made up of shares financed by redundancy payments of its Muslim members, and therefore constitutes an Islamic way of putting these sums to good use, since Islam prohibits them from investing them in credit loans, which are associated with usury (*riba'*), and therefore their savings would simply 'evaporate' in a bank account. Second, the business (which employed around forty people in 1993) provides jobs for the youth of the community who would otherwise be threatened with unemployment. Third, it is a shop where Muslims 'can buy with confidence, knowing it is halal', unlike the other local supermarkets.[32]

Communalism is expressed here in market segmentation: halal meat provides the opportunity for a community to function more or less autarkically by investing its capital in companies 'in an Islamic way', thereby creating 'Islamic' jobs for veiled check-out assistants and at the same time eating 'Islamic' food. The enactment of religious taboos and the organization of communal networks around the first mosques thus allowed the immigrant Muslim communities to set in train a process of identity differentiation affecting all aspects of daily life. The campaign for strict observance of halal procedures in the provision of school meals for Muslim children later served as a lowest common denominator uniting the different currents of Islam in Bradford. Their leaders could therefore move from a situation of defensive communalism and fragmentation (characterized by the mosque-building programme) to demands for a publicly recognized separate identity. This process began in the 1970s as a result of mass education of immigrant children, and turned into a battle in which community leaders succeeded in many cases in imposing their views at the local level. The Rushdie affair later shifted the battle for Islamic identity into the national arena.

The fight for Islamic education: the first rounds

Once again, a Franco-British comparison helps to illuminate the distinctive features of the British system. In France, the Republican model of education sees the school as the melting-pot of national identity in which cultural differences between children are subsumed in shared membership of the secular nation. The educational system is meant to mould citizens with equal rights and a shared set of values. Religion is kept completely separate and outside the public sphere. The British educational system, on the other hand, obeys a different logic, based on the dissociation of citizenship and nationality.

State schooling is not 'secular' in the French sense of the term. The curriculum includes religious education, as befits a state with an established religion, whose head of state is also head of the Church of England. The 1944 Education Act (passed at a time when Muslim immigration to Britain was negligible) required that the school day should start with an 'assembly' using Old and New Testament readings, thus making Christianity one of the basic elements of civic education and perpetuating a Christian identity in the public sphere. Parallel to the state education system there are also voluntary-aided schools, semi-private religious schools belonging to the Church of England, the Catholic Church or to Jewish associations, which have entered into a contract with the state under which the state finances most of the running costs and lays down certain conditions. The independent schools, including the famous public schools, are financed privately.

When the first children from Muslim families arrived in the British educational system in the late 1960s, workers' mosques and local Islamic associations found themselves facing a sizeable cultural challenge: what would be the consequences of the socialization of these children within an 'open society' where they would meet children of their own age from different cultural backgrounds, whilst their families remained within the immigrant community, recreating values and attitudes inherited from the internal hegira of the Raj? Was there not a risk that the Islamic identity would be adulterated and eroded through contact with the dominant non-Muslim society (this time British rather than Hindu)?

As early as 1966, the British state attempted to answer these concerns. Roy Jenkins, then home secretary in the Labour government, declared that there was no question of assimilating the immigrants and that the United Kingdom was a pluralistic society which could only be enriched by cultural diversity. In Section 11 of the Budget, money was granted to local authorities to finance all aspects of multicultural development, particularly the teaching of native languages and activities designed to foster immigrant traditions and customs. The multiculturalist viewpoint was then considered left-wing and progressive, in opposition to the attitude of the conservative right whose perceived racism included disrespect for the 'inferior' culture of immigrants. However, in a longer-term perspective, the glorification of multicultural society in many ways resembled the communalism of empire, however progressive the intentions of the Labour leaders at the time (and indeed Roy Jenkins was later, at the height of the Rushdie affair, publicly to regret his earlier policy). Multiculturalism encouraged the rise of community leaders who acted as intermediaries between their religious or racial kin and the state and strengthened the sense of 'otherness' felt by these communities in their dealings with the outside world.

It was no coincidence that 1966 also saw the birth of the Muslim Educational Trust. The Trust, arising from Mawdudi's movement, is led by a Bengali university lecturer in business studies, who devotes his energies to the propagation of Islam throughout the world. Its many publications define the content and form of education designed to perpetuate a specific Islamic cultural identity and to prevent the assimilation of Muslim children into British society.[33] The Trust represents a unified standpoint, which formed the basis for the various Islamic associations in their early negotiations with the British educational authorities.

This standpoint may be summarized as follows. The Trust sees it as vital at the outset to 'safeguard and defend the distinct Muslim identity of Muslim children' exposed to Western 'permissive society' marked notably by the 'flood of obscene publications'. According to this view, Muslim children are torn between two worlds: the home, where in theory at least they live in accordance with the rules of Islam, and school, where they are in contact with 'materialistic Western society, broken homes, sexual promiscuity, alcoholism and relaxation of morals'. The teaching of Islam in the United Kingdom, which could be expected to keep the distinct identity of Muslim children out of the reach of permissive, materialistic Western society, is in fact inadequate. In the mosques where children are sent in the evening and at weekends, imams try their best, but they struggle to meet the children's needs, since they themselves speak little or no English and are often strongly influenced by the cultural environment of the subcontinent and therefore unable to understand the children's experience of British culture. In state schools, Christianity permeates the curriculum, especially in history and English. Moreover, many British schools are co-educational, whereas 'Allah did not make man and woman identical, and consequently Islam requires girls and boys to be educated separately.' Muslim parents should therefore, according to the Trust, put pressure on the authorities to maintain as many separate girls' schools as possible. School uniform requirements should allow Muslim girls to wear Islamic dress (trousers, tunic and veil) in the school colours. School meals should not only allow Muslim children not to eat pork, but should include halal meat from animals killed according to Islamic ritual. Finally, schools should provide a prayer-room to allow their Muslim pupils to make their obligatory daily prayers at midday and in the afternoon (*Zuhr* and *'Asr*), and on Fridays children should be allowed to stay away from school in order to attend the main prayer congregation, except where an imam can lead prayers in the school.[34]

The Muslim Educational Trust puts forward two types of demands here: first, demands for specific arrangements to allow Muslim children to observe Islam rigorously, by excepting them from several general rules; second, demands for a revision of the content of the curriculum itself, since this is seen as steeped in permissiveness and Christianity. Where Islamic associations have been most successful in obtaining their demands, they have had to organize themselves to lobby local authorities. Issues associated with Islamic education, starting with campaigns for halal food in the first instance, have thus become a major axis for the development of community identity. A later stage of the communal identity-building process has involved linking these demands to the entry of 'Muslim minority representatives' into politics at local level. In many cases, these representatives emerged from the mosque networks and went on to play an important role as power-brokers, bringing the votes of their electorate to a given party in exchange for support for demands which reinforced Islamic cultural specificity.

Communalism and electoralism

Communal demands found conditions in Britain particularly propitious because of the decentralized nature of the educational system (at least until the reforms undertaken by Margaret Thatcher's government in the late 1980s) and the way in which the Muslim populations were able to influence political parties at local level.

Local education authorities (LEAs) are responsible for the education budget, the choice of teaching materials and the organization of studies, and the recruitment of teachers. To a large extent they depend on local councils. In turn, the political parties seeking to win control of local councils speculated on the mass vote of Muslim communities in cities with large immigrant populations, especially as the Muslim communities appeared susceptible to the instructions of leaders within the mosque network. Muslim leaders addressed a population which had problems communicating in English, and were therefore able to gain recognition as intermediaries and to filter the basic elements of the British political debate into issues which would help them to boost their own role.

Within the Muslim populations, the traditional image of the Conservative Party was that of an 'anti-immigrant' party responding to the concerns of a white working-class and lower middle-class electorate, as illustrated in the violent outbursts of Enoch Powell. As a result, 'minority' voters generally tended to vote for the Labour Party throughout the 1980s.[35] Labour needed the 'minority' vote to compensate for the erosion of its traditional working-class electorate. In Birmingham and Bradford, the 'ethnic minority' vote essentially meant the Muslim electorate, although in other cities it could be Hindu, Sikh or West Indian. Figures from the 1991 census (the first to register data on race) indicated that 6.9 per cent of Birmingham's population declared themselves Pakistanis and 1.3 per cent Bengalis, out of a total proportion of 21.5 per cent of 'non-whites', which also included an undefined number of Muslims among the 5.3 per cent of Indians. In seven of the inner-city wards, Pakistanis and Bengalis made up between 23 per cent and 43 per cent of the population.

Until 1984, Birmingham city council was led by the Conservative Party. Labour took over in 1984 having received strong support in its campaign from the 'ethnic minorities', as a result of its manifesto promises to them. The new council set up a Race Relations and Equal Opportunities Unit with the task of establishing contact with the various 'black' associations (the term 'black', used in anti-racist discourse to denote any person who suffers discrimination on grounds of ethnicity, race, religion or colour, includes Eastern and Southern Europeans as well as West Indians, Africans, Indians and Pakistanis). The aim was to compile a list of these associations' demands and to promote positive discrimination measures in favour of the minorities. In particular, the council set a target quota of 20 per cent of Blacks for its own job recruitment.[36]

The 1985 Handsworth riots, which saw ugly confrontations between young West Indians and Asian shopkeepers, dented the idea of unity of interests within a single 'black' community. But it made the council all the more anxious to find intermediaries among the 'minority' populations whose precarious social conditions threatened to disrupt civil peace. In the case of the Muslim populations, the local authorities turned in particular to the network of mosques.

Thus, in Dudley in the West Midlands, the Muslim association, belonging to the Barelvi movement, had in 1977 bought a former Church of England school, thanks to support from a Kuwaiti benefactor. The building was converted into a mosque and community centre, satisfying all the needs of the local Muslim population and thus uniting it from the cradle to the grave: from an Islamic crèche to an Islamic morgue. The mosque itself is financed by donations from the congregation, as is religious instruction for children, apart from the minibus which takes them to and from the classes, which along with the driver's salary is paid for by public funds. The charitable activities of the community centre are financed out of the public purse (to the tune of 75 per cent) and by Dudley council. One of the centre's employees (who also happens to be a local councillor) works as a legal adviser, acting as a mouthpiece for the community in all matters related to the law, such as immigration law. Another employee acts as educational adviser to local schools, explaining the Islamic rules which the pupils, particularly the girls, must obey. Their command of English as well as the language of the pupils' parents, who often speak very little English, gives them a vital role as intermediaries. In 1993, the head of Birmingham city council's Race Relations Unit had formerly been secretary of the committee of the Dudley mosque, thus providing the network of Islamic community associations with a direct line into the council offices responsible for the 'minority' populations.

On a new road complex in the Golden Hillock area of Sparkhill (in the constituency of former Labour deputy leader Roy Hattersley), overlooking the main road leading to Birmingham airport, the dome of a spectacular mosque rises up above a complex of buildings housing various social and cultural activities. The mosque is controlled by a Barelvi *pir*, Sufi Abdallah, a charismatic figure with an impressive physical presence. Sufi Abdallah began to build his mosque complex in the early 1980s to counteract the hegemonic tendencies of the 'central' mosque in Belgrave Road. In the buildings surrounding the mosque, he set up sewing workshops and training centres, heavily subsidized by the city council, which attract young people, women and unemployed workers from the immediate vicinity of the mosque. These social services correspond to a local need, filling as they do a gap in state service provision. The mosque centre also includes a 'job club', replacing the services of the local job centre. When the author visited the mosque, it was being swept by a Muslim prisoner on day release, who had been allowed out by the prison authorities to carry out odd jobs for the Islamic association.

The local parliamentary representative Roy Hattersley has put forward this type of initiative, which uses a mixture of public finance and private community management, as the best solution for individuals still heavily influenced by their traditional culture to acquire skills and knowledge and to gain access to support and services they would not be able to get from the usual British institutions. He cites the case of a rundown health centre in his constituency which he wanted to close, so that his constituents would seek health care in the big modern hospitals in the city centre. He had to rethink his plans, because, despite the low quality of its facilities, the local health centre at least employed Muslim nurses and doctors who spoke the same language as the local people and knew their customs, notably rules relating to sexual propriety. Similarly, proposals to rehouse Muslims in better-quality accommodation in other districts with a majority of non-Muslim residents have often failed because immigrant families prefer to remain together; in the community ghetto, however poor the housing, women (who in most cases do not speak English) can leave the house, go shopping and visit each other. However, Hattersley notes that behaviour will change, since younger generations all speak English.

Nevertheless, the close relationship between mosques and social services has encouraged the emergence of a certain type of leader who has an interest in perpetuating the community boundary, since it makes them indispensable as intermediaries. Moreover, the official policy of multiculturalism actively promotes cultural specificity. In the realm of party politics, too, communalism exerts a strong influence. In Roy Hattersley's constituency, 600 of the 800 local Labour Party activists are 'Muslim', in a population that is only 40 per cent Muslim (Pakistanis and Bengalis), according to the 1991 census.

This disproportionately high rate of activism within the Labour Party is, according to Mr Hattersley, 'non-ideological': most of the Muslim activists in his local party could not define the programme of the Labour Party or what it represents. They have joined the party en masse because they see that it defends their specific interests as regards housing, employment, or immigration policy. As for the Muslim local councillors in Sparkbrook, they are elected not on the basis of policies or party affiliation but on the basis of networks of support their family used to enjoy in the district of Mirpur in Pakistan. The old networks have been transposed onto the structures of a Labour Party which has gradually lost its white working-class support and therefore welcomed the new blood with its command over the mass immigrant vote. But according to Hattersley, the local MP is not necessarily the prisoner of a community bloc vote, since the interests of imams, mosque leaders and association officials diverge too widely to form a unified lobby.[37]

In the neighbouring constituency of Small Heath, which has a similar ethnic mix, the local Labour Party selected a Muslim councillor, the treasurer of the Belgrave Road mosque, as its parliamentary candidate for the 1987 elections. Small Heath was a safe Labour seat. But the party's statutes at that time gave trade unions a say in the selection of candidates, and the local trade union delegates decided to choose a white candidate instead. The white Labour candidate was elected, defeating his Muslim Conservative rival. Anxious to win the support of the local Muslim population, the new MP brought in from outside then set up his office on the ground floor of a Bengali mosque run by disciples of Mawdudi, who were known to be on bad terms with the Belgrave Road mosque.

The close links between politics and religion are evident in the sign announcing the 'political office' of the local MP on the front of the Bengali mosque on Coventry Road, one of Birmingham's main thoroughfares. They are all the more striking because the MP belongs to the Labour Party, and the mosque is the headquarters of the Bengali branch of Jama'at-i Islami (Dawat ul-Islam, founded in 1976), an Islamist movement which has always abhorred any form of socialism. The 'non-ideological' nature of Muslim support for the Labour Party, which Roy Hattersley observed in his own local party, is apparent in this seemingly contradictory situation. It sums up perfectly the interrelationship between religious communalism and electoral clientelism which comes into play when parliamentary candidates need to seek the support of one mosque against the candidate of another mosque.

For most Islamic community leaders, access to the political sphere was not an end in itself but simply a means to reinforce positions of power and influence over the maximum number of their fellow believers, at least until the Rushdie affair broke out in late 1988. One of the most important issues in this respect has been education. Community leaders needed to control education in order to perpetuate Islamic communal identity across the generations and prevent this identity from dissolving into dominant Western culture, because a breakdown in the generational reproduction of Islamic culture would have threatened their ability to mediate and thus the very basis of their power within British society. During the 1987 general election campaign, a leaflet entitled 'The Muslim Vote' was distributed in Britain, particularly in Birmingham.[38] The leaflet, printed in English, Urdu, Gujerati and Bengali, asked Muslims to vote only for candidates who agreed that UK Muslims should be governed by Islamic behavioural codes and who supported the educational demands expressed by the Muslim Educational Trust.

This explicit linkage of educational demands and the Muslim vote goes to the heart of the civic function of education. In a non-secular schools system, is the only solution the total or partial separation of pupils from different religious backgrounds? In Bradford, the educational issue led to the creation of the most effective Islamic pressure group in England, the Council of Mosques. The setting-up of the Council of Mosques marked an important stage in the communal organization of Islam in Britain, and was to play a major role in the Rushdie affair.

The Bradford Council of Mosques

In 1991, one in nine Bradford residents was Muslim; 9.5 per cent of the Bradford electorate came from the Indian subcontinent.[39] The Muslim population is concentrated in the inner-city districts. In 1992, eleven Muslim city councillors were elected, all belonging to the Labour Party. One of them, Mohammed Ajeeb, had been elected the first 'coloured' Lord Mayor in Britain in 1985. The new city councillors were aware that their voters attached the utmost importance to educational matters. Back in 1973, an 'independent Muslim' candidate had campaigned for the maintenance of girls' schools, and had won so much support in an 'ethnic' area of the city that the Labour candidate who was expected to win the seat lost out to his Conservative rival.[40]

The Council of Mosques was set up in September 1981 to give the 'Muslim community' a voice and to achieve demands aimed at preserving its distinct identity, as defined by the Islamic associations and the local mosques. The Council was composed of representatives mandated by each of the associations and mosques, so as to transcend divisions between Barelvis, Deobandis and others by putting forward Islamic demands which would be acceptable to all groups. In its negotiations with the local authorities the Council was recognized as a representative interlocutor. As such it received a sizeable subsidy and the council gave it responsibility for the running of social services aimed specifically at the Muslim populations, employing a total of fifty people (a rest home for the elderly, employment services, advisory centres in mosques and Islamic associations and so on).[41] As in Birmingham, the local authorities thus delegated social services targeting a specific population, identified as a community, to a religious organization.

In return for acting as an intermediary, the Council of Mosques was able to transmit its own ideas about the education imparted to Muslim children in Bradford's schools. In 1982, the Metropolitan Council for Education laid down instructions for pupils from ethnic minority communities. These instructions gave legal force to the Islamic associations' demands for the recognition of Muslim children's specific needs: schools attended by Muslim children would have to set up a prayer-room approved by the Council of Mosques, where an imam could come to say Friday prayers. Parents would have the right to keep girls over ten years old away from any mixed school activities which in their view contravened Islamic laws (physical education, dance, drama, swimming). Children could wear Islamic dress as long as it was in school colours. Lastly, the local authorities promised to examine the possibility of providing halal meals for Muslim children.[42]

The question of halal meat was to provide the Council of Mosques with the opportunity to make its first public show of strength. In January 1983, an 'Association of Muslim Parents' – a separate organization which was more radical than the Council – had demanded that five state schools in Bradford with a majority of Muslim pupils should become Muslim schools with 'voluntary-aided' status. Under this agreement the Association would control the curriculum and the organization of teaching. The local authorities, keen to keep the five schools under public control but worried by the support given to the Association among the Muslim population, hurriedly conceded some of the Council of Mosques' demands. At the beginning of the next school year, school meals were already including halal meat on the menu. This provoked a campaign by animal rights activists who described the Muslim ritual slaughter of animals as cruel. They were supported by various figures who, it was claimed by anti-racist campaigners, had suddenly developed a love for animals only as a disguised means of spreading their message of race hatred.

The question of halal meat was thus blown up into a major local issue, and in March 1984 it was debated at a plenary meeting of the city council. The Council of Mosques marked the occasion by organizing a school boycott by Bradford's Muslim pupils. Ten thousand schoolchildren failed to attend classes that day, and many took part with their parents in a demonstration in front of the town hall during the debate. The demonstration served to amplify the warning given by one Muslim councillor during the discussions, that if the council 'went back on its decision [to provide halal meat in schools] it would be regarded as unworthy and biased by the Muslim community'. The outcome was a majority vote in favour of halal meat.[43]

The battle over education

The Council of Mosques did not have time to savour its triumph over halal meat before it became embroiled in another controversy, this time spilling out beyond local politics. The protagonist was a Bradford headteacher, Ray Honeyford.[44] More than 90 per cent of the pupils in Honeyford's school were of Indian or Pakistani origin, mostly Muslims.

Ray Honeyford himself came from a poor background. He had to leave school to work, and became a teacher, then headmaster, by studying at evening classes. In 1982, this 'self-made man' found himself under orders to implement local authority recommendations laid down in the 'Education for a multi-cultural society' document. He was totally opposed to the measures proposed by the LEA. In his view, all children should receive the same education; cultural relativism could only set back their chances of successful social integration. He was not prepared to compromise either on Christian religious instruction or on school meals, since halal slaughter seemed cruel and therefore contrary to the values education was meant to promote. Honeyford therefore refused to apply the LEA recommendations in his school, and outlined his beliefs in several newspaper articles, as well as in the *Salisbury Review*, a publication associated with right-wing Conservative think-tanks.

In March 1984, the local newspaper the *Yorkshire Post* published extracts from one of these articles, 'Education and Race: an Alternative View'.[45] In the article, Honeyford protested against Muslim parents' habit of taking their children out of school for several months at a time, in order to travel to Pakistan to visit relatives. This practice was tolerated in the name of 'multicultural education' which was then fashionable in Bradford, but according to Honeyford it had disastrous consequences on pupils' educational attainment. Moreover, visits to Pakistan could only harm the children since it was 'obstinately backward', corrupt, and the 'heroin capital of the world', 'ruled over by a military tyrant who, in the opinion of at least half his countrymen, had his predecessor judicially murdered'. How could parents prefer to keep their children out of school and subject them to the influence of such a place? Honeyford asked.

The publication of these ideas in the local press sparked a heated debate. The immediate consequence was the formation of an 'anti-racist front' bringing together leaders of the Council of Mosques and various far-left groups, who called for Honeyford's dismissal by the LEA. They organized a petition which was signed by half of the parents of Honeyford's pupils, kept their children away from the school and set up a 'pirate' school in the nearby Pakistani cultural centre, having first summoned the television cameras to record the event. On the opposing side, a Honeyford support committee was formed, and organized its own petition which collected 10,000 signatures, mainly from white local residents. Margaret Thatcher later gave her support to the embattled headmaster, by inviting him to Downing Street to take part in a meeting of educational experts.

The Honeyford affair split the nation down the middle, with Conservative opinion and the government (whose own powers of intervention in education remained limited since this was a matter for LEAs) taking Honeyford's side. In opposition, the Council of Mosques mobilized the faithful, organizing demonstrations and a school boycott, but found its campaign being taken over by more radical groups: Islamist figures who were later to be seen at the side of Colonel Gaddafi, or leftist campaigners who set the tone for the 'anti-racist' struggle. After various legal actions, Ray Honeyford eventually agreed to take early retirement in December 1985, at the age of fifty-one. He received a 'golden handshake' of £161,000, the largest ever awarded in British education.

The Honeyford affair pushed to their limit the contradictions of the British multicultural model, in the most sensitive area of education, the interface between family and civil society. Is school the melting-pot where inherited family identities merge into a homogeneous whole, or should it preserve cultural heterogeneity? The 'laisser-faire' logic of community heterogeneity was at that time seen by part of the Conservative establishment as threatening and pernicious, since in many of Bradford's schools 'native' English children had become the minority. The attitude of the Conservative administration was profoundly ambiguous. On one hand, it seemed to be looking for factors of homogenization in the school system, as seen in the 1985 report presented to the government by a committee headed by Lord Swann, which redefined multiculturalism as genuine pluralism and social integration: 'diversity within unity'.[46] But the 1988 Education Reform Act stressed the Christian character of education, whilst allowing non-Christians to opt out of some obligations.

The Swann report, motivated by the persistently poorer performance of children from the ethnic 'minorities', identified racism and discriminatory practices as one of the causes. In order to solve the problem, the report advocated the development of minority cultures as long as they did not clash with the 'current laws of the country' and 'commonly accepted values, practices and procedures'.[47] But the emphasis placed in the report on educational pluralism aroused the wrath of the Islamic education lobby. A seminar organized under the aegis of a Saudi diplomat, the statutory leader of the London Islamic Cultural Centre, served as a forum for the grievances which were expressed in the name of the 'Muslim community'. The published report of the seminar proceedings makes it clear that 'The Muslim community cannot accept the secular philosophical basis of the report, and thus commit itself to follow "all current laws", however anti-religious those laws may become through democratic means. The community thus reserves its right to withdraw its children from courses and practices in schools which it regards as anti-religious or anti-Islamic.' Fundamentally, 'The ultimate aim of Muslim education lies in the realization of total submission to God on the level of the individual, the community and humanity at large.'[48] Whereas the Swann report had declared that 'one of the major aims of education should . . . be to broaden the horizons of *all* pupils to a greater understanding of the diversity of value systems and lifestyles which are now present in our society',[49] the Islamic Academy interpreted this objective as an imposition of relativist values: 'by multicultural education the Swann Committee wants to impose on Muslim children what it considers of educational value – such as autonomy and a critical approach to their own faith and culture.'[50] Cultural relativism, which is welcomed when it allows

Muslim children to opt out of music, dance and drama lessons, cannot be applied to unconditional compliance with the laws and injunctions of Allah, as they are interpreted by community leaders.[51]

Whereas the Swann report was concerned with the educational attainment of ethnic minority children and sought to achieve a balance between pluralism and integration, the 1988 Education Act aimed to reform the whole education system and centralize it in line with the wishes of the Conservative government. It maintained and strengthened the place of religion in the curriculum. In particular, the 1988 Act stipulated that all schools should arrange a daily session of collective worship for all pupils and that the 'majority of these collective worship sessions should be exclusively or mainly Christian in character.'[52] The Christian identity of schooling in Britain is thus explicitly and forcefully asserted. However, parents wishing their children to be excused from these acts of daily worship may do so by applying in writing to the head of the school. In other words, they must identify themselves and their children as 'different' by deliberately exempting them from classes.

The Muslim Educational Trust sets out to encourage parents to take this step. In a 1989 booklet aimed at Muslim parents, the Trust advises that if they remain passive, their children 'would pray to Jesus as the "son of God", learn about the "Trinity", and thus commit the awesome sin of *shirk*, associating others with Allah. This is the worst thing a Muslim can do.'[53] Muslim parents should therefore take their children away from acts of Christian worship and insist on alternative acts of collective Muslim worship as well as Islamic religious instruction. Where Muslim pupils form the majority within the school, it is possible to obtain funding in the school budget for alternative Islamic instruction. Where they are in the minority, the parents must pay for the alternative teaching. The 1988 Act effectively places the onus on those who do not identify themselves as Christian to make a point of stating their cultural difference. By promoting Christianity to the status of cultural norm, the Act erodes education's ability to integrate pupils from different backgrounds. On the contrary, it encourages communalism by favouring community institutions which have the necessary resources to promote separate religious identities.

Throughout the years, the community institutions have produced a large number of publications in order to meet the demand for textbooks to be used in religious instruction classes and acts of collective worship. As well as the Muslim Educational Trust, several other associations have devoted their efforts to this particularly useful means of spreading their influence. Their first step has been to criticize most of the publications on Islam written by non-Muslims as hostile or ill-intentioned.[54] Instead they recommended alternative texts written by Muslims and therefore regarded as authentic. For example, *The Muslim Guide*, aimed at 'teachers, employers, community workers and social administrators in Britain', was produced by the Leicester Islamic Foundation, an offshoot of Mawdudi's Jama'at-i Islami. The *Guide*, with its glowing preface by the head of the Commission for Racial Equality, presents the Jama'at-i Islami's radical Islamist stance as the norm accepted by all Muslims. As well as the sacred texts, the book puts forward as 'recommended reading' the writings of Mawdudi and various authors closely associated with the Muslim Brotherhood, and omits any reference to publications which present an alternative view of Islam, even those written by Muslims. Barelvi Sufist writers are absent from the list of recommended texts, despite the importance of the Barelvi movement in Britain, as are Muslims who eschew a communalist or Islamist approach.[55] Similarly, in 1992 the same organization created an Islamic computer game (Personal Computer Islamic Quiz) 'in order to provide an Islamic alternative to the "Trivia" game mania which has been sweeping many countries for many years now. It has considerable educational value, as it highlights areas where one's knowledge may be weak, and provides a stimulus for learning.'[56] By investing in publishing and computing, the Islamic Foundation has made real inroads into the youth communications market and through its command of new technologies has been able to promote its own view of Islam.

At the same time as Islamists have been devoting efforts to 'Islamizing' education in state schools and capturing the publications market resulting from these campaigns, around twenty private Muslim schools have been formed. In Birmingham, for example, a secondary school with boarding facilities for Muslim boys, Darul Uloom, was opened in September 1985 in one of the buildings belonging to the Bengali mosque on Coventry Road, another branch of Mawdudi's Jama'at-i Islami. The head of the school, who also runs the mosque, has a doctorate in economics from the University of Glasgow. In 1990 the school had around seventy pupils on its books, and aimed to attract 300. The school's pupils, dressed in grey *qamis* (long, loose tunics) down to their knees and grey trousers, and wearing skullcaps on their head, start their day with prayers, then follow a programme of Islamic studies which combines language instruction (Arabic, Persian, Urdu, Bengali) with various subjects which form the background to study of the sacred texts, from memorization of the Koran to Islamic law. In the afternoon, they receive secular instruction: special attention is paid to English, mathematics, applied sciences and computing. When the author visited the school, one of the pupils was using desktop publishing techniques on his personal computer to put together the school magazine. History, however, is limited to the life of the Prophet and the 'beliefs and teachings of Islam'. 'Having all sorts of Islamic atmosphere', the school aims to 'prepare its pupils to be good Muslims and responsible citizens' as well as preparing them for their A-level examinations.[57]

However, a Department of Education and Science inspector's report found in 1990 that 'Standards of work are less than satisfactory. With some notable exceptions, teachers' expectations and pupils' achievements are low. Many lessons are insufficiently challenging and, in many subjects, pupils lack opportunities to achieve their potential ... Important subjects are omitted from the curriculum ... There is a lack of staff expertise in a number of subjects, including science, geography, art, and design and technology.' There are other basic criticisms of the facilities, hygiene and the overcrowded boarding rooms. Nevertheless, the report notes that the major positive feature of the school is 'the quality of [its] community life to which all pupils and staff contribute'.[58]

One of the various reasons which explain the problems encountered by Darul Uloom is the lack of public funding. In order to get round this problem, several Islamic associations have attempted to obtain voluntary-aided status for their schools.[59] Under these agreements, all of the school's operating costs (salaries and so on) and most infrastructure costs (repairs and maintenance) are publicly financed. In 1993, several thousand voluntary-aided schools were in operation, mainly Anglican and Catholic, with some Methodist and Jewish schools.

The flagship school of the Islamist associations is the Islamia School in London, whose chief promoter and benefactor is Yusuf Islam, formerly known as singer Cat Stevens. The school was founded in 1983 in the borough of Brent, over a third of whose population is originally West Indian or Indo-Pakistani. The primary section of the school is mixed, and the secondary section takes girls only. Girls wear the Islamic veil as part of their uniform from the age of seven. In secondary school, eight teachers instruct them in both secular (English, geography, mathematics, science and physical education) and Islamic subjects (Islamic studies, Arabic, Islamic art and history, memorization and commentary of the Koran).[60] As at Darul Uloom in Birmingham, only Islamic history is taught. A major difference here is that the languages of the Indian subcontinent do

not appear on the curriculum, as if to emphasize the school's intention to move beyond conceptions of Islam inherited from the country of origin and towards an ideal community entity, using Arabic as
the vehicle.

The Islamia School project had its problems getting off the
ground. In 1986, Brent borough council gave its support to the
school's application for voluntary-aided status. The Labour-
controlled council had been one of the first in Britain to set up a formal recruitment policy of 'positive discrimination' in favour of
'non-whites'. However, the school's application was turned down by
the Department of Education in 1990. But the High Court overturned this decision in 1992. In support of their cause, the school's
advocates were able to call on several right-wing pressure groups set
up to campaign for private religious education. These groups were
in favour of separate Muslim schools as a means of segregating
black and white pupils. Their campaign for a kind of educational
apartheid also overlapped with the Islamists' demands for separate
Muslim education in that, in the words of one of the pressure
groups' leaders who defined himself as a 'Christian fundamentalist',
'we are fighting a common enemy: secularism. And [the Muslims]
believe in a moral education.'[61]

Despite the sympathy shown in the right-wing press for the
Islamia project, and a visit to the school in the spring of 1993 by the
education secretary John Patten, voluntary-aided status was once
again refused in August of that year. The Department of Education
argued that a number of unfilled places remained in the borough's
existing state schools. The school's advocates were all the more disappointed because they felt that by allying their cause with right-
wing educational groups they had strengthened their application.[62]
A section of the Conservative establishment and its electorate were
strongly in support of the idea of separate Muslim education.
Undoubtedly, common concerns linked the two lobbies: a preoccupation with moral issues and the common struggle against secularism going back to the Enlightenment. On the part of the Islamists,
the alliance revealed the old logic of communalism which had given
the Muslims of the Indian empire a separate status from their Hindu
fellow citizens.

But the demand for separate status had a political cost in Britain
after the Rushdie affair, which profoundly affected the image of
Islam. Could the right-wing establishment really entrust the education of young Muslims to community leaders, some of whom had
fanned the flames of unrest over *The Satanic Verses*, and given
Ayatollah Khomeini the opportunity to pronounce his famous fatwa

on Rushdie, a British citizen? In order to look more closely at this uneasy relationship between Muslim community leaders and political power in Britain, the following section will examine the Rushdie affair in the light of Islamic communalism and the power struggles within it to gain control of the Muslim populations and their relations with the British state.

3

The Rushdie Affair

At the time of the publication of *The Satanic Verses*, in September 1988, Islam in the United Kingdom was at a turning point. Effective pressure groups had been set up to lobby councils in several key cities, and they had proved themselves capable of achieving their demands on 'Muslim education' and of managing a network of social services closely linked to the mosques. In addition, several city councillors and officials responsible for race relations policy were themselves originally members of various mosque management committees, whether Barelvi or Deobandi. In many towns, this form of Islamic representation, based on local notables who had established themselves as the chief intermediaries between Muslims and the British political authorities, had come to dominate the political and cultural expression of the populations of Muslim origin.[1] The local leaders created and shaped an Islamic 'religious field', to use Pierre Bourdieu's term,[2] which established its hegemony over their followers. They had the ear of their flock, to whom they could preach social peace in exchange for the fulfilment of a certain number of demands which they themselves set out, Islamic education being the most potent of these. They also had access to the local authorities and were able to influence their decisions in the direction most favourable to the Muslim populations they represented, since they were able to guarantee social peace despite the unfavourable social situation of the populations concerned, notably the persistently high unemployment.

However, the goods and services to which the Islamic community leaders had access remained limited. The charitable centres attached to the mosques could at best only provide some relief to the marginalization of the elderly generation. Employment quotas for 'non-whites' within positive discrimination policies opened up jobs for Muslims in the city council and council contracts, but only within the limits set for each ethnic/racial group, so that these opportunities had to be shared with West Indians, Africans, Indians and others.[3] Finally, the way in which the community itself was structured and its separation from the surrounding society perpetuated lifestyles and consumption patterns imported from the subcontinent. For the older generations, this meant that practices and customs were protected, but in dealing with younger English-speaking Muslims, directly exposed to the cultural world of television soap operas and electronic games, community structures faced a challenge of an entirely different scale. Thus, separate Muslim education, which had been achieved in some cities, had to go beyond artificially preserving Islamic lifestyles and practices from the subcontinent and presenting British society in simplistic terms as a forbidden territory of permissiveness and loose morality.

Whatever the problems they encounter in integrating socially and economically, Muslim youth know British society from the inside and have mastered some of its cultural codes. From their viewpoint, the Islamic critique of British society should no longer speak the language of exteriority; nor should it seek to protect the Muslim community in the way that the first generation of immigrants mobilized. This does not mean, however, that their criticism of British society is any less radical.

It was in this context that the Rushdie affair burst out. By violating the community taboo and ridiculing the Prophet, his wives and his companions, Rushdie laid bare the inherited Islamic identity and exposed it completely to the factors of destruction and cultural reconstruction present in postindustrial Britain. The network of traditional Muslim notables lacked the intellectual resources to respond to *The Satanic Verses*, which expressed in fictional form the identity problems faced by young people of Muslim origin born and educated in Britain, albeit in an extreme way. On the other hand, the affair provided the opportunity for other, better educated and more sophisticated actors from Mawdudi-inspired Islamic groups or loyal to the Ayatollah Khomeini to challenge the traditional notables' domination of the religious field, by presenting themselves as better able to formulate a credible response and defend the community. The violence which came to characterize the affair arose not only from the confrontation between Rushdie's supporters and opponents, but also from the rivalries and one-upmanship of the various groups competing for control of Islam in Britain.

Rushdie himself was already well known to the populations originally from the Indian subcontinent. Two of his earlier novels, *Shame* and *Midnight's Children*, had already made him one of the stars of the up-and-coming generation of 'non-white' British writers like Hanif Kureishi or Kazuo Ishiguro. In addition, Rushdie's anti-racist statements and outspoken criticism of Margaret Thatcher and her policies had established him as a leading figure among left-wing cultural circles. His rise to prominence made him someone of whom middle-class Indians and Pakistanis could feel proud, a symbol of success who had managed to overcome British society's racial prejudices. Admittedly, Rushdie himself had never had to contend with class prejudice: as the son of an Anglophile Indian businessman, he had got to know Britain through the exclusive establishment of Rugby public school.

Rushdie has often told of the way he was mocked by fellow pupils for not being able to eat the traditional breakfast kippers without choking on the bones. Suddenly, in England, he discovered he was Indian, he was later to recall.[4] His identity was thus formed in reaction to the disparaging eye of the Other, within a cultural system of differences and reciprocal perceptions. This complex construction of identity in the postmodern world of immigration was to form the leitmotiv of *The Satanic Verses*. It reflects an image of the world where the legacy of tradition blends into a universe of interplanetary migration, electronic communication and satellite transmissions. From this cocktail of cultural influences, a new individual emerges: a kind of mutant. The hybrid migrant characters in *The Satanic Verses* are a deliberately heightened embodiment of this view.

For those who present themselves as the defenders of the Islamic community identity, the world view represented in Rushdie's novel (which they took literally, instead of entering into the 'fictional agreement', as Umberto Eco has it) meant the dissolution of the Muslim community through the adulteration of its faith and ultimately the complete elimination of the Believers. One Islamist newspaper commented sarcastically on Rushdie's anecdote about kippers, noting that 'apparently he had no problem with pork, ham or bacon.'[5] Rushdie's melting-pot vision is thus stigmatized and reduced to a new form of Islamic adulteration akin to the earlier political crises stretching back to the nineteenth century, against which the internal hegira of the various Deobandi, Barelvi, Tabligh and Jama'at-i Islami movements had formed in imperial India.

Rushdie's work was bound to upset the religious leaders who had managed to establish their control over the populations of Muslim origin in Britain. By undermining the very basis of an Islamic community identity, it threatened their cultural, social and political domination of their flock. But the language used by Rushdie in relation to Islam and the Prophet aroused the anger of a much wider Muslim population. By using ironic names for figures held in reverence by pious Muslims, especially the Prophet (referred to as Mahound, a name used by medieval Christian polemicists) and his entourage, and placing these characters in obscene or morally degrading circumstances, Rushdie alienated a great number of ordinary Muslims outside the inner circle of mullahs and Islamic association leaders. Paradoxically, the controversy surrounding the book brought together those who felt that their closest beliefs had been attacked, reinforcing many Muslims' sense of community and making them even more receptive to the mullahs and Islamic leaders.

Rushdie himself does not seem to have realized the extent to which Muslims felt aggrieved at his treatment of the Prophet until after the Ayatollah's fatwa condemning him to death. On 18 February 1989, four days after the fatwa, he stated: 'As the author of *The Satanic Verses*, I recognize that Muslims in many parts of the world have been genuinely upset by the publication of my novel ... I deeply regret the hurt that this publication has caused to the sincere followers of Islam. For those of us who live in a world where faith is plural, this affair reminds us that we must all be aware of the sensitivity of others.'[6] His apologies came late in the day for the main orchestrators of the campaign against *The Satanic Verses* and had little effect. For the various Islamic organizations involved, the campaign had moved beyond the novel itself and was now about a fierce struggle for the leadership of one of the most important mobilizations of religious community politics of the late twentieth century.

Even before the publication of *The Satanic Verses*, controversy had arisen in India in response to interviews given by Rushdie to the English-speaking Indian press and to rumours concerning the manuscript of the novel. In a secular country with some 120 million Muslims living on its soil (despite the creation of the Pakistani state in 1947),[7] Islamic issues are politically very sensitive. The party in power takes care to mobilize Muslim voters on its side, especially in the run-up to elections. There is also a public order issue since the resurgence of tensions between Hindu, Muslim and Sikh communities which have flared up from the mid-1970s onwards, which means that the public authorities must pay close attention to national cohesion. In 1987, in the old city of Delhi and the nearby town of Meerut, inter-religious riots left hundreds dead, many of them burnt to death.[8] For these reasons, Prime Minister Rajiv Gandhi, facing difficult elections in late 1988, banned the book from Indian territory. Rushdie sent him a bitterly scathing open letter, and in return was vituperatively criticized by various Indian Muslim politicians who were quick to present themselves as the mouthpiece of an 'offended' electorate (in anticipation, since these Muslims had not had the chance to read the banned book) in order to attract a community block vote, following the tradition developed during the Indian empire.[9]

After the first shots in the campaign had been fired on the Indian subcontinent, the Rushdie affair started up again in Britain. The first moves were made by the Islamist movement inspired by Mawdudi's Jama'at-i Islami, whose secular arm was the Leicester-based Islamic Foundation. The movement, strengthened by a strong international back-up through Saudi Wahhabism, led the campaign until mid-January 1989, when the Bradford Council of Mosques took over with its spectacular burning of the book, which captured the world's attention. On 14 February 1989, the Ayatollah Khomeini's fatwa upped the stakes and encouraged a new protagonist onto the scene, the Muslim Institute, later to become the 'Muslim Parliament'. With this development, the logic of community action was pushed to its limit by the establishment of a separate self-styled 'parliament' of British Muslims, sitting in parallel to the Westminster Parliament.

Besides these movements which aimed to overcome the fragmentation of British Islam and establish themselves as the national spokespeople of a homogeneous community, the anti-Rushdie campaign also attracted to its front line young English-speaking Muslim intellectuals. Both sets of protagonists constituted a major threat to the domination of the mullahs and local notables, whose influence did not reach beyond the local council. The campaign against *The Satanic Verses* required more *savoir-faire*; it required leaders able to operate at a national or even international level and to represent the feelings of the young generations of English-speaking Muslims born in Britain and radicalized by their experience of race. In other words, this exceptional affair allowed Islam in Britain to move from a communalism of management, which at best perpetuated a traditional Islamic order transplanted from the subcontinent to local British politics, to a communalism of radical mobilization.

The first round: Mawdudiites and Saudis

On 3 October 1988, in the week following the publication of *The Satanic Verses*, the Leicester Islamic Foundation sent a circular to all the Muslim organizations, mosques and Islamic figures in Britain. The circular denounced the 'blasphemous' book, 'thinly disguised as a piece of literature', which 'portrays in the worst possible colours the very characters of the Prophet Abraham and the Prophet Muhammad (peace be upon them)'. The authors included 'relevant extracts from the novel, quite painful to read, ... for your perusal and an early action', and asked all the Islamic organizations to lay siege to the publishers by post and telephone, in order to have the book withdrawn from sale and to obtain a public apology to Islam and Muslims because of the 'sinister nature' of the book and the 'irreparable damage it would inflict on the image of Islam' if it remained in circulation.[10]

The leaders of the Leicester Islamic Foundation had been encouraged to launch this initiative by their brothers in the Madras Islamic Foundation in India, who had informed them of the campaign for a ban on *The Satanic Verses* in their country and suggested they might take it up in Britain,[11] as if the former imperial mainland, through a reversal of perspective, had become a cultural dependence of its former colony. Above all, the speed of the operation showed the efficiency and perfect coordination of the 'Islamist International' created by Mawdudi's disciples, which was able to run parallel campaigns in India and Britain. By being the first to launch the campaign, the Mawdudiites had a real chance of taking over the leadership of a movement which promised to mobilize large numbers and thus considerably extend their influence over British Islam.

Until the Rushdie affair, in fact, the groups belonging to Mawdudi's Jama'at-i Islami movement were only weakly established in Britain. Headed by the UK Islamic Mission, founded in 1962, the movement also included a youth organization, Young Muslims UK, and the research institute set up in 1973, the Islamic Foundation, which had considerable funds at its disposal. The UK Islamic Mission defined itself as 'an ideological organization. It believes that Islam is a comprehensive way of life which must be translated into action in all spheres of human life. The Mission, therefore, aims at moulding the entire human life in accordance with Allah's will ...' The means used by the Mission to achieve its ends 'include the propagation and projection of the true teachings of Islam, the exposure of wrong concepts and innovations introduced in Islam, and a continuous campaign for the establishment of Muslim family laws and Islamic education for Muslim children in the U.K.' In the final analysis, 'the purpose of the Mission, according to its constitution, is "to establish Islamic social order in the United Kingdom in order to seek the pleasure of Allah".' To this end, it does not seek 'to quickly gather a large group of people nominally committed to Islam, but rather to develop a core of dedicated workers as a vanguard to spearhead a life-long struggle in the cause of Allah.'[12]

From the outset, the objectives set by the UK Islamic Mission were on a completely different scale from the modest ambitions of the Deobandi or Barelvi associations which had sprung up in the working-class areas of Birmingham or Bradford, aimed at preserving an Islamic identity carried over from the rural social networks of the Indian subcontinent. In line with the policy of the Jama'at-i Islami (the creation of an Islamic state where the sharia would be applied), the Mission sought from the beginning to promote 'the Islamic social order in the UK', without specifying whether this would apply to just the Muslim population or eventually to all of society. The Mission prides itself on the numerous conversions it has made among the 'indigenous' British population, and has issued several publications which remind readers that one of the central objectives of Islam is the conversion of non-Muslims. Thus Khurram Murad, an engineer who trained in the United States and who was director of the Leicester Islamic Foundation in the early 1980s before returning to Pakistan to become one of the main leaders of the Jama'at-i Islami, wrote a handbook on how to convert non-Muslims to Islam, which was published by the Foundation.[13] Statements on the Mission's ambition to convert non-Muslims were *de rigueur* in the glossy presentation brochures, illustrated with colour photographs;[14] like the bilingual text in Arabic and English, they were designed mainly to impress their Arabian benefactors and confirm the latter's conviction that Islam, in its most intransigent version, would subjugate the whole world, with the Mission forming an avant-garde. But on the other hand, the Mission's extremely radical, political and exclusive view of Islam could hardly be understood and accepted within the mass of workers of Muslim origin, except by a relatively small circle of radicalized and dedicated Islamists.

In order to widen its audience, the Mission set up more 'targeted' organizations: the Muslim Educational Trust, established in 1966, was one of the first. But the most ambitious undertaking was undoubtedly the Islamic Foundation. Established in 1973 in Leicester, it moved in 1976 onto a ten-acre campus, with buildings named after leading Islamist figures ('Mawdudi Hall', 'Hassan el-Banna Hall', 'Ibn Taimiyya Block'),[15] a large library, accommodation for students and visitors, an impressive computing unit, and sizeable translation and publishing activities dedicated to spreading the work of Islamist thinkers and activists. The Foundation is today one of the most important centres for the propagation of militant Sunni Islamist thinking in the world. Its main feature is that it publishes in English, in order to transmit its message into the universally dominant language and to challenge Western cultural hegemony (whether 'secular' or 'Christian') on its own linguistic territory.

The first two directors of the Foundation were officers of the Jama'at-i Islami. The third, M. M. Ahsan, places his mandate in a wider context: 'We belong to the international Islamic movement – neither to Jamaat [-i Islami] nor to Ikhwan [Muslim Brotherhood] nor to the Refah Party in Turkey – but all of them are our friends.'[16] Its main objective is to preach 'true' Islam to the educated younger generation, in a situation which, according to him, is characterized by sectarian conflicts between Deobandis and Barelvis, popular 'tribal superstitions' imported from the Indian subcontinent, which all but turn mosques into a battlefield. The Foundation also organizes seminars, for which it charges fees, for non-Muslims: social workers, teachers, and especially police officers. The seminars form part of the permanent multiculturalist training which has become an obligatory part of these public-sector jobs. In this way, according to Mr Ahsan, the public-service workers can rid themselves of the hostile prejudices spread by the British media and the 'superstitions going on in the Muslim community in the name of religion'. The fact that Islamic-awareness training of British police officers is carried out by the Foundation's Islamist activists demonstrates their ability to fit into a political system which seeks to find community interlocutors, whatever their ideological attachments. These training courses also constitute a vital element in the movement's strategy aimed at achieving hegemony within the Islamic field: by 'targeting' English-speaking Muslim youth on one hand, and state employees on the other, the Foundation has prepared the way for transition from a fragmented, locally based communalism towards community activism on a national scale.

Thus, by launching the campaign against *The Satanic Verses*, the Foundation hoped to mobilize around its own set of demands the mass of Muslims whom it had not yet succeeded in purging of their popular 'superstitions'. The first blow was struck with the circular sent on 3 October 1988 to the Islamic associations. The following week, the Islamic Cultural Centre in London, headed by a Saudi diplomat, Dr Al Ghamdi, hosted a meeting of representatives of nine organizations, which formed the UK Action Committee on Islamic Affairs (UKACIA). The committee was set up to combat the circulation of *The Satanic Verses* and gave itself the task of guiding 'the Muslim community in their efforts to express their anger and hurt, through democratic means, and to ensure that their protest stayed within the framework of the law'.[17]

In Britain, the campaign was limited to collecting signatures for a petition calling on the publisher of *The Satanic Verses* to withdraw the book and organizing a letter campaign to the Prime Minister to ask her to alter the British law on blasphemy. The British law on blasphemy concerns only the Anglican Church as the state religion. UKACIA's aim was to have the law amended to include Islam. Neither of these two demands was achieved. But the campaign for the amendment of the blasphemy law demonstrated the way in which Islamic communalism operated within the logic of a non-secular political system. In education, the Muslim associations had successfully demanded that their children be organized into a separate community in order to exempt them from the assemblies and collective acts of worship which according to the 1988 Act were supposed to be of a 'predominantly Christian nature'. Similarly, in the legal sphere the Muslim organizations demanded equal treatment of communities, that is, the extension of the blasphemy law to Islam.

The blasphemy initiative aroused several different reactions among British public opinion. Some were sensitive to the discriminatory nature of the law and called for its outright repeal: this was the position of the International Committee set up to defend Salman Rushdie. On the other hand, some Anglican priests, keen to keep the crime of blasphemy on the statute books, declared themselves in favour of the principle of extending the law to other religions, whilst stressing the practical difficulties involved.[18] In the event, the Conservative government decided to maintain the existing law, thus reinforcing the definition of British identity based on the established state religion, to the detriment of a secular conception of national identity.[19] The decision followed the same logic as the 1988 Education Act, which had emphasized the Christian nature of education in state schools. In this way, people of Muslim origin, however strongly they held their beliefs, could be forgiven for thinking that the only way to create their own political identity was through reference to their religious affiliation.

Despite the failure of their efforts to ban the sale of *The Satanic Verses* and extend the blasphemy law to protect their own religion, the organizations led by disciples of Mawdudi and supported by Saudi Arabia achieved success in the international arena, which was much more open to this kind of campaigning. In October 1988, a pro-Saudi organization based in London, the Islamic Council of Europe, telexed the governments of Muslim countries to ask them to ban the book – which was done. On 5 November, the Organization of the Islamic Conference, which assembles forty-six states and is strongly influenced by Saudi diplomacy, decided to take measures against the publisher and author of *The Satanic Verses* unless the book was withdrawn from sale.

Such achievements, which extended the protest of British Muslims to the scale of the whole *Umma*, were beyond the means of the local Muslim notables of Bradford or Birmingham. The local community leaders now had to explain to their flock that their best defenders against the novel which had offended them were the 'political' Islamist activists of the Leicester Islamic Foundation or similar organizations, which propagated 'true Islam' and had access to Saudi political and financial back-up.

However, the expectations raised by this international mobilization were disappointed. The British state did not give way to the entreaties of the Mawdudiites and the Saudis. Disappointment was all the greater because in June 1980 the Saudi regime had succeeded in obtaining satisfaction over the *Death of a Princess* incident, when the screening of a film on adultery within the Saudi royal family had caused a serious diplomatic incident. The British Home Secretary had to fly to Saudi Arabia to present an apology. On that occasion, the Saudi leaders had pulled out all the stops, since the honour of their own royal family was at stake. Their failure to defend the honour of the family of the Prophet therefore aroused trenchant comments from those who challenged their leadership of the anti-Rushdie campaign. The Barelvis attributed this lack of zeal to the Wahhabi monarchy's old hatred of popular forms of devotion which give the Prophet and his companions a role of intercession. Others more vindictively proclaimed that the Saudis cared only for the honour of their own royal family, exploited Islam with the sole aim of perpetuating their own power, and therefore had no claim to lead the defence of the Islamic faith.

Round two: the *auto-da-fé*

Parallel to the international campaign of the Mawdudiites and their Saudi backers, the Deobandi and Barelvi associations organized their own mobilizations, albeit a little later and at the local level. Once again, the early warnings came from India: the Bradford Council of Mosques received correspondence from a Deobandi organization based in Blackburn which included extracts from *The Satanic Verses* translated into Urdu, called the author an apostate of

Islam and urged the recipients to petition the Queen and the British government to have the book banned.[20] Sher Azam, as president of the Council of Mosques, responded by writing a letter to Margaret Thatcher on 12 November, his unsophisticated style contrasting with the more worldly-wise missive sent by the Islamic Foundation.[21]

Photocopied extracts from the novel relating to the Prophet, accompanied by commentaries, circulated among most of the grassroots Muslim organizations and became the theme of sermons in the mosques. Among working-class Muslims, the sense of outrage inflicted by *The Satanic Verses* on the honour of the community was of a different order from that of the Islamic Foundation activists. It found expression on two levels: on one level, the sense of belonging to a proletarianized social class, humiliated by the disdainful gaze of the London intelligentsia suddenly bearing down in it, and on the other the indignation felt at the scornful attitude towards the Prophet in the photocopied extracts, which deeply offended the intense popular devotion to the Prophet typical of the Barelvi movement. Their sense of humiliation found expression in a heightened sense of honour ('izzat) which covered the indignities of the younger generations unable to find work and encountering racism, as well as the frustrations of the parents' generation whose object of devotion was now exposed to ridicule.

During the Honeyford affair, the coalition which had led the campaign in Bradford against the headteacher brought together the various Islamic associations under the leadership of the Council of Mosques, but also various secular groups linked to the Indian/Pakistani anti-racist movement as well as the British far left. The Rushdie affair broke up this coalition: the far left and the secular anti-racist groups refused to associate themselves with demands for Margaret Thatcher's Conservative government to ban a novel by an author known to hold progressive, anti-racist views.[22] The only option for the Indian/Pakistani youth of Muslim origin, born in Britain, who had distanced themselves from the modes of reproduction of the Islam of their parents' generation, and wore jeans, T-shirts and trainers, but who felt culturally attacked by *The Satanic Verses*, was therefore to sign up for the campaign organized by the Bradford Council of Mosques and the other local Islamic associations. The young Muslims, with the distinctive symbols of their mixed culture, were present and very visible in the rallies and processions against the novel, and later in the large demonstrations held in London – mobilized behind the demands of the Deobandi or Barelvi Islamic associations.[23] Ironically, *The Satanic Verses* also tried to express a similar kind of hybrid culture, but it presented Muslim youth with an image of themselves they could not recognize.

As well as youth mobilization, it is the particular dynamism of the Barelvi associations in Bradford which explains why the city came to symbolize the opposition of British Muslims to Rushdie's novel. The Barelvis revere the Prophet to the highest degree. He is seen as the perfect being, who has access to the world of occult realities and can bless believers and intercede through the brotherhood leaders or *pirs*, who dispense grace (*baraka*). In the city where as prestigious a *pir* as Pir Mahroof lives, any attack on the person of the Prophet could only be received by him and his disciples as a direct assault on their beliefs and their socio-religious community. In Bradford as in Pakistan, reference to the Prophet is deeply ingrained in daily life and is expressed in the many poems, songs and hymns in his honour which are recited on any important occasion: for example, the poems of Imam Raza (1856-1921) to the glory of the Prophet can still be heard in the mosques of Yorkshire or the Midlands.

> *It is in his light that all things shine.*
> *It is in his person that the secret lies hidden.*
> *His body is not one, which the rays at dawn illuminate*
> *And which is controlled by the position of the sun.*
> *He is God's light and God's shadow.*
> *Everything is due to him; everything is for him ...*
> *Majestically, you walk in the sky,*
> *Yet watch the things on earth, far and near.*
> *There is nothing hidden from your eye,*
> *In the celestial and temporal sphere.*[24]

For those with such reverence for the Prophet, Rushdie's novel directly attacked their most intimate beliefs, beyond the general accusation of blasphemy against Islam. It destroyed the individual, mystic relationship held dear by even the most humble Pakistani unemployed worker in Bradford between himself and him to whom 'everything is due', the being who would give meaning to his life when all else failed.

In the anti-Rushdie campaign, the Council of Mosques deployed all the talents of mobilization and lobbying of local politicians it had used to good effect in its campaigns for halal meat in school dinners and against Ray Honeyford. It had the support of local Indian and Pakistani city councillors, but they did not have access to the national political arena, which was where the Rushdie affair was being played out. One of Bradford's Labour MPs, Max Madden, whose constituency was home to a large number of Muslim voters, expressed his solidarity with the campaign, but stopped short of calling for the book to be banned. A small number of his colleagues took up similar positions, the most influential being the deputy leader of the Labour Party, Roy Hattersley. They had little impact. The failure of the traditional tactic of lobbying local politicians therefore led a group of 700 Muslims to perform an initial public burning of copies of the novel in Bolton on 2 December 1988, but the event went largely unreported in the media. The following month, the Bradford Council of Mosques decided to repeat the operation, this time making sure of media attention.

On 14 January, the book was burnt in Bradford town hall square in front of a crowd of around a thousand people. The secretary of the Council of Mosques placed the large blue-covered tome (previously doused with petrol) onto the flames. Then Muhammad Ajeeb, who had been Britain's first 'coloured' mayor in 1985–6, addressed the crowd, saying that the gathering demonstrated the extreme anger aroused by the book among the Muslim community and congratulating them on their peaceful protest. He pledged to ask his colleagues on the city council to have the book withdrawn from Bradford's public libraries.[25] A few local journalists and photographers were present to record the scene, but the national press and television did not show up, despite the Council of Mosques' briefings. The organizers therefore had an amateur video shot, which they subsequently sent to the television stations in the hope that their dramatic representation of Muslims' outrage would attract public attention and put pressure on the government to act. The result surpassed all the organizers' hopes, but not quite in the sense they had foreseen. The power of the images, transmitted across the globe over the next few days, did not produce feelings of solidarity and sympathy among the non-Muslim public. On the contrary, the *auto-da-fé* evoked images of Nazism or the Inquisition and aroused hostile reactions against the protagonists.

Among Muslims, the book-burning ceremony temporarily made the Bradford Council of Mosques the undisputed leader of the anti-Rushdie campaign, at the expense of the Mawdudiites and their Saudi backers. The two camps represented different campaign styles: on one hand, state-level diplomatic pressure, which had proved ineffectual; on the other, a grassroots protest movement, whose direct emotional appeal made it attractive to the media. The officials of the Leicester Islamic Foundation did not appreciate having the limelight taken away from them, and declared that 'It is now amply documented that the Bradford incident was staged by certain sections of the media and a London solicitor was behind the "management"', in order to spread a negative image of Islam.[26]

The Bradford Council of Mosques acquired international notoriety overnight. Years later, they still recall with some pride how they were interviewed by journalists from all over the world, from New Zealand to the United States. They were not necessarily disturbed by the hostile reaction in the British press to the Muslim demonstrations. External criticism could only reinforce community cohesion and further legitimize the religious leaders, now given added recognition by the international media. The campaign intensified. On 28 January, aggrieved Muslims marched on the London offices of Rushdie's publisher, and an important bookshop chain instructed its outlets to take the book off the shelves and sell it under the counter.

The final round: from Khomeini to the Muslim Parliament

The ascendancy of the Bradford Council of Mosques was short-lived. One month to the day after the *auto-da-fé*, the anti-Rushdie campaign found its ultimate champion in the Ayatolloh Khomeini, who announced from Tehran: 'I inform all intrepid Muslims in the world that the author of the book *The Satanic Verses*, which is against Islam, the Prophet and the Koran, and all those who have published it knowingly are condemned to death. I call on courageous Muslims to execute them as soon as possible, wherever they may be, so that in future no one may dare to insult what Muslims hold sacred.'

In order to explain this exceptionally notorious fatwa,[27] we need to look at the international context in early 1989. The previous year, Khomeini had been forced to accept a ceasefire in the war against Iraq, and his stock fell in the Muslim world. He needed to find an opportunity to reassert his ideological hegemony as champion of Islam, especially as his Saudi rivals had mobilized their international networks of influence in the anti-Rushdie campaign. The fatwa was above all a blow in the power struggle inside the Islamic world.

In fact, according to Islamic law, the fatwa should have concerned only the Shiites who recognized the Ayatollah's spiritual authority and respected his interpretation of Islam. By addressing all the Muslims in the world in his judgement against Rushdie, Khomeini was effectively proclaiming himself the spiritual guide of all Muslims and thereby wresting the leadership role from the Saudis. Moreover, no precedent existed for a fatwa condemning to death, in the name of Islam, an individual who lived outside the Muslim world. Here, too, Khomeini was demonstrating that, for him, the universal mission of Islam did not stop at national frontiers, but included populations who had emigrated to Europe and who were seen as Islamic enclaves, the bridgeheads of the Muslim nation (*Umma*).

For the Muslims living in Britain, the fatwa meant that control of the campaign had now slipped away not only from the Islamic Foundation, but also from the Bradford Council of Mosques. The latter's officers had the feeling that the Ayatollah had 'pulled the rug from under our feet',[28] even though two of its leading members responded approvingly to the fatwa – only to retract their words when they later appreciated the full consequences in Britain of incitement to murder. Whilst the British media and non-Muslim public opinion unanimously condemned the Ayatollah's death sentence on Rushdie, many different shades of opinion could be observed among the 'Islamic community' in Britain.

Most of the associations which aspired to the role of intermediary between their followers and the authorities had no choice but to dissociate themselves from incitement to murder. But at the grassroots level, many Muslims, especially the young, were deeply involved in the campaign against Rushdie and saw the fatwa as a logical next step after the book-burning. On 20 October 1989, more than a year after the book's publication, a survey carried out for the BBC indicated that four out of five British Muslims still supported the campaign, and a 'significant' proportion approved of the fatwa.[29] In the demonstrations against *The Satanic Verses* which took place throughout 1989, slogans calling for Rushdie's death and posters depicting him covered in blood were a natural part of the proceedings. The more non-Muslim opinion was shocked and outraged by the sight of British Muslims hanging effigies of Rushdie, the more the media and politicians indiscriminately blamed 'Muslims'. The communalism which had previously been valued as a factor of social peace now became an object of stigmatization. The more the outside world heaped opprobrium on Muslims, the more the Muslim community closed ranks. It was a vicious circle.

Amid such an escalation of tensions, Ayatollah Khomeini embodied the harbinger, the defender of the faith at any price, the scourge of the West. The gap between the impassioned reactions of the grass roots and the tactical caution of the recognized Islamic associations opened up a free space in the political representation of British Islam. Into this space moved an organization which proclaimed support for the fatwa in order to capitalize on the anger of Muslim youth: it pushed communalism to the extreme in setting up a 'Muslim Parliament' intended to counter the Westminster assembly.

The instigator of the project, Kalim Siddiqui, had arrived in Britain in 1954. The son of an Indian landowner who had fled to Pakistan in 1947, he began a career as a journalist, which took him to the *Guardian*. He had studied Islamist political thinking through Mawdudi's writing, and whilst studying for his doctorate in conflict studies at the University of London he was in contact with other Islamist students from the subcontinent. The 1971 war in which Bangladesh gained independence from Pakistan put his political and religious affiliations to the test. The Pakistani state had originally been set up solely to bring Muslims together in one state. Now, once again, Muslims were divided into two states. Kalim Siddiqui and his friends blamed the leaders who had come to power after independence for this disaster: instead of being guided by Islam in their political affairs, they had reproduced what colonialism had taught them. They belonged to the West culturally, politically and economically. Only the colour of their skin set them apart: the white master had simply been replaced by the 'brown sahib'.

In order to respond to this problem, an Islamic alternative – both political and intellectual – was needed. This was the objective of the Muslim Institute, founded in 1972, which sought to find a way to liberate Muslims from the Western concepts of democracy and other liberal doctrines, and to promote an Islam-based revolution in ways of thinking and organizing political power. The ideology of the Egyptian Muslim Brotherhood and the Jama'at-i Islami interested the Institute's members, but they distrusted these groups because of their close ties with the oil dynasty of Saudi Arabia, which seemed to rule out any chance of a radical departure from the Western-dominated world order.[30] The Iranian revolution provided them with an ideal model. Several of the Institute's members were Iranian students who went on to occupy important posts in the new Islamic republic. They relayed the message back to their comrades in Britain. However, despite being in favour in Tehran, the Muslim Institute remained largely unknown among the Muslim workers of Bradford or Birmingham until the Rushdie affair. It remained a think-tank for students and intellectuals, and did not carry out any social work.[31]

At the start of the anti-Rushdie campaign, Kalim Siddiqui did not organize any major activities.[32] However, he soon became a sought-after speaker on radio and television, because the former journalist knew the tricks of the trade and performed well in debates, unlike the apparatchiks of the Islamic Foundation, who came across as rather dry and uninteresting, and the often self-educated leaders of the Islamic associations, who spoke English with difficulty. In the weeks following the fatwa, Siddiqui provided the British media with the 'bad guy' they wanted, since unlike the leaders of the associations he was happy to endorse the Ayatollah's pronouncement. His flamboyant rhetoric and quick wit ensured he appeared regularly in front of the cameras, although he did not represent an organized movement. He then set about building a movement to back him, hoping to capitalize on the spontaneous and very personal identification with the Ayatollah felt by a number of young Muslims after the fatwa.

To this end, Siddiqui first needed to delegitimize the other campaign leaders, by stressing their ineffectualness and attributing it to 'complicity' between the Saudis and the West. He poured scorn on the 'Saudi lobby' embodied in the UK Action Committee on Islamic Affairs, 'led by a diplomat from the worst "moderate" and pro-Western regime in the world', and declared that the campaign had been so weak it had actually helped to publicize the book: 'Salman Rushdie was enjoying himself tremendously rushing from one television studio to another, and from one party to another, while his bank balance, and his publisher's profits, reached for the sky, far beyond their wildest dreams ... Had Ghamidi, the Saudi diplomat, been leading an effective campaign of mobilizing Muslim opinion in Britain against Salman Rushdie, the British government would have declared him *persona non grata* and expelled him.' Instead, Ghamidi's continued presence in Britain meant that UKACIA and the Saudi diplomat were simply 'Saudi fronts and acceptable to the British government as "leaders" of Islam in Britain'.[33]

In fact, the Saudis and their allies started to show concern when the Rushdie affair escalated beyond control after Ayatollah Khomeini's pronouncement. The affair threatened to force a confrontation between Islam and the West, whilst many Arab states had a stake in maintaining good relations with the United States and Europe. Thus, foreign ministers of member states of the Organization of the Islamic Conference meeting in Riyadh on 13–16 March 1989 decided to reiterate their condemnation of the book and declare its author an apostate (a crime punishable by death in Muslim countries and therefore not applicable to Rushdie as long as he remained in the West), without endorsing the Ayatollah's death sentence. This stance was seen as an admission of weakness by the members of many Islamic associations in Britain, not just by the pro-Iranian groups. Pro-Khomeini sentiment was much in evidence at the biggest anti-Rushdie demonstration, held outside the Parliament buildings on 27 May 1989.[34]

Unlike many of these organizations, however, Siddiqui's strategy was to bring him into open conflict with the British authorities. In his view, outright opposition to Rushdie meant

> taking on the British government, opposition, media, and even the police and the judiciary in a prolonged campaign which may at times amount to confrontation and open conflict. The fact is that the presence of 2 million angry Muslims in a post-Christian secular society represents a major source of potential social conflict. If we refuse, as in my opinion we must, to allow the amoral and largely immoral, secular society to destroy our moral values, then we are too, ipso facto, in long-term conflict with our environment, including the British government.[35]

In order to provide long-term management of this conflict and offer the Muslim populations an alternative allegiance to the British state, Kalim Siddiqui set about bringing together all those who had supported the fatwa. He convened a series of meetings all over Britain in 1990 to discuss a text which he himself had drafted, the *Muslim Manifesto*. The objective was to establish 'a body that can speak with authority on behalf [of Muslims]' and operates like a 'parliament', although 'community-wide institutionalization and organization will have to reach a very advanced stage before an "electoral" process can be introduced.' The 'MPs' would therefore be coopted from within the groups set up to discuss the *Muslim Manifesto*.

This 'Muslim Parliament' was to 'consolidate the Muslim population in Britain into an organized community in pursuit of the goals set by Islam', which took precedence over all others. Thus, the acquisition of British nationality through birth or naturalization 'does not absolve the Muslim from his or her duty to participate in the *jihad*; this participation can be active service in armed struggle abroad and/or the provision and material and moral support to those engaged in such struggle anywhere in the world.' Finally, reminding readers that conversion of non-Muslims is a basic duty of all Muslims, the *Manifesto* notes that 'Muslims have come to live in the West in large numbers at a time when Western civilization is beginning to develop disorders of the mind, body and soul as a direct consequence of unmitigated secularism.' The best way of converting non-believers is to preach by example, by leading a life worthy of pious Muslims: 'but this will only happen if we succeed in arresting the "integration" and "assimilation" of Muslims themselves into the corrupt bogland of Western culture.'[36]

The 'inaugural session' of the Muslim Parliament took place in London on 4 January 1992. At the inaugural session there were 155 'Members of Muslim Parliament', who used the initials MMP in their title, following the practice of British MPs. In his opening speech, Kalim Siddiqui declared: 'We have called ourselves a Parliament because, above all, we are a "political system" in every sense and meaning of that term. We want to take our place among the primary institutions of Great Britain. The inauguration of this Parliament transforms the disparaged Muslim minority in Britain into a political community with a will and purpose of its own.'[37] Noting that the diverse ethnic, linguistic and social origins of British Muslims were well represented by the MMPs, Siddiqui reminded his audience that the common language of the Muslim parliamentarians was English, reflecting the aim that its members should form an Islamic community enclave established on British soil. The MMPs were no longer likely to return to their country of origin, neither would they integrate or assimilate; rather, they would strengthen their Islamic identity and eventually convert non-Muslims.

The constitution of a separate Muslim 'parliament' or legislative body marked a break with the British judicial system and logically entailed a selective approach to the law of the land: 'Let us make it quite clear that Muslims in Britain will oppose, and if necessary defy, any public policy or legislation that we regard as inimical to our interests.' Siddiqui's remarks won an immediate rejoinder from Mr John Patten, then secretary of state at the Home Office, who called on law-abiding Muslims to reject such 'nonsense'.[38] Siddiqui's many enemies within the various Islamic associations also took up the charge, describing his separatist initiative as unduly provocative and mocking the unrepresentative nature of his 'parliament' which had no mandate from the majority of British Muslims.

Siddiqui's aim in giving an embryonic organization the grandiose title of 'Muslim Parliament' was of course to obtain maximum publicity for his schemes. However, in so doing he ran the risk of reinforcing stereotypical views portraying all Muslims as 'fundamentalists'. But manipulation aside and even in its most caricatural aspects, the initiative is rich in significance. It is no accident thatit took place in Britain. The 'Muslim Parliament' initiative represents the union of two fundamental patterns of organization: the political communalism inherited from the Raj, and British multiculturalism. The logic of Siddiqui's project fits in with these patterns, and only because they are pushed to the limits do the caricatural aspects arise.

The contradictions of communalism

The structuring of civil society through communalism (ethnic/racial or religious) remains a basic component of British political culture. The 'Muslim Parliament' rejected integration or assimilation into the 'bogland' of decadent Western civilization. But only the rhetoric distinguishes Kalim Siddiqui and his friends from other Islamic groups, such as the UK Islamic Mission and its offshoot the Islamic Foundation, whose aim of 'establishing the Islamic social order in Britain' is not fundamentally different. The standpoint of these organizations constitutes a response to the existing political system in which the inequality of citizens before the law – as illustrated by the discriminatory legislation in favour of the established Anglican Church – finds compensation in specifically targeted 'positive discrimination' measures. Compromises can be found by conferring special exemptions: as, for example, to Sikhs, who may ride motorcycles without helmets. In the case of education, too, recognized minorities may 'opt out' of the universal commitment to Christian education: thus, the 1988 law obliges schools to provide religious education of a predominantly Christian nature, but suggests that 'minorities' may opt out of these provisions, thus encouraging communalist leaders to exercise control over the populations concerned.

However, the Rushdie affair rekindled the debate among British politicians about the meaning of integration. In 1965, the Labour home secretary Roy Jenkins had defined integration as a combination of equal opportunities and cultural diversity, 'in an atmosphere of mutual tolerance'. In March 1989 (having meanwhile left the Labour Party to found the Social Democratic Party), he annoyed the multiculturalist lobby by publicly questioning the results of his earlier policy. In his view, Muslims had clearly not succeeded in blending their culture, let alone their religion, into British society, and multiculturalism seemed to him now to produce undesirable effects.[39]

But the British state seemed to find it difficult to change direction. The legacy of empire and later the institutionalization of multicultural society (with residents identified according to racial origin) embedded communalism into the political system. Moreover, communalism presented several advantages to the British state: not least, its economic cost was low, since it allowed the state to farm out many social services to the community leaders in exchange for subsidies. In a context of state budget-trimming, such contracting-out of services was viewed favourably by government, especially since it promoted the Thatcherite message of 'rolling back the frontiers of the state'. However, the Rushdie affair revealed that communalism could have a high political cost if overseas support networks intervened to exacerbate internal conflicts. Even more damagingly, rivalry for leadership of the community could create a spiral of confrontation, culminating in the case of the Rushdie affair in the creation of a 'Muslim Parliament'. The political cost of this exacerbation of community tension, based around religious and therefore non-negotiable values, is potentially very high indeed.

We saw earlier that, in the United States, Louis Farrakhan's Nation of Islam first pushed the rhetoric of separatism to its logical extreme, then later tried to find a compromise with the postindustrial social system. In *A Torchlight for America*, published in 1993, Farrakhan presented the community model of the Black Muslims as an example for the whole of the country, which he envisaged as a series of communities living side by side. But grassroots social discontent led some within the movement, notably Farrakhan's lieutenant Khalid Abdul Muhammad, to intensify the confrontational aspects of communalism in anti-Jewish outbursts, which opened up conflicts between the Nation of Islam and B'nai B'rith and led to clashes between Blacks and Jews. In the United States as in Britain, the logic of communalism has come up against the same dilemma: when the leadership wants to preach social peace to the flock in order not to upset existing social hierarchies, the grassroots uses the language of communalism to express revolt against its living conditions. Religion guarantees the common values and identity, but underlying social contradictions will always find a way through to the surface.

PART III
France, Land of Islam

On 5 February 1994, some fifteen hundred school and university students took part in a mass sit-in in Grenoble. At times the atmosphere and the activists' enthusiasm recalled the youthful left-wing protests of May 1968 and the early 1970s. There were many similarities: the age of those taking part, the vehemence of their protest against the national education administration, the mocking attitudes towards the authorities (with a sketch parodying the headteacher) and even a hunger strike by one of the school's pupils, who had been excluded from her school. The demonstration had been organized in her support, with coaches arriving from all over France.

But the issue was not support for anti-colonial wars in Vietnam or Cambodia, as it had been twenty years earlier, or even the anti-racist campaign of SOS-Racisme, which had taken off in the 1980s. At the Grenoble demonstration, the participants were Muslim, and the female demonstrators wore headscarves and were kept separate from their bearded companions by stewards who wore black arm-bands with a yellow crescent and the words 'When will it be our turn?' as a reminder of the yellow star imposed on Jews in Nazi Germany. The sketch showed five people turning up at the school gates. The first four were welcomed in by the headteacher: a punk with multicoloured hair, a rasta handing out joints, a Catholic wearing a cassock and a Jew wearing a kippa and locks. When 'Schérazade' arrived, with her head covered with an Islamic veil (*hijab*), she was refused entry. The audience of protesters took up the refrain: 'Secular education – my veil too!' and 'France is my freedom – my veil too!', punctuated by cries of 'Allah Akbar!'

Schérazade, of Moroccan parentage but herself of French nationality, was in her final year of secondary school. She had been excluded from school for refusing to take of her headscarf during physical education lessons, thus contravening the establishment's 'safety rules', according to the local education authority in Grenoble. As during the first conflict over Islamic headwear, which had taken place in Creil (just north of Paris) in the autumn of 1989, negotiations between the pupil and the headteacher had broken down. However, some concessions had been made: Schérazade was allowed to wear her head-covering during other classes, in line with the Council of State's constitutional ruling of 2 November 1992 that 'the wearing by pupils of insignia by which they intend to show allegiance to a religion is not in itself incompatible with the principle of secularity [*laïcité*].' But Schérazade and the various associations of young Muslims for whom she became an emblematic figure wanted to make an example of the case and mobilize young French citizens of North African origin around issues of Islamization. Associations which promoted the Islamic aspect of second-generation North African youth identity now moved into the gap left by the anti-racist and *beur* integration movements of the 1980s.

The Grenoble demonstration revealed a significant shift in the self-perception of a number of young people of Muslim origin born or at least educated in France, many of them French citizens. In 1983, during the 'march of the *beurs*' for equality of treatment and against racism, one of the young marchers had publicly stated his allegiance to Islam. At a time when the movement represented a mixture of anti-racism, anti-imperialism, solidarity with the Palestinian cause and other left-wing, non-religious ideologies, this young marcher stuck out like a sore thumb and one of the movement's magazines published an article on him under the heading 'A UFO has landed'.

Ten years later, a growing number of young French people of North African origin defined themselves in relation to Islam. In most cases, the allegiance is specific to that particular generation and only partly draws on the 'traditional' Islam of their parents' generation. Unlike in Britain, where Muslim immigrants from the Indian subcontinent brought with them tight and durable community structures, North African immigrants in France only really started to set up Islamic associations and open mosques in the mid-1970s. The Islam expressed at that time belonged mainly to the generation of the first immigrants, who in the 1970s were settling down in France and bringing over their families just at the time when unemployment started to bite. The younger generation at that time, still young children and adolescents, the Islam of their parents seemed old-fashioned and remote from their experience of urban life. The only Muslim activists of a slightly older age (between twenty and thirty years) at that time were Islamist students from North Africa and the Middle East, who attended French universities (usually science departments) and were exclusively concerned with recruiting student sympathizers who would later return home to 'clean up' the country and establish an Islamic state.

One such activist admitted to the author in 1985 that, as far as he and his colleagues were concerned, the *beurs* were permanently lost to Islam because of their integration into French culture. Similarly, the imams of the prayer-halls in workers' hostels were concerned not to imperil the position of immigrants in France, which was seen as a land of refuge, and consequently preached to their flocks on the dangers of strike activity. In terms of Islam, France was neither *dar el islam* nor *dar el harb*: neither land of Islam nor a land open to war and conquest. Instead, France was seen as *dar al 'ahd* (land of negotiated peace): a situation where Muslims are not in conflict with the 'ungodly' but not openly hostile state.

It was not until the mid-1980s that some second-generation youth began attending mosques, in the Lyons suburbs. At first, the pietistic Jama'at al Tabligh exerted the most influence over these new followers, notably at Chasse and Givors (just outside Lyons), through community help for young in the multifaceted crisis in which they found themselves: unemployment, xenophobia, the disintegration of the family unit and a wider identity crisis. A few initiatives got off the ground here and there, and by 1987 a small but significant number of young people could be seen in Paris mosques, where three years earlier there had been none.[1]

In this respect, the year 1989 constitutes something of a watershed for Islam in France. The international background had changed significantly. In particular, for those of Algerian origin, the rise of the Islamic Salvation Front (Front Islamique de Salut, or FIS) considerably altered their perception of Algeria and their relationship to the country and to the legacy of French colonial presence. Their relationship to Islam and indeed their very definition of Islam were both profoundly affected by rapidly acquired hegemony of the FIS over the Algerian religious field. Until then, Islamism had concerned only a few relatively small, esoteric groups of activists who remained on the fringes of the major power struggles of the day. From 1989, it came to the forefront of public interest, since it was now bound up with the present lot and probably the future of all Algerians, living north or south of the Mediterranean.

In addition, 1989 was the year of the 'veil affair' in France, which divided the country down the middle after three schoolgirls were excluded from their secondary school for wearing headscarves in class. The affair marked the start of a new strategy for Islamist activists, who acted as 'advisers' to the parents of the pupils concerned: France was now to be regarded as *dar el islam*, as Rached al Ghannouchi, leading intellectual of the Tunisian Islamist movement Al Nahda and its French networks, proclaimed at the congress of the Union of Islamic Organizations in France (UOIF) (then the main Islamist grouping in France) the following year. His declaration laid down the objective of the re-Islamization of the populations of Muslim origin resident in France, rather than an immediate Islamization of the entire population. From this moment, the Islamist movements in France took into account the inescapable fact of the immigrants' permanent establishment in the host country, which previously they had ignored. The events of that year led them to conclude that the ability of the young populations of Muslim origin to speak French and their status as French citizens did not necessarily alienate them from Islam, any more than it assimilated them into the French population. Nor did it mean they had to accept the secular republican model which rejected religion in the private sphere.

From that time, Islam *in* France began to operate as Islam *of* France, whilst at the same time undergoing some important changes. It increased its hold over the grass roots by highlighting the religious dimension. In this, it was helped by the growing visibility of Islam in the international sphere and by a heightened sense of identity following the Rushdie affair and the veil affair, then later the Gulf War. These events helped people who up until then had not paid any great attention to that part of their identity to discover that they were Muslim, by realizing their solidarity with fellow believers whom they saw demonized by the Western media. Djida Tazdaït, president of the association of Young Arabs of Lyons and its Suburbs (Jeunes Arabes de Lyon et Banlieue, or JALB), MEP and leading light of the *beur* movement in the 1980s, remarked in 1989: 'French society thought it could do without a debate on Islam, despite the presence of several million Muslims on its soil. Since the Rushdie affair, instead of going to the heart of the problem it engages in an inquisition: "Are you for or against fundamentalism?" ... This is a real attack on Muslim consciousness; Muslims are forced to take up a position on something that is a purely French fantasy.' On the subject of the Creil affair, she notes: 'How do you expect Muslims to respond, after two weeks of abuse? With a knee-jerk reaction: "Of course we're in favour of the veil!"[2] This redis-covery of Islam took many, often diffuse and contradictory forms, but the result was to give 'Islam' (however defined) a much greater part in the definition of identity than had previously been the case.

From another perspective, the search by young second-generation immigrants for alternative models of society to which they, as vic-tims of labour-market discrimination, could relate,[3] was encouraged by the patent crisis of French identity, as revealed in the veil affair. At the end of the 1980s in France, Jean Marie Le Pen's National Front (FN) attracted not inconsiderable political and media atten-tion by blaming 'immigrants' for unemployment and rising crime rates, and calling for their and their children's expulsion from the country. Around the same time, the remarkable electoral success of the FIS in Algeria brought the hope of a '*doula islamiyya*' – an Islamic state. This goal, with its utopian overtones and its promise of social justice for the Algerian dispossessed, found support among some of Algeria's children living in miserable conditions in France's cities, with little hope for the future.

Two crises – the crisis of French identity and the crisis of social integration and employment – combined to create a favourable environment for re-Islamization movements among many young *beurs*. The new strategy correspondingly developed around two main concerns. First, the young *beurs* reasserted an Islamic community identity, notably around the issue of girls' right to wear the *hijab* at school, in order to counter the crisis of French identity. The French state's management of each conflict that arose over the veil worked in the Islamists' favour, enabling them to present them-selves as the best defenders of young Muslims against 'the racism of the French'. Second, the activists sought to recreate self-managed networks of social solidarity to combat the social problems of city life, replacing the old associative structures (youth clubs, youth cen-tres and so on) which the Catholic Church, trade unions, left-wing parties or city councils had formerly provided but which had fallen into disuse or disappeared entirely. In their activities, the Islamists thus fulfilled a function of supervision and social peace covering everything from educational back-up services to the fight against drugs. This made them potentially important interlocutors for the public authorities, who were now faced with a dilemma: on one hand the authorities themselves knew that they had difficulties com-municating with a youth that was changing, but on the other hand their Islamic intermediaries demanded subsidies which the republi-can principle of separation of church and state seemed to rule out.

These trends reflect a similar process to that observed in

the United States and Britain, although not on the same scale. However, the context here is completely different in that the notion of communalism is rigorously combated in the French republican model of social organization, even if in practice republican equality through citizenship fails to deliver the goods. As a result, the demands of the more established Islamist movements in France show some ambivalence, mixing the republican discourse of human rights, liberty and even integration with a set of ideological references inspired by the Muslim Brotherhood, the Islamists of the Tunisian Nahda or the various currents of the Algerian FIS.

To some extent, the contradictory logic of Islamic communalism is similar to that of another movement which developed out of underprivileged, subjugated social groups: French communism. The struggle to establish the dictatorship of the proletariat had not prevented communist activists from standing in elections, particularly local elections. This strategy allowed communist-run local councils, in the peak of their influence, to become the mouthpiece of their working-class constituency and thus claim representativeness beyond party membership. A similar dynamic is also at work in the re-Islamization movements of North African youth, although it is still at an early stage. Following the decline of the traditional working-class subculture and its network of associations, and the loss of impetus of the anti-racist movement of the 1980s, the new movements seek to fulfil a 'mouthpiece' function (*'fonction tribunicienne'*) to express the frustration, hopes and demands of marginalized youth.[4] They offer the youth a means of collectively negotiating with an apparently impenetrable or even hostile French state for a place in future French society.

In the following pages, we will analyse the ways in which the re-Islamizing movements have created and asserted an Islamic community identity in France, and its significance. In order to assess the importance of the changes taking place in the last decade of the twentieth century, we need to start with the year 1989 and examine its consequences – including the Algerian dimension – for the Islamic presence in France.

We saw earlier that the assertion of Islamic identity in Britain can only be understood within the context of the relationship between Islam and British rule in the Indian empire. Similarly, Islam in France in the 1990s has developed within a wider context marked particularly by events in Algeria. The appearance and staggering success of the FIS have shaken up the whole system of values associated with Islam, not only in Algeria but also more generally in France, whose Muslim populations come mainly from Algeria and its neighbours. Even before the FIS set up its support networks in France (whose influence has sometimes been exaggerated), its impact on the organization of Islam on the former 'mainland' was enormous. The example set by the FIS – the new relationship it defined between Islam and political power, the social work projects it carried out to combat the poverty and despair of the young, and the cultural war it waged against French values – imposed a mass 'Islamist alternative' which strongly promoted an Islamic identity based on rejection of the West.

This transformation fundamentally altered the close relationship and mutual perceptions which had been built up between France and North African Islam. This changing relationship will be the focus of our next section. We will then go on to look at the way in which Islam *in* France became Islam *of* France through the veil affair in the autumn of 1989, and identify the leading protagonists in this process. Finally, we will examine how this Islam *of* France linked up with the youth movement of discontent and social protest, in the aftermath of the Gulf War, just as the civil war started in Algeria. We will see how far French Islam fits in with new international social, cultural and religious cleavages, which the Black Muslim movements in the United States and the 'race relations' approach in Britain reflect to some extent, and how far it has followed its own distinctive path.

I

The FIS versus the 'Sons of France'

The creation of the Islamic Salvation Front (FIS) was proclaimed one Friday in March 1989, in the Ben Badis mosque in the Kouba district of Algiers.[1] Four months had passed since the popular uprising of October 1988, during which the authoritarian regime (controlled since independence by the National Liberation Front (Front de Libération Nationale, or FLN)) wavered. In a record space of time, the Islamist party came to wield undisputed hegemony over the Islamic field, conquer a remarkable social following and dominate the political scene. It won the vast majority of mosques and preachers over to its cause and managed to eliminate all interpretations of Islam other than its own. In the social sphere, the FIS capitalized on a strategy already put in place by the grassroots Islamic associations which had gone before it: through an exceptional number of charitable services it was able to take on responsibility, at least temporarily, for a large part of the problems of daily existence confronting Algerians in the absence of state initiatives. The FIS stepped into the gaps left by the state, reorganizing society around mosques where goods and services were dispensed. The party's social base gave it a landslide victory in the local elections of June 1990, when it won most of the local councils, and then in the first round of the legislative elections in December 1991, prompting the regime to cancel the second round of elections and outlaw the FIS in March 1992.[2]

The unprecedented scale of the FIS's electoral success represented the culmination of the Islamist activists' work in Algeria, partly underground, partly within the ruling National Liberation Front itself, where a 'bearded' tendency had agitated for Islamization of society and a break with 'the values of France'. In 1989, this long-

term activism joined up with the widespread unrest which had earlier found expression in the October 1988 revolt. The uprising had
revealed the extent of popular anger and frustration at the regime,
but at the time no effective political alternative emerged.

Only the FIS proved able to transform popular discontent into a
radical project of transformation of society. Its world vision, which
until then had been confined to a few thousand bearded activists,
suddenly acquired a mass following. This vision carried with it a
redefinition of Algerian identity involving the rejection of any
French influence. By blaming all the country's ills on French cultural
influence, the FIS heightened a sense of 'pure' Islamic identity, from
which the party wanted to exclude all the intellectual and linguistic
contributions made by France, from the beginnings of colonization
to the latest television serials made available by satellite dishes. It
thus sought to erect watertight barriers between Algerian community identity, redefined by belief in and strict observance of Islam, and
the Other world of (French) ungodliness and wickedness.

The 'poisonous milk of France'

The eviction of French culture had, together with Arabization and
Islamization, been the official policy of the FLN during the whole of
the Boumedienne era. In the area of linguistic policy, the results had
been controversial, producing the generations of 'bilingual illiterates'
satirized by Algiers wit. But beneath the authoritarian blanket of the
state, the Algerians had constructed a mixed political and cultural
popular identity, rooted in 130 years of shared history with France.
It was this cultural cross-fertilization which the FIS's ideology
sought to eliminate. This necessitated an Islamist rewriting of the
whole history of the war of independence (out of which the FLN
had emerged victorious), now depicted as a 'jihad against the Cross'.
In this way the FIS could attack FLN rule since 1962 by portraying
it as the 'party of France'. By demonizing France and all the values
associated with it, the FIS refined the frontiers of allegiance to Islam
on the basis of a rhetoric of radical separation.

When the Algerian war broke out on 1 November 1954, Islam
was present as a reference, but played a minor role in the ideology
of the young revolutionaries.[3] The call to insurrection on
1 November 1954 was made in the name of Allah, but this must be
interpreted merely as the expression of the sociological identity of the
future independent Algeria. By invoking Islam, the insurrectionists

meant to draw a sharp distinction between the future Algerian people – defined as Muslims – and the 'pied-noir' settlers and Jews who
would not belong to the new society. But they did not thereby
express an intention to apply the sharia, in the sense used today by
the FIS. For most of the rural Algerians who provided the troops for
the battle for independence, Islam's traditional sociopolitical vocabulary, as conveyed by the religious brotherhoods and the marabouts,
translated the ideals of justice and equity into pre-colonial categories. On the other hand, the urban Islamic scholars of the
Association of Ulema (founded in 1931 by Sheikh Ben Badis), which
embodied the drive for Islamization of customs and behaviour, and
from which the FIS claims to be directly descended, at first remained
aloof from the young revolutionaries, whose programme seemed full
of irreligious ideology.

The Islamists' distrust of the socialist-oriented independentist
movement, in its various forms under the leadership of Messali Hadj
(the Etoile Nord-Africaine, then the Algerian Popular Party and later
the Movement for the Triumph of Democratic Freedoms),[4] had
remained constant since the 1920s. The *ulema* (doctors of Islamic
law) had developed a way of thinking and an educational system
which took colonial political domination into account. Not that
they were satisfied with the existing state of affairs – but unlike their
Indian counterparts who had organized an independent Islamic
identity away from the 'ungodly' regime, Ben Badis and his disciples
conceived of their preaching and their desire for change as
autonomous and therefore unaffected by the *fait accompli* of French
colonization. It was only in 1956, when it became clear that the
FLN had become a political force to be reckoned with, that the
ulema rallied to the independence cause, bringing with them the lit-
erate, Arabic-speaking urban social strata over whom they wielded
authority and influence.

At the time of independence, the Islamic tendency was marginalized among the new leadership circles in favour of socialists and
Marxists, especially during the brief presidency (1962–5) of Ben
Bella. During these early years, the stigma of disapproval surrounding the fraternal associations and marabouts, accused of collusion
with the colonizers and of blocking social progress, attached itself
more generally to anything perceived as 'reactionary clericalism'.
But the religious leaders were not the only ones excluded from
power. The combatants who had suffered the heaviest losses in the
independence war – the leaders of the central regions of the country
(Mitidja, Kabylia and the Algiers region) and Aurès – found themselves ousted by the men of the 'frontier army' which had remained

in Tunisia and Morocco until 1962. Colonel Boumedienne, the supreme embodiment of the 'frontier army', replaced the first president, Ahmed Ben Bella, in a *coup d'état* in July 1965.

When they imposed the single-party dictatorship, the Algerian leaders also eliminated all of those who had brought more democratic ideals to the anti-colonial insurrection, such as Muhammad Boudiaf, Hocine Aït-Ahmed or Mohammed Harbi, all imprisoned or exiled. What is more, under Boumedienne a small ethnic group was allowed to tighten its hold over the country: the Arab families of the east (nicknamed the 'BTS' after the initials of the three towns which constituted the geographical limits of the region, Batna, Tebessa and Souk-Akhras), who provided the FLN with the core of its leaders, to the detriment of Berber- and French-speaking Algerians, as well as the veterans from the centre and the west.

In this way, a diffuse sense that the '1954 revolution' and the 'November principles' had been appropriated, hijacked, even betrayed, continued throughout the history of independent Algeria, but since it was strictly forbidden to express such feelings, they remained confused and clandestine. The great strength of the FIS's idelogy has been to adopt this feeling of betrayal as its own and to present a single ideological interpretation of it. According to the FIS, the jihad for independence should have opened the way for the establishment of an Islamic state, but was led astray by the 'children of France'.

For the younger generations, who did not live through the events and had access only to the official history, the betrayal of the independence struggle remained a 'confused certainty' because of the deliberate obfuscation of memory and the silencing of the insurrection's main protagonists during the whole period of single-party rule.[5] This made it easy for the Islamists in the late 1980s to substitute their version of Algerian history for the censored memory of the FLN, especially as at a time of deep social unrest there was room for a 'rectifying' ideology which would attribute all society's problems to the betrayal of the original ideals of 1954. The FIS's great achievement was to limit the betrayal to that of the 'original *Islamic* ideals' (leaving aside the question of democracy) and to link the other usurpations – by the frontier army or the eastern Arabs – to this central issue.

'The Algerian State of 1962 no longer corresponded to the aspirations of 1 November 1954, for which we took up arms: an independent State founded on Islamic principles,' declared Abbassi Madani, leader of the FIS. 'The state which emerged before our eyes was based on secular socialist foundations. This was a serious deviation

... We were entering an era of despair, failure and disaster.' Ali
Benhadj, the FIS's star preacher, put the point more forcefully still:
'My father and my brothers (in religion) may have *physically*
expelled the oppressor France from Algeria, but my struggle,
together with my brothers, using the weapons of faith, is to banish
France *intellectually* and *ideologically* and to have done with her
supporters who drank her poisonous milk.'[6]

This ideology has acquired great mobilizing power in Algeria
today. The party's organ, *Al Munqidh*, regularly took up the theme.
Thus, for example, in issue number eighteen, a group of mujahaddin, veterans of the Algerian war, recall that 'the war of holy liberation was not a jihad for the devil (*taghout*) but a jihad for Allah
... The first words to sound after the first shots were 'Allah
Akhbar', and we knew we were waging war against the Cross,
which wanted to annihilate Islam by all means possible.'[7]
Consquently, the authors call on Muslims to vote for the FIS at the
local elections: Islamic domination of local councils will finally
achieve the aims of the war of liberation against France. In the same
edition, another article explains that the maintenance of French cultural institutions in Algeria, guaranteed in the Evian agreement
granting the terms of Algerian independence, was intended to prevent the implementation of the Islamic principles of 1954, and that
the Algerian leaders in power, having been educated in French
schools, are pillars of cultural colonialism.[8]

This series of arguments offers a simple response to the still unan-
swered question about the causes of national collapse. Conveniently
for the FIS, Algerian historians have been unable to make their
voices heard except in exile on the other side of the Mediterranean,
which is an illegitimate place in the eyes of the Islamists. At the heart
of the FIS's ideology, there is the irrepressible desire to replay the
moment of separation from France, which was botched the first time
round. But this time, it is no longer simply a question of winning
back national territory: the combatants must reconquer hearts and
minds, by depicting France as an evil entity and an enemy of the
Islam of which the FIS claims to be the supreme representative.

From Arabization to Islamization

In order to propagate its world view among wider Algerian society,
the FIS appropriated those elements of the FLN's ideological heritage which related to 'authenticity', Islam and the goal of

Arabization. At the same time, it justified its attacks on the ruling party (its former ally in the war of independence) by designating its leaders as 'children of France', in order to attract support from all those who resented the FLN for one reason or another.

The FLN's Arabization policy had since independence been riddled with contradictions. In the beginning, the policy was aimed mainly at strengthening links with the Arab states of the Middle East which shared the elite's socialist ideals, such as Nasser's Egypt. From the mid-1970s, however, the main promoters of the policy were groups which saw Arabic not as the language of Nasserian socialism, but as the language of the Koran and of the Muslim Brotherhood. At that time, Boumedienne's regime saw the 'Islamic' factions within the FLN as a useful support in its struggle against the far left and the Algerian communists who had taken over the implementation of socialism in the countryside. But the key to understanding the FIS's success in creating an Algerian identity around community-based Islam is to be found in the way in which the FLN's mass Arabization policy backfired, creating resentment among those who should have been its beneficiaries but who felt themselves to be victims. The FIS was able to exploit this popular resentment.

Boumedienne's *coup d'état* in July 1965 had made the Arabization policy irreversible. In April 1968, it was decreed that the civil service would be completely Arabized by 1971 – a 'Stakhanovite' measure, since almost half of the civil servants recruited in 1969 could neither read nor write Arabic. This policy, which was gradually extended to cover all public life, was also meant to give the ruling administration ideological control over 'authenticity' and thus the ability to police any attempts to challenge the regime in the name of Allah.

An association called 'Al Qiyam' ('The Values') had been set up in 1964. The association was close to the Muslim Brotherhood, at the margins of what the FLN was prepared to tolerate. In September 1966, it protested to Nasser about the hanging of the Islamist thinker Sayyid Qotb, and as a result was banned. In order to avoid repression, its leaders then decided to pursue a policy of 'entryism' into the civil service, where they devoted their efforts to total Arabization as the prelude to Islamization.[9]

From that moment, state institutions with a religious mission became a meeting point for all those who wanted Algeria to enforce strict application of the injunctions of the Koran and the Sunna, either by reforming the system gradually or rejecting it outright. In this context, an important role was played by the *Al Asala* journal

('Original Purity'), launched by the minister for religious affairs and original education in 1971. The journal gave the regime some Islamic legitimation, but also gave column space to writers like Abbassi Madani who used it to develop a vision of society which closely resembled that of militant Islamism, as promoted by Banna, Qotb and the Muslim Brotherhood.

Some of the ruling elite felt quite comfortable with this Islamism. In January 1979, the minister for religious affairs, Mouloud Nait Belkassem, wrote in *Al Asala*:

> The Islamic state derives its superiority over other regimes from the fact that the others, as monarchies or republics, receive their constitutions from kings and parliaments, whereas the Islamic state receives the power to legislate from God. Establishing the state, in Islam, means implementing the sharia which God inspired in His envoy, and submitting to it ... Long live Khomeini, may his example be multiplied in all Islamic countries![10]

Thus, beyond the FIS's rhetoric stigmatizing the FLN as the 'party of France', a number of important links were created between a pro-Islamist faction within the ruling party and members of the Islamist movement in opposition but culturally on the same wavelength as the 'establishment', such as Abbassi Madani, the future leader of the FIS. The two groups shared a vision of society which did not seriously disrupt existing social hierarchies, so that once it became a question of addressing the discontented urban poor, towards the end of the 1980s, they could not compete in terms of social programmes, but instead engaged in a competition to outdo each other in Islamic 'authenticity' and Francophobia.

From the campus to the guerrilla underground

Outside the pro-Islamist faction within the ruling party, several initiatives sprang up in civil society which were also favourable to the re-Islamization movement. In 1967, the first prayer-hall was set up in the central faculty of Algiers University. The students behind this initiative were mainly followers of Malek Bennabi (1905–73), an electrical engineer who wrote his many books in French. Until the 1950s a close associate of the Muslim Brotherhood, Bennabi had in his 1954 book *Vocation de l'Islam* written in praise of Hassan al Banna, whom he saw as the thinker the most able to transform the contemporary world through Islam. Sayyid Qotb referred approvingly to Bennabi in his book *Signes de piste*, the best-selling Islamic equivalent of Lenin's *What is to be Done?* But Bennabi later distanced himself from the Brotherhood. His concern was to examine from within the causes of the weakening of Muslim civilization, which he termed 'colonizability', whereas the Brotherhood placed the blame mainly on the damaging influence of the colonizing West.

The 'Bennabite' science and technical students who set up the mosque were for the most part French-educated. Bennabi's thinking offered them the possibility of retaining Islam as their world view without thereby rejecting their Francophone culture, unlike most of the Islamist activists in Algeria who associated Islam with Arabization and the rejection of French cultural influence. Bennabi's disciples included some Berber-speaking Kabyle Islamists, who felt uncomfortable with the prevailing glorification of Arabic and denigration of other languages.

Bennabi's influence has waned over the years, but it left behind a legacy in two main areas. First, many of the young 'Islamic technocrats' who controlled the FIS after June 1991 and led it to success in the December 1991 legislative elections had earlier been active in the student movement. Second, the same reluctance to denigrate languages other than Arabic would later be found among second-generation immigrant youth in France, whose first language was French. The aim was not to reject the French language, but to dissociate it from its ideological connotations and 'ungodliness', from its association with the values of the Enlightenment, Voltaire and Rousseau,[11] and to make it the vehicle for propagating the faith, just as the Islamists of the Leicester Islamic Foundation in Britain used English in their publications to gain as wide an audience as possible and transform it into the language of Islam.

In 1982, the Algerian Islamist Movement began to make its presence felt, both in public – in the universities – and in the underground. The first large-scale demonstration of Islamist opposition to the regime took place in November 1982 in the central faculty of Algiers University. Arabic-speaking students, dissatisfied with their mediocre career prospects (since the most highly valued disciplines required command of French), started a strike, which turned into a confrontation between French-speaking leftists and Arabic-speaking Islamists. After one of the latter was stabbed, thousands of people turned up to a protest prayer in the faculty mosque. Abbassi Madani, who taught at the faculty, headed the protest and later presented the government (led since 1979 by Chadli Benjedid) with a fourteen-point set of demands, the first draft of an Islamic manifesto for Algeria.[12] The document demanded a purge of state bodies to rid them of 'elements hostile to our religion', the abolition of mixed education and respect for the sharia in all legislation, and denounced 'the policy of France, aimed at the disintegration of the family unit and the loosening of morals'.

This was the first Islamist-inspired public demonstration to challenge the regime and put forward a set of specific demands. The movement's earlier strategy had consisted of entryism into the ruling elite. One or two direct-action operations had been planned, but were quickly abandoned.[13] The government reacted in two ways to the November 1982 demonstration: it had Madani arrested (he remained in jail for two years) and rounded up the main leaders of the movement. Sheikhs Ahmad Sahnoun and Abdellatif Soltani, representatives of the older generation of Islamist preachers who had signed the manifesto alongside Madani, as well as Abdallah Jaballah[14] and various other future leaders of the FIS such as Ahmed Merrani, the Kabyle translator of the 'fourteen points' into French. The government was determined to show that it would tolerate no pressure for Islamization which came from outside the ruling elite and therefore represented a political threat.

Outside the universities, Islamist opposition was engaged in a long-term clandestine operation aimed at penetrating society and creating support networks, using various pietistic and charitable associations. After a fruitless first attempt in 1965, the Jama'at al Tabligh movement succeeded in establishing itself in Algeria in 1970, thanks to Pakistani, Moroccan and Syrian missionaries working from Morocco. Ahmed Merrani belonged to the first groups which set out into the villages and the poor urban neighbourhoods, preaching Islamic moral values, the need for collective prayer at the stipulated times and rejection of everything that deviated from Islam in its strictest sense. In the poor districts of Algeria, as all over the world, the Tabligh played a role of instigator, 'relighting the flame of Islam' from the embers buried under the ashes of Western materialism.

When Ahmed Merrani left the Tabligh in 1975, he founded an Islamic mutual help association in the Sidi Muhammad al Sharif mosque in the Algiers kasbah, collecting alms (*zakat*) from the tradespeople and redistributing it to the needy. Similar networks would emerge in many poor neighbourhoods in order to compensate for the lack of state provision. The charitable networks were intended to serve as a link between the people and those Islamist activists who took up armed struggle in order to escape repression.

The first Islamist underground organization in post-independence Algeria, the Armed Islamic Movement (Mouvement Islamique Armé, or MIA), was set up by Mustafa Bouyali in 1982. Its saga forms the link between the 1954–62 war of independence and the civil war which broke out in 1992, appropriating the collective imagination of resistance and insurrection against France and imbuing it with Islamic significance. In a way, it was a dress rehearsal for the conflicts which would follow the disbanding of the FIS in 1992 and the subsequent formation of Islamist 'liberated zones' in the mountains. With hindsight, then, the armed resistance of the 1980s appears to have had a great impact, but at the time, it was portrayed in the press and in official pronouncements, as the work of a tiny, marginal and aberrant faction.

The MIA was created in July 1982, a few months before the events at the University of Algiers. The exact sequence of events remains hazy (even to the extent of confusion over the organization's name), but it apparently grew out of the merger of several preexisting groups. Mustafa Bouyali was nominated 'emir' not because of his knowledge of Islam, which by all accounts was superficial, but because he had become something of a legend during the five years he had spent on the run after the police assassination of one of his brothers, dodging the police and carrying out a number of daring raids. His extremism appears to have been backed up by a literal interpretation of the sermons of radical imams, from which he took the idea that armed struggle was the only way of bringing about an Islamic state. Bouyali was ambushed and killed in February 1987 but remains an important reference point for Algerian Islam because he worked closely in the clandestine movement with some of the most virulent activists of the post-1988 period, both inside and outside the FIS. The cover of the first edition of Al Munqidh (5 October 1989) carried a demand for the immediate release of the last members of the Bouyali group still in gaol.

From 1982, the Islamist movement had thus gained a foothold in Algeria. Its presence had many forms, from penetration of the ruling elite through community services and university agitation to armed resistance. It included conservative notables as well as the poor in search of social revenge. This heterogeneous mixture later resurfaced in the FIS, held together by the doctrine of separation depicting France as the archetype of evil and ungodliness. In France in 1982, however, no one had any inkling of the Algerian Islamists' existence. The socialist government under Pierre Mauroy courted the FLN government and approved the appointment as head of the Paris mosque of one of the FLN's representatives, Sheikh Abbas Bensheikh Lhoussine, a leading member of the Islamist tendency within the party – thinking that he would act as a bulwark against 'Iranian fundamentalism'.

Pure and impure

The most famous of Mustafa Bouyali's accomplices was no other than Ali Benhadj, the most charismatic leader of the FIS and a powerful public speaker with whom many of the young Algerian dispossessed (*hittites*) identify.[15] Born in December 1956 in an Algerian refugee camp in Tunisia, Ali Benhadj was the son of a *shahid* ('martyr' of the war of independence) and his mother also died, leaving him orphaned. He had a difficult time at school and failed his *baccalauréat* 'because he was extremely weak in French, which he never liked',[16] but went on to become a secondary-school teacher, an entirely Arabic-speaking profession where the Islamist movement was well represented.[17] Influenced by the preaching of Sheikhs Soltani and Sahnoun, he practised as an 'independent preacher' in various mosques which were outside the control of the Ministry for Religious Affairs, before joining Bouyali's group. He was arrested in 1983 and remained in detention until 1987, spending most of his sentence in the high security Lambèze jail.

Ali Benhadj became the brightest and most eloquent spokesman for a group within the Islamist movement called the 'salafists' (*salafiyyun*), which developed in the early 1980s. The term refers to the 'pure' tradition of the 'pious ancestors' of primitive Islam (*salaf*) and has acquired many different meanings across the Muslim world. In contemporary Algeria, it designates the group of young preachers including, as well as Benhadj, Abd al Hadi Doudi (who has been an imam in Marseilles since 1987)[18] and Al Hachemi Sahnouni, one of the founders of the FIS. Many of the group's members spent some time in Bouyali's underground movement. The group rose to prominence in Algiers in 1980 with the construction of the Sunni mosque of Bab el Oued (which became one of the FIS's 'cathedral mosques' after 1989), whose imam was Sahnouni.

The salafists may be distinguished from the Muslim Brotherhood (represented in Algeria in the 1980s by Mahfouz Nahnah, who was released from prison in 1981) by a more all-embracing view of Islamic preaching. According to Sahnouni,[19] the Brotherhood felt that the basic beliefs and religious doctrine of the people were sound, so preaching should address the political dimension in order to convince the faithful of the urgency of the need to establish the Islamic state. The salafists on the other hand thought that the Muslim faith of the Algerian masses remained marred by superstitions inherited from the marabouts and heterodox practices mixed with French influences, so that preachers needed to eliminate all false ideas and return to basics, to the letter of the Koran and the Sunna.

Their call for the return to a lost 'purity' echoes what we observed earlier in the context of British India: the 'internal hegira' movements of Deobandis, Barelvis and Tablighis in response to the loss of political power and the fear of acculturation to dominant non-Muslim society. But the salafists also wanted at the same time to reform the individual, transform society and establish the Islamic state. They represented a desire to break with the cultural cross-fertilization of post-colonial Algeria, with its mixture of Arabic, Berber and French influences, and marabout, socialist and secular tendencies.

In the early 1980s, the Sunni mosque and other prayer-rooms in the poor urban areas where the young salafist imams preached faced an influx of rural populations, who brought with them their peasant beliefs and their distress at living conditions. The salafists' preaching suited the sense of anguish and anomie and the poverty and uncertainty felt by these uprooted peasants. Their first objective was to reconstitute the individual identity within a wider, unassailable Islamic identity. By blaming misery and injustice on the ungodly political regime, the preachers provided the despairing youth with a solution to their problems.

One of the young activists closest to Sahnouni, who himself experienced the frustrations of urban poverty, recalled the happy teenage years he spent with his friends attending the sermons of the salafist preachers, who helped him through the transition to adult life. When he was sixteen years old, a neighbour of the same age 'who had attended the mosque for several years, and had gone to remedial classes, Islamic classes there, formed a group with some others: they all came first in their class ... One Friday, I went along with them to the mosque ... I saw that the educational programme they were providing was very good ... I started to attend lessons at the mosque. During the summer holidays, they organized month-long excursions ... they organized competitions and you could win prizes of Islamic books ... it was superb.'[20]

This experience not only helped the adolescent to structure his own identity but also provided him with an ideal way of life and social organization: 'I would like to relive the century of the ancestors (*salaf*). They were really the golden centuries. At that time, they were the strongest in the world. Islam was brought to several European countries. Islam conquered Spain. I would love those days to return.' In order to achieve this, the young activists would like to live 'in a neighbourhood where my neighbours were practising

Muslims who say their prayers ..., a neighbourhood where Islam was really practised: that's what we read in the books about our ancestors, not what some people practise now. But to have that real fraternity, to help each other, to not be always thinking about material things.' He would like to marry 'a practising Muslim woman who could found an Islamic family', 'a little Islamic state in the home'. In comparison with Western countries, he remarked, 'I feel I have an advantage: even if I don't have the material means, I feel very relieved on the moral front ... I see them living like beings who have no path to follow. They work, they laugh and joke, but they don't have a fixed path to follow.'

This is a – no doubt extreme – example of community restructuring of identity, the 'fixed path to follow' marked out by the salafist preachers, from the tiniest details of daily life to their vision of Algeria and the world modelled on the most uncompromising interpretation of 'pure' Islam. This vision was at the heart of the creation of the FIS. Although it was combined with other elements, represented by the 'Islamo-technocrats' of the *djazara* ('Algerianists'),[21] it appears to have dominated the popular expression of Islamist activism. But the separatist identity promoted by this vision of Islam did not necessarily entail violent confrontation with the public authorities: Sahnouni and other salafists left the FIS in 1991 and, despite their continued opposition to the regime, refused to join the armed resistance movement which they saw as directionless.

Beyond the divergences between the founding tendencies of the FIS, the issue which fundamentally divided the 'pure' and the 'impure' was that of French influence. The party's organ, *Al Munqidh*, shows the way in which 'France' was constructed as the symbol of anti-Islam and evil. This France, conceived 'in the heads' of the colonized people, must be expelled in order for Algerians to recover their lost purity, for it is more dangerous than the enemies traditionally reviled by the Islamic rhetoric of the Middle East – Judaism and Freemasonry.[22]

The publication of the first issue of *Al Munqidh* coincided with the day when the first articles on the 'Islamic veil affair' in Creil appeared in the French press (5 October 1989). Two weeks later, *Al Munqidh* took up the subject in its second issue, under the title 'France: three sisters are forbidden to continue their studies'. The article notes that 'in French schools, which are secular, clothing must follow secular principles!' but asks whether 'the French regime is not itself extremist and hostile in its attempt to force the sisters to wear "secular" clothing: where are the individual freedom and human rights which the regime invokes? Or does it just mean the freedom and the right to alienate Muslims from their religion?'[23]

The question of the veil also arose in some Algerian schools in 1989. The third issue of *Al Munqidh* presents a long open letter from veiled secondary pupils to the Ministry of Education, protesting against the pressure they have to endure by being forced to wear non-Islamic clothing in physical education classes: 'what do education and science mean when we are forced to take off our *hijab* (veil) and *jellabah*, which God the Most High ordered us to wear in His Law and forbade us to remove, except at home and in front of our *mahram* relatives?'[24] The article presents a foretaste of the bitter conflicts which later arose over the wearing of Islamic clothing during PE lessons in a number of schools in France in the early 1990s, with an important difference: in Algeria, it was God's law which was invoked in the girls' plea to the Ministry of Education, whereas in France arguments of individual freedom and human rights would be put forward in defence of the *hijab*. In Algeria, defence of Islamic dress placed the Islamists in direct conflict with the French values of freedom and human rights. The last issue of *Al Munqidh* reminded readers that 'the Koran (and the veil) are stronger than France', recalling that in June 1958 the colonialists themselves had been forced to this conclusion when faced with Algerian girls who deliberately wore their veils to sit the *baccalauréat*, in defiance of the official ban.[25] This act of heroism against the anti-Islamic French colonizers was held up as a lesson for contemporary Algeria.

The veil concerns two fundamental issues: secularism and the place of women in society. In both cases, *Al Munqidh* adopted an unequivocal position. An article written in French rejects the Western notion of the 'emancipated woman', using a crude play on words to imbue the term with pejorative connotations.[26] Anything resembling demands for 'women's liberation' and therefore entailing a change in Algerian family law, codified in 1984 on the basis of the sharia, is depicted as *fitna* or internal sedition leading to the ruin of the Muslim community.[27] As for secularism, it represented a major threat to Islam, especially at school. Thus, the withdrawal of an examination on Islam at the end of primary school was attributed to 'a new plot dreamed up by the men of secularism and the agents of colonialism with the aim of destroying our children's generation' and revealed 'the ignominy of the souls of the secular enemies, grandchildren of France'. *Al Munqidh* therefore called for the teaching profession to be purged 'of these intruders who continue to swoon before "overseas" [France]'.[28]

Throughout *Al Munqidh*'s three years of publication, France was

denounced both for its pernicious influence which lasted beyond colonization (since 'French occupation was above all a policy of cultural Westernization, marked by the spirit of the Crusades, with the
aim of destroying Islam')[29] and for the plots it was supposed to be
continually hatching to combat the FIS as the incarnation of Islam.
The legislative elections of 1991 were therefore presented as a battle
between 'the party of Arabic, Islamic civilization, which represents
the majority of the people' and the 'French language party' which
had been in power since 1962.[30]

'Smashing open the head of democracy'

In the battle between the West, symbolized in all its evil by France,
and Algerian 'authenticity', represented by the FIS's interpretation of
Islam, the main dividing-line concerns notions of democracy. The
pages of *Al Munqidh* consistently execrated the concept of democracy, but at the same time the FIS was willing to play the democratic game by taking part in the two first free elections in
post-independence Algeria. This ambivalence was to some extent
dissipated in a speech by Ali Benhadj: 'I assure you, brothers, that
we have no need of Parliament, if the goal of Parliament is to silence
us on the religion of Allah! Will God judge us tomorrow, on the day
of the last judgement, on our success or failure in Parliament? For
us, Parliament is a means, not an end, our end is the application of
the Law of God (*tahqiq shar'Allah*).'[31]

The FIS's most developed explicit view on the question of democracy is a long text by Ali Benhadj, published in three parts in *Al
Munqidh* under the title 'Smashing open the head of the doctrine of
democracy'.[32] The expression originates in a sentence from the
Koran: 'Nay, we hurl the true against the false, and it doth break its
head and lo! it vanisheth.'[33] This quotation, presented at the head of
the article, allows Benhadj to assimilate the aberrent 'doctrine of
democracy' and 'falsehood' in relation to God. 'One of the most
dangerous calamities which have beset Muslims in the course of
their long history, especially in our time,' writes Ali Benhadj,

> is that they have taken as their own impious doctrines and dangerous
> intellectual heresies, in which God has invested no power ..., because
> they did not measure what was being put to them against the yardstick
> of the Koran, the Sunna, and the Pious Ancestors (*salaf*). And they began
> to repeat slogans ... resembling a tomb: the borders are filled with flow-
> ers, but the rot is buried beneath ... And among these sickening intellec-

tual heresies which subjugated the minds of people and took hold of their hearts, so that young and old, innocent and debauched all applauded, was democracy – which they praised from dawn to dusk, without taking heed of its moral poisons and its ungodly origins.

Benhadj's radical critique of democracy uses a whole range of arguments borrowed from both 'Western thought' and Islamic tradition.[34] He points out that the Westerners, who invented the term, are incapable of agreeing on a definition, and that in any case true democracy does not exist. From the Islamic point of view, as interpreted by Benhadj, democracy as the doctrine of the sovereignty of the people contravenes the doctrine of 'sovereignty of God', which is the political credo of radical Islamist activists. Democracy must therefore be rejected wholesale.

But although the doctrinal standpoint of Ali Benhadj is unequivocal in its condemnation of democracy, its practical application and particularly the way in which it has been received at grassroots level are much less easy to pin down. A young Algerian who subscribed to Benhadj's views on democracy explained to one researcher that the Islamic state he hoped for would be characterized by the *shura*, 'that is, democracy'.[35] Despite the claim that parliament constitutes a means rather than an end, the FIS's participation in elections in the early 1990s caused some of the more militant activists, many of them former members of Bouyali's groups or former jihad fighters in the Afghan war, to refer to the party's leaders as 'ungodly' (*takfir*).

To add to the confusion in Algeria surrounding the notion of democracy, the regime – which prided itself on its democratic virtues – interrupted the legislative elections after the first round in order to prevent the FIS from claiming victory. The FIS was about to win power by purely democratic means.[36] The outlawing of the Islamist party, which had polled the highest number of votes, and the imprisonment of its leaders and activists (including many of those who had been legitimately elected in the first round) was approved by many parties, movements and associations which claimed to be 'democratic'. Those electors who voted for the FIS may well have been confused about the meaning of democracy. With hindsight, we can see that the term served as a figleaf for the authoritarian practices of the ruling party, and its meaning was lost in the disrepute which fell on the state. For Algerian youth faced since the onset of the civil war with worsening living conditions and even less hope for the future than before, the 'democratic' strike of January 1992 had the effect of discrediting not only the regime which clung to its money and privileges, but also the 'democracy' to which it laid claim, as well as all those who professed a democratic world view 'imported from the

West' and who used the language of the West (French) or its cultural references.[37]

These are some of the characteristics of the radical transformation which took place in Algeria at the start of the 1990s. The desire for change which exploded in the October 1988 uprising was later channelled by the FIS towards its own vision of the world, which was massively approved in the elections of 1990 and 1991. The Islamist vision was associated with a discourse of separation from France, one of its main objects of execration. In the Algerian political field, ritual denunciation of France fulfils a rhetorical function, which allowed the FIS to compete with the FLN as the 'authentic' voice of Algeria and to appropriate to its own ends the betrayed ideals of the independence movement. But it also fulfilled another objective: it masked the contradictions within the wider Islamist movement between the conservatives who simply wanted to dress up existing social hierarchies in the sharia, and the rebels for whom the sharia represented a utopian social justice.[38] Between the Islamist entryists within the ruling elite who took over the colonizers' vacant villas in 1962, the notables who aimed to protect their vested interests by a show of piety and the dispossessed urban youth anxious to attack those who had accumulated wealth and power and 'thought only of their bellies', the common ground was small and the alliances fragile. By demonizing France and making it a scapegoat for all Algeria's ills, the movement was able to hold its disparate elements together.

However, France was not only the mythical demon of *Al Munqidh*'s articles or the sermons of FIS imams; it was also a real place with a language, a culture and political institutions which made their presence felt in Algeria, and where millions of Algerians lived. Every Algerian has a relative who lives or has lived in France at some time, so every Algerian has access directly or indirectly to its market of goods and services. Conversely, every person of Algerian origin living in France has a close or distant relative who voted for the FIS in 1990 or 1991. In the interpenetration of these two worlds, what does the demonization of France mean in reality? How are the Islamists' diatribes against secularism, democratic doctrine, the language of Voltaire and Rousseau, or emancipated women transposed from one side of the Mediterranean to the other?

Threats hang over the future. For people of Muslim origin living in France, the situation in Algeria is close to their hearts. Some look forward to the victory in Algiers of a group emerging from the FIS, whilst others find the very idea abhorrent; whatever their view, it is in everyone's minds. At another level, a FIS victory could well result in renewed antagonism against France, leading to virulent anti-Muslim reactions in France, an upsurge in xenophobia and a right-wing political backlash equating 'foreigners' with crime. The signs have not been slow in coming: the second round of the 1995 presidential elections began with the drowning of a Moroccan man by two skinheads during a National Front demonstration in Paris, and the June 1995 municipal elections saw the National Front take three local councils. In 1958, events in Algeria triggered off the fall of the Fourth Republic. Although they will not reach the same scale in the 1990s, the situation in Algeria is likely to cause similar shock waves in end-of-millennium France.

2

Behind the Veil

In France, the year 1989 was marked by the 'Islamic veil affair'. In his column in the weekly *Nouvel Observateur*, Jacques Julliard noted ironically that on 9 November 1989, the same evening that the Berlin Wall fell, conversation at the dinner party he attended had revolved around the three veiled pupils excluded from their school in Creil.[1] Next to the Berlin events, the Creil affair was a parochial incident, and press comment abroad dismissed French preoccupation with the headgear of three adolescents as proof of 'French exceptionalism' or downright idiosyncracy. On the historic occasion of communism's collapse, when Eastern Europe regained its liberty, was it not ridiculous to concentrate instead on the battle between secularism and 'fundamentalism'? Or was something more sinister at work, using the 'veil' as the cover for an unspoken racism which emphasized 'fundamentalism' all the better to promote the rejection of populations of North African origin, particularly in the context of fears about the Algerian situation?

Despite the sarcastic comments, there was nothing ridiculous about the debate on the veil. Far from revealing France to be a declining, backward-looking country worried about its fragile identity, it set France's horizon firmly on the future organization of post-modern society. The old organization of society had been marked by cleavages between left and right, which the collapse of communism in the east now stripped of their meaning. In France as elsewhere, the social solidarities constructed by the labour movement, which had taken charge of the fate of poor, working-class areas and expressed their demands on the political scene, were weakening. New groups of dispossessed appeared, especially among the young

people of foreign, notably North African origin. What new collective identities would express their opposition to the norms and values of the dominant classes and help them to negotiate an
improvement of their lot? Amidst such uncertainties, was the wearing of the Islamic veil at school not the precursor of the emergence
of an Islamic community identity, against a backdrop of unemployment and social exclusion? How would the secular state and society
respond to this challenge? All of these questions were posed in the
welter of viewpoints and counter-opinions surrounding the Creil
affair.

In many ways, the affair marked the end of an era for the anti-
racist movement which had characterized the 1980s in France.
Throughout the decade, a myriad of associations had sprung up in
France's cities, to voice the demands of immigrant youth and help
their integration into civil society through the redistribution of
goods and services. At the time of the Creil affair, this network of
associations was suffering a credibility crisis. Many of the small
urban associations had not succeeded in integrating the youth they
were targeting or significantly improving their chances in society.
They lacked resources and, more importantly, did not have access to
public- or private-sector employers. (The associations linked to the
labour movement, socialist or communist, had on the other hand
always been credible in this regard because through the 'red' local
councils in particular they could control public-sector labour-market
demand.) Even the clearest-sighted associations, like SOS-Racisme,
were incapable of fulfilling this function, and frustration at their
lack of success was all the greater because of their proximity to the
ruling Socialist Party, to which they had helped to channel the *beur*
vote (notably in the presidential election of 1988).[2]

The anti-racist associations' loss of influence left a vacant space in
which the veil affair could maximize its impact. In any case, it took
on a national dimension when the leader of SOS-Racisme himself,
Harlem Désir, carried it into the public arena. On 6 October 1989,
he protested against the exclusion of the three girls, which he
described as 'a punishment meted out because of their faith'. His
intervention was intended to situate the debate in a wider context of
discrimination and racism, which his association had been set up to
combat. But events quickly moved beyond this simple categoriza-
tion, transforming the campaign for 'the right to be different' (which
Harlem Désir had championed as head of SOS-Racisme) into a campaign for 'different rights for different groups', on account of the
special injunctions of Islam.

During the months leading up to the Creil incidents, Islam in

France had undergone various phases of tension in relation to its environment. Three events of unequal impact stood out: the fallout from the Rushdie affair, in February 1989; the death of Sheikh Abbas, rector of the Mosque of Paris, and his replacement by Tedjini Haddam, in May–June; and finally the bulldozing of the Charvieu-Chavagneux mosque, in the Isère department, in August, whilst around the same time the mayors of Lyons and Marseilles announced that great mosques would be built in their cities. Each of these events expressed the complex and erratic relationships between Islamic associations and French institutions, as well as the internal tensions reflecting power struggles within Islam in France.

From Bradford and Algiers: the Rushdie affair and the Mosque of Paris

The direct impact of the Rushdie affair remained limited in France, compared with the huge mobilization it aroused on the other side of the Channel. On 26 February 1989, around a thousand people marched through Paris, including, alongside North Africans and converted French Muslims, Turks and Pakistanis belonging to Pir Mahroof's Bradford-based World Islamic Mission, who distributed leaflets in Urdu (probably the first time this had happened in France). The marchers chanted maximalist slogans: 'We are all Khomeinists' and 'Death to Rushdie!', but they were scarcely representative of Islam in France. The event had been organized by a tiny group, the Voice of Islam, which had published a few issues of a journal of the same title, partly financed by Saudi Arabia. Thanks to the march, the Voice of Islam succeeded in gaining maximum publicity for its activities. For a few weeks the group's charismatic leader, Abdul Farid Gabteni,[3] to whom the association's statutes gave the title 'founding father', became television's favourite Muslim bogeyman.

Only a small minority of Muslims in France rallied behind Gabteni's group. As in Britain, however, the publication of *The Satanic Verses* was considered by many ordinary Muslims in France to be an insult to the Prophet and to their faith. Many believers, especially the less well-off, saw the affair as yet another pretext by the West for discrediting Islam. This widened the gulf between them and the secular Arab intellectuals who organized rallies in Paris to condemn Khomeini in the name of human rights and express their solidarity with Rushdie. The intellectuals supported Rushdie because they feared a similar fate, in the event that their writings too might be accused of blasphemy by any imam who felt like issuing a fatwa.[4] A few years later, their fears would prove justified with the murders of the Algerian civil war.

Throughout the Rushdie affair, the two main rival Islamic organizations, the Mosque of Paris (since 1982 under the direct control of the Algerian regime) and the National Federation of Muslims of France (FNMF, founded in October 1985 with the express aim of taking over from the Mosque as the sole representative of Islam in France), both adopted a cautious strategy, torn between the need to express the views of their outraged grassroots audience and their desire to present themselves as a respectable partner for the French authorities. In a meeting on 15 March with minister of the interior Pierre Joxe, the rector of the Paris Mosque, Sheikh Abbas, echoed 'the insult received by Muslims, who had been offended in their faith', and expressed the wish that Salman Rushdie be charged with defamation in a British court.

In addition, an *ad hoc* coordinating committee was set up on 2 March, bringing together the FNMF, the Union of Islamic Organizations of France (Union des Organisations Islamiques de France, or UOIF) and the Association of Islamic Students in France (Association des Étudiants Islamiques en France, or AEIF); the latter two organizations were close to the ideology of the Muslim Brotherhood. The Mosque of Paris overcame its reservations concerning the FNMF and joined the committee. The committee set about trying to appeal to the French courts to stop the publication of the French translation of the novel. On 30 May, four of the member associations applied for a summary judgement to be heard, but the case was rejected on 8 June on the grounds of 'the constitutional right of each citizen to freedom of expression'. A second attempt on 19 July to have the book withdrawn after publication also failed.

For the French state, the Rushdie affair served as a reminder that problems linked to Islam could easily escalate out of control, in the absence of an interlocutor recognized both by the public authorities and by the grassroots Muslim populations. Since 1982, the socialist government had accepted the Algerian government's control of the Mosque of Paris, which it had treated as the unofficial representative of Islam in France. But Algiers had expressed support for Jacques Chirac in the 1988 presidential election, following the first period of 'cohabitation' between the socialist president and a right-wing government under Chirac's premiership. A few weeks before the first round of the presidential election, Sheikh Abbas welcomed Chirac's minister of the interior (responsible for religious affairs), Charles

Pasqua, amid great pomp at the Mosque of Paris, thus indicating to those French voters who shared his religion the best way to vote, as far as Algiers was concerned.

The suggestion did not have much effect, since the mass of 'sociologically defined' Muslim voters (mainly young people who in 1988 remained unconcerned by the message of the imams) chose François Mitterrand and the Socialist Party, largely because they considered the right-wing parties to be hostile to immigrants.[5] Nevertheless, the re-elected President Mitterrand and his government saw the Algerian government's intervention in French political life, through its 'religious embassy' in the Paris Mosque, as a threat. The French government was also now beginning to fear, after the 1988 uprising and the rapid rise of the FIS, that Islamists might come to power in Algeria.

For these reasons of home and foreign policy, the socialist Interior Minister Pierre Joxe decided to cultivate links with a body which would serve as intermediary between the public authorities and Islam in France and take responsibility for solving any problems relating to Islamic affairs. This body needed to be free of foreign control, and would prevent extremist groups from taking over Islam in France. On 15 March 1989, the minister convened a meeting with Sheikh Abbas, intended as 'the first of a series of consultations to be held with Muslim personalities, experts and theologians, on the problems of the French and foreign community living in France'.[6]

The consultation process was carried out with great caution, but came under strain with the death of Sheikh Abbas. The rector of the Muslim Institute of the Mosque of Paris was taken ill at the Crillon hotel, where he was awaiting an interview with Yasser Arafat during the PLO chairman's visit to Paris, and died shortly afterwards on 3 May. Besides being the representative of Algiers among French Muslims, Sheikh Abbas had been a popular and well-liked religious leader, especially among the older and poorer members of his flock who appreciated his unaffected manner and his generosity. The appointment of his successor revealed the omnipotence of the Algerian government and the inability of the French government to have any say in the leadership of Islam on its territory. As a result, the French government redoubled its efforts to set up a Muslim body free of Algerian influence.

Although the former rector of the Mosque of Paris (from 1957 to 1982) Si Hamza Boubakeur and his associates had 'handed over' control of the mosque to the Algerian authorities with the appointment of Sheikh Abbas, they had nevertheless remained influential within the Society of Habous and Holy Sites of Islam (whose president is also rector of the Muslim Institute of the Paris Mosque).[7] Si Hamza Boubakeur had regularly clashed with the governments of the North African countries, but in the 1980s he saw the tactical wisdom of allowing Algerian influence to predominate in the management of the mosque. On 10 June, the same day that Pierre Joxe declared publicly that 'we could soon see the Muslims in France organizing', the Society of Habous elected another Algerian politician, Tedjini Haddam, to replace Sheikh Abbas. Whereas his predecessor had been a non-French-speaker, a member of the inner circle of the Association of Algerian Ulemas and then a leading Islamic official within the FLN party-state, Tedjini Haddam was a polyglot surgeon, very modern in his appearance and speech, but nevertheless just as much involved in the Algerian power structures. He had been minister of religious affairs and minister of health, and had been ambassador several times. Haddam's appointment made the Algiers government's control over Islam in France crystal clear. However, the French government was later able to pressurize the new rector into making important concessions, once the Algerian government was weakened by the growing protest movement at home and the continued success of the FIS.

Mayors and mosques

The third 'hot' issue concerning Islam in the months preceding the veil affair was the question of mosques. Throughout the 1980s, the fact that most people of Muslim origin did not have French nationality and were therefore ineligible to vote meant that many mayors used everything in their power to ensure that no mosques were built in their commune. They were usually responding to pressure from 'anti-mosque committees' made up of residents close to the planned site, who were voters and therefore demanded attention. Some candidates in the municipal elections had campaigned on an anti-mosque platform. Once in office, they exercised their pre-emptive powers to block the mosques, thus putting aside the spirit of the 1905 law guaranteeing religious freedom.

On 16 August 1989, one mayor went much further. At Charvieu-Chavagneux, thirty kilometres from Lyons in the Isère department, a disused factory housing a prayer-room was bulldozed in the small hours of the morning. The RPR (Gaullist) mayor, M. Dezempte, had ordered the demolition of the building in order to allow the redevelopment of the site. He claimed that the prayer-room had been demolished by mistake, and the other part of the building should have been destroyed instead.[8] Several people, including children, had been inside the prayer-room at the time, and one was severely injured. The incident hit the headlines in France and abroad, especially in the Arab world. Not only had a holy, consecrated site been demolished, but the sacrilege was compounded by the fact that the perpetrators were not Muslim. Under Pierre Joxe's orders, the prefect for the Isère department summoned the mayor before him to remind him of the 1905 law. He expressed 'the government's disapproval and [his] personal indignation at the destruction of a Muslim place of worship, presented as an accident', reminding the mayor that in 1989, 'the year of the bicentenary of the declaration of the rights of man, such displays of intolerance and violence damage our country and public peace; they should be outlawed in the future and put right today.'

Beyond the symbolic significance of this clash, the Charvieu affair revealed an intricate set of interests emblematic of the transformations of contemporary society. It illustrated the changes taking place within a small industrial town: on one hand, the immigrant workers who had taken up permanent residence there; on the other, the 'native' Lyonnais who had settled there with their modest incomes to fulfil the dream of buying a small suburban house. The latter, who had triumphally elected Dezempte into the mayoral office, opposed the mosque because it would decrease the value of their houses. The immigrants, however, saw the destruction of the mosque as an aggressive act and were traumatized by it. Prior to the bulldozing of the mosque, the mayor had expressed his hostility to the permanent presence of immigrants in his commune. The incident provided one member of the local immigrant community claiming to belong to the FIS (which had been set up that year in Algeria) with the chance to make a series of public statements.

The prayer-room at the heart of the controversy had been established in 1981 in a former Moroccan café, to provide a service to the many Muslim workers at the factory. But in 1983 the factory closed down the buildings, which were then to have been demolished as part of a neighbourhood renovation scheme. A regular exchange of correspondence between the mayor and the president of the local Islamic association then ensued, with a view to rebuilding the mosque on another site, subject to planning permission. However, during the March 1989 municipal elections, the mayor made it clear that 'I do not wish to grant planning permission for this "mosque", because I believe ultimately that it is the future of our town which is at stake, the balance of our population which is under threat.' His campaign committee distributed leaflets claiming that 'a mosque would bring all the Islamics [sic] in the region down on us, including Islamic fundamentalists.'

On the day when the mosque was demolished, 16 August 1989, the local Islamic association had organized a public prayer-meeting outside the town hall as a mark of protest. The arrival of television cameras to capture the event exacerbated the power struggle between the Association of Algerians in Europe and the Moroccan chairman of the Islamic Association. The leaders of the two organizations, long-standing rivals, were ultimately left in the shade by a newcomer, Muhammad Yahiaoui, who castigated their weakness and inefficacy against the mayor. Yahiaoui defined himself as an Islamist activist who had been 'tortured and imprisoned in Algeria' and as such claimed to be better placed to speak on behalf of aggrieved Muslims. In his self-proclaimed capacity as 'member of the FIS delegation in France' he gave an interview to a national magazine, although the FIS later apparently denied any association with him.[9] The Charvieu affair, which started out as an electoral issue, thus ended up encouraging the emergence of a radical Islamist spokesman, who saw the chance to take advantage of the grievance felt by a number of Muslims after the destruction of their place of worship.

In the neighbouring city of Lyons, during the summer of 1989, the question of the construction of a mosque also became a major electoral issue for the newly elected mayor, Michel Noir. Unlike his former party colleague M. Dezempte, Noir was in favour of the construction of a great mosque in his commune. By making it a central issue, he hoped to make a national impact beyond the bounds of Lyons and thus serve his political career. Noir had already created a public image for himself and staked out the political centre ground by his firm stance against any local alliances with Jean-Marie Le Pen's National Front, declaring that 'it is better to lose the elections than to lose our soul.' During a high-ratings television programme which he hoped to use to establish himself as a potential future presidential candidate, the new mayor of Lyons announced that a great mosque would be built in his city on a prestigious site as originally planned, rather than the down-market site previously offered. The project had been conceived years earlier but had got nowhere.[10] 'Muslims have the right to have their own place of worship,' he declared. On the choice of the site, he was adamant: 'No question of a rubbish-tip mosque deep in the ghetto.'[11] Planning permission was granted on 29 August.

Whether motivated by ethical concerns or political strategy,

Michel Noir certainly took the opposite direction to that of most French mayors on the question of mosques. However, after the initial publicity, the issue was badly handled. A very active residents' committee had been set up to block the plans, but the main obstacle arose within the Muslim association responsible for the mosque project, the Lyons Islamic-French Cultural Association (Association Culturelle Lyonnaise Islamo-Française, or ACLIF). Two former French army officers, a professor of medicine and a local government official of the Greater Lyons conurbation were the leading figures in the association and had played a major role in the mosque negotiations in the 1980s. Their status as French Muslim notables, which they highlighted in order to reassure the hostile residents (in vain), did little to hide their lack of representativeness of the wider Muslim population of the city.

Plans for a 'cathedral-mosque' were welcomed by many Muslims living in Lyons, a city dominated by the Catholic cathedral perched on the Fourvière rock. But many Muslims also feared that the mosque would be controlled by an association which seemed foreign to their concerns. One of the ACLIF officers had argued the case for the mosque by saying that it would be 'the best way of avoiding the multiplication of little prayer-rooms where no one knows who's doing what.'[12] Those involved in the 'little prayer-rooms' were not best pleased, and the imam of one of them, when asked for his view on the plans, noted simply that 'Some want it [the mosque], others don't.'[13] The financial appeal launched among the 130,000 Muslims of the Rhône department to cover construction costs (estimated at fifty million francs) had brought in only around 100,000 francs by the beginning of 1990.[14]

In February 1990, the general secretary of the ACLIF, Colonel Chabaga (also deputy to the socialist mayor of the Lyons suburb of Villeurbanne), resigned from the association, alleging incompetence on the part of some of his colleagues. His resignation threw the association into a crisis which revealed the internal conflicts linked to the ACLIF's lack of representativeness and its relationship with Muslim countries of the Arab peninsula. Only the Arab countries could contribute the necessary funds for the building project, but in return they expected to exert control over the running of the mosque. The project seemed doomed when Kuwait, which was 'among the leading backers',[15] was invaded by Iraq in August 1989. Later that year, Saddam Hussein's ambassador in France, hoping to set up a support network in the country, offered Iraqi funding for the mosque through an association of former *harkis* (Algerian soldiers who fought on the French side during the war of independence). If the proposal had been accepted, Lyons would have had a grandiose 'Saddam Hussein mosque' like the one in Birmingham. But it was not taken up, and eventually a gift from Saudi Arabia allowed construction plans to go ahead.[16] The first stone was laid on 14 June 1992 in the absence of Michel Noir, who by now had become dissatisfied with the financial uncertainties of a project he had wanted to present as the flagship of his social concerns and his political ambitions. In addition, the problems he had encountered within his own party and his later brushes with the law over allegations of corruption afterwards weakened Noir's position to the point where in 1995 he was effectively excluded from the political scene. In these political power games at local, national and international level, the Muslim associations were left feeling as helpless as the public authorities.

Similar intrigues formed the backdrop to plans for a grand mosque in Marseilles. On the feast of Eid (13 July 1989), the mayor Robert Vigouroux followed Michel Noir's example by announcing his approval of plans for 'the construction of a grand mosque, the size of a cathedral or the Paris Mosque, which will be a symbol for the Muslim population of Marseilles'. In November, proposals for a building holding 15,000 people were submitted by a local wholesale butcher, Mustapha Slimani, 'the king of halal meat'. After years of local policy aimed at blocking planning permission for mosques, French mayors now seemed to be competing to see which of them could inaugurate the most splendid mosque in their city. But in Marseilles as in Lyons, the mayor's publicity coup did not result in any concrete action. Slimani's proposals were thwarted by fierce opposition from the already established Islamic associations.[17] The veil affair and then the Gulf War, by dramatizing the question of Islam in France, would in any case make mayors much less ready to commit themselves to support for mosques, as their voters increasingly identified Islam with 'fanaticism' and 'violence'.[18]

In the summer preceding the veil affair, an era came to an end. The 1980s were characterized by the growing visibility of Islam in France, but this Islam belonged to the older generations. Political expression revolved around the construction of mosques, dependent on the policies of local councils. At national level, the Rushdie affair, followed by the appointment of a successor to Sheikh Abbas as head of the Paris Mosque, helped to convince the French government that it needed to encourage the emergence of a new body to represent Islam in France, free of outside influence. But just as Pierre Joxe was beginning the consultations leading to the establishment of such a body, and city mayors were about to go ahead with grandiose schemes for cathedral-mosques, the veil affair shifted the basis for discussion. It was no longer a question of mosques, but schools; no longer a question of foreign interference, but of a new kind of Islam which had become a reference for youth born or at least brought up in France. The state's efforts to institutionalize Islam came too late to be able to defuse the conflicts and the social problems of the 1990s.

Liberty, veil, community

On 5 October 1989, the French national press reported that three schoolgirls wearing Islamic head-coverings had been refused entry to classes in the Gabriel Havez secondary school in Creil. Pupils had already been wearing headscarves to school for some years without causing major conflicts. In some cases, contacts between the school administration and parents had led to the pupil agreeing not to continue wearing the *hijab*. But elsewhere, pupils carried on without receiving any official reprimand. By prohibiting pupils wearing headscarves from attending classes, the headmaster of the Creil school adopted a traditional tactic of putting pressure on the parents to persuade their daughters to take off their veil. But by announcing his decision to the local press, he opened up the problem outside the confines of the school.[19]

The incident escalated when SOS-Racisme and the Movement against Racism and Anti-Semitism and for Peace (Mouvement contre le Racisme, l'Antisémitisme et pour la Paix, or MRAP) took up the defence of the three schoolgirls and placed the veil question within the wider context of anti-racism and the 'right to be different'. The anti-racist associations hoped to de-dramatize the image of Islam in France and play down the specific aspects of Muslim identity by presenting the veiled schoolgirls as victims of discrimination like any others. The girls should be allowed to attend school as a means of warding off fundamentalism: 'Where will their exclusion from state schooling lead to? To their enrolment in Koranic schools ... Whether they wear a veil or not, these children will best learn how to resist obscurantism in the school of Rousseau, Voltaire and the Enlightenment', declared Harlem Désir.[20] But instead of being diluted in the anti-racist melting-pot, the assertion of a separate Islamic identity managed to appropriate many of the themes of the earlier anti-racist movement and its appeal to the youth of North African origin who had identified themselves as *beurs* or as supporters of SOS-Racisme. In this respect, the transition from anti-racist movement to re-Islamization echoed the earlier shift from participation in the trade union movement to attendance at factory mosques in the late 1970s.[21]

Despite the press attention, the Creil affair at first seemed set to calm down. On 8 October, the headmaster and the families had come to an agreement, thanks to the mediation of a local Tunisian association leader: the girls would remove their head-covering in class but wear it in the corridors and playground. They could thus return to school. But five days later, the head received a visit from Abdallah Ben Mansour, the general secretary of the Union of Islamic Associations in France, and Mokhtar Jaballah, an officer of the Union's Paris branch, the Islamic Group in France, both close to the ideology of the Muslim Brotherhood.[22] They explained that Islam, as they interpreted it, stipulated that women should wear veils. On the other hand, Daniel-Youssouf Leclercq, the main organizer of the National Federation of Muslims of France (an association founded in 1985, which challenged the domination of the Paris Mosque), expressed his solidarity with the schoolgirls and was in constant contact with the Moroccan father of two of the girls.

For the re-Islamization movements, the controversy surrounding the affair made it an excellent mobilizing ground. Many young Muslims, whatever the strength of their belief, felt uneasy about the arguments of the secularists and saw their hostility to the wearing of the *hijab* as discriminatory. They argued that the authorities had never reacted to prevent Jewish pupils from wearing the *kippa*, or when they failed to attend classes on Saturdays. Nor was there any reaction to the wearing of crosses and chains around pupils' necks. The young Muslims felt that Islam was being singled out because of a fear of 'fundamentalism' which hid a racist, xenophobic hostility towards those who were no longer referred to as 'young', 'immigrants' or '*beurs*', but 'Muslims' (that is, 'fanatics'), all the better to reject and exclude them. The feminist writer of Algerian origin Leila Sebbar wrote: 'Is it not possible for those in a position of strength and power to tolerate young girls, who are attached to the external and internal forms of their religion, wearing a headscarf which does not cover the face, just as other girls wear ribbons in their hair?'[23] Imperceptibly, the ground shifted during the veil affair so that those who were stigmatized as 'Muslims' (that is, fundamentalists), began to turn this pejorative label into something of value and dignity – an assertion of their identity. The Gulf War, a few months later, was to make this attitude even more widespread.

From the Islamists' viewpoint, the veil affair triggered off a cycle of provocation–repression–solidarity which worked considerably to their advantage. Following the collapse of the 8 October compromise, the girls started to keep their hair covered in class. They were again excluded from school. The television cameras followed every tiny development in the saga. At this point, the President's wife Danielle Mitterrand herself intervened in the debate, stating: 'If the veil is the expression of a religion, then we should accept all traditions, whatever they are.' The next day, 22 October 1989, the Voice of Islam group, which had come to public notice with its anti-Rushdie march in February, organized a demonstration attended by a few hundred people, where veils were conspicuously worn, to shouts of 'Our veil is our honour.' Although the protest was disavowed by the National Federation of Muslims of France, who saw it as a provocation,[24] it showed that the radicals were capable of escalating the campaign.

The new rector of the Mosque of Paris, Tedjini Haddam, was forced to comment publicly on 23 October. He deplored the excesses of the previous day's demonstration and appealed for calm, and also cited Danielle Mitterrand's words to demand freedom for Muslims to obey the prescriptions of their faith. He attributed the escalation of the affair to the shortcomings of French academic specialists in Islam.[25] Whilst the rector of the Paris Mosque sought to find a scapegoat, his rivals in the National Federation of Muslims of France and the Union of Islamic Organizations of France had meanwhile outmanoeuvred him, and succeeded through their active participation in the Creil events in radicalizing the situation.

As far as they were concerned, their radical stance could not fail. No less than Lionel Jospin, the education minister, declared on 25 October: 'If, following discussions with the families, they do not agree to give up any religious signs, the children should be admitted back to school.' The minister's carefully worked-out statement noted that 'it would be a serious mistake to adopt a rigid attitude and thereby unite the whole of this [Muslim] community around a few isolated elements, by stimulating a solidarity reflex.' However, he also supported 'the absolute refusal of any proselytizing'.[26] Jospin's statement, coming from the minister in charge of the question, provoked a heated reaction from many intellectuals who took it to mean that the government was going back on the principle of secularism. They expressed their indignation in a manifesto entitled 'Teachers, let's not give in!', signed by such well-known figures as Elisabeth Badinter, Régis Debray and Alain Finkelkraut.[27] The debate took on huge national significance, focusing on wider questions of French identity at the end of the twentieth century and almost leaving to one side the Creil affair which had triggered it.

The Islamists hailed Jospin's statement as a victory: they had made the state yield, imposed the opportunity to wear the veil in state schools and thereby taken several steps forward in asserting Islamic communalist identity in the public arena. Their 'victory' had immediate consequences for the balance of powers within the various strands of Islam in France. Two national-level associations were particularly active in the Creil affair: the National Federation of Muslims of France (FNMF) and especially the Union of Islamic Organizations of France (UOIF). Meanwhile, as we have seen, the rector of the Paris Mosque, recently arrived from Algiers, remained in the background. On 21 November, the president of the UOIF, Ahmed Jaballah, wrote an open letter to Prime Minister Michel Rocard, who had recently made a speech against the wearing of the *hijab* in schools: 'You claim that the Koran does not impose the veil. In fact, the Holy Book of Muslims is very clear and very explicit, and leaves no doubt about the duty of all Muslim women to wear the veil.' Rocard's view that the veil 'is less the sign of a faith than of alienation' was attacked by Jaballah, who remonstrated that 'the Muslims of France could not accept such attacks on their dignity' and countered ironically: 'Must we understand [from Rocard's remark] that the citizens who cover their heads with a veil suffer from mental illness?' With this open letter, the UOIF challenged the French state for the first time. The Islamist organization signalled to Muslims that it was the supreme defender of their Islamic duty to wear the veil, and to the government that it was now a force to be reckoned with.

The day before Jaballah's open letter was sent, Pierre Joxe had received at the Ministry of the Interior 'six Muslim personalities' who would form the core of a future Discussion Group on Islam in France (Conseil de Réflexion sur l'Islam en France, or CORIF). As well as the rector of the Mosque of Paris, two Lyons representatives and one each from Lille, Marseilles and the Paris area were present. As well as representing the major cities with significant immigrant populations, each of Joxe's guests represented different groups of interest: Algeria, Morocco, the Muslim Brotherhood or former *harkis*. One of the participants was close to the UOIF, but this did not stop the association from marking out its territory in the open letter and making clear that it would be a tough negotiator.

On 27 November, the Council of State published its judgement, which Lionel Jospin had requested on 4 November, on the 'compatibility or incompatibility of the wearing of signs of affiliation to a religious community with the principle of secularism' in state schools. The Council ruled that 'the freedom ... granted to pupils includes the right for them to express and display their religious beliefs within educational establishments, whilst respecting pluralism and the freedom of others, and without prejudicing teaching activities, the curriculum and the duty of diligence.' However, it set limits to this freedom by prohibiting anything which could constitute 'an act of pressure, proselytizing or propaganda', threaten 'the dignity or freedom of the pupil or of other members of the educational community', endanger health and safety or cause disruption.

The Council of State was very firm in its restatement of the principles of individual freedom, including for minors, and ruled that attendance at state school could not in itself limit that freedom. In this it remained within the limits of the question that had been set by the education minister. Jospin had in fact formulated the question in a rather curious way; he had referred to 'affiliation to a religious community', an expression with no legal status. He took for granted the notion of communalist affiliation – but this was precisely the central issue in the debate: did the state education system recognize the notion of 'communities'? Was this the prelude to the recognition of a whole series of communalist identities which would differentiate the French from one another and form the basis of differential rules, as in Britain? The minister's question and the Council of State's response gave legitimacy to the assertion of communalist identity within the state system, as an expression of individual freedom.

The prohibition of constraints which could limit this freedom – pressure, proselytizing, provocation, propaganda – opened up the way for subjective interpretations of signs of religious affiliation. Was the wearing of the *hijab* Islamist propaganda? Was it an act of provocation? The ultimate test, according to the Council of State's ruling, was the effect on public order. In concrete terms, the decision belonged to heads of schools. The fundamental rule was freedom of the pupil, and it was up to the head to prove that any undesirable conduct constituted a threat to public order. Jospin circulated a memorandum to head teachers spelling out the responsibility which the Council of State ruling placed on them.

But by delegating responsibility to head teachers, the education minister created two new problems. First, he opened up the possibility that the law might not be the same for everyone: there would be schools which permitted the wearing of the veil, and others which did not. Second, he exposed head teachers to discipline by administrative tribunals. 'For a long time,' Councillor of State David Kessler has written, 'judges accepted that what happened in schools did not concern them ... A gradual change took place ... and later it was felt that if it was a matter of the clothes worn by pupils, if it was a matter of the organization of school life, it was a matter of rights. Pupils are subjects who have rights.'[28]

'Will Muslim families appeal to justice? This is one of the questions on which the future of this debate hangs,' noted Robert Solé in his commentary on the Council of State ruling.[29] It was not long before one family did just that. On 2 November 1992, the Council of State overturned the decision by a secondary school in Montfermeil (a suburb of Paris) to exclude three veiled pupils.

'Symbolizing Islam'

The veil affair had created a complex problem for the state authorities, which the French institutions were badly equipped to resolve. The assertion of Islamic communalist identity was rapidly becoming a major political issue, even though the main protagonists had not been clearly identified. The Mosque of Paris, supposedly the representative of Islam in France, had been overtaken by other movements which sought to dominate the Muslim associative scene. The state, worried by the rise of the FIS in Algeria, wanted more than ever to cut the umbilical cord between Algiers and the Mosque of Paris. Pierre Joxe's attempts to create an alternative network became ever more urgent.

The six Muslim personalities who had met with Joxe in November 1989 reported their conclusions in March 1990. They recommended the creation of a Discussion Group on Islam in France (CORIF), widened to include fifteen members so as to represent the different origins, itineraries and leanings of Muslims in France. Despite the similarity of the title to that of the Representative Council of Israelites in France (Conseil Représentatif des Israélites de France, or CRIF), the CORIF was not intended primarily to represent Muslim demands, but as a study and discussion group. It did not have institutional status but was established by virtue of a ministerial letter entrusting it with a specific mission. Its success would depend on its ability to change its status and become a representative body – but here it came up against the very obstacle it had been set up to avoid: the intimate relationship between Algiers and the Mosque of Paris. As a result, the Discussion Group never achieved its objectives.

Joxe, explaining his motives in setting up the CORIF, said: 'I could not find the interlocutor I was looking for, I therefore looked for this interlocutor to exist. ... I took up a suggestion by Jacques Berque, who told me it was possible to symbolize Islam, if not to represent it.'[30] This state initiative, which had no precedent in any other European country, reflected a centralizing tradition going back to Napoleon, who had organized Jewish and Protestant councils. Likewise, the Republic, as a colonizing 'Muslim power', had constructed the Mosque of Paris in 1926, in order to create an interlocutor between the state and the minority religion.

The objective of the CORIF, a consultative body with no power of decision, was, according to Joxe, 'to help [him] to manage as well as possible the concrete situations created by the practice of the Muslim religion in France'.[31] A wide range of Muslim personalities were coopted onto the CORIF in order to play an intermediary role and thus resolve any problems linked to Islam (which the affairs of the Charvieu-Chavagneux, Lyons and Marseilles mosques had highlighted) and avoid any major conflicts such as those which had marked the anti-Rushdie campaign and the veil incidents.[32]

The composition of the Group reflected these objectives: it included Islamist activists, such as the UOIF representative and a Turkish supporter of Milli Görüş (the immigrant offshoot of the Muslim Brotherhood-inspired Refah Partisi or Party of Prosperity), and included them in all their work, thus avoiding any complaints of exclusion from the Islamists. Missing from the CORIF were Daniel-Youssouf Leclercq, president of the National Federation of Muslims of France in 1990–1, and the Tablighis, always reluctant to get involved with any state initiative. Leclercq became a merciless critic of the CORIF; his news-sheet *L'Index* described it as 'a post-colonial institution which will sanction all anti-Islamic standpoints for reasons of state.'[33] But few others criticized the CORIF so harshly. A survey carried out in 1990 among leaders of Islamic associations in the Île de France region showed that the CORIF was 'judged favourably, even by those who were not involved in its creation'.[34] However, the CORIF had difficulty getting itself known, let alone recognized as an official representative, by grassroots Muslims.[35]

The members of the Group itself fell into two main categories. The first was made up of Muslim academics, businessmen or top civil servants whose legitimacy stemmed from their personal success rather than their networks among fellow Muslims, which were weak. The second category included association leaders who, now that they had been introduced to the Interior Ministry, could benefit from this contact in their dealings with parliamentary representatives or the administration. The CORIF thus gave the second category greater legitimacy in their status as notables, encouraging the emergence of a class of individuals for whom the expression of Islamic piety was endowed with respectability, just as participation in parish councils can fulfil a similar function for provincial Catholic doctors or lawyers.

The CORIF was able to boast three main achievements in influencing government policy. First, a ministerial circular of February 1991 recommended the general practice of 'Muslim plots' in cemeteries, thus saving Muslim families the cost of burial in the home country. France became a part of *dar al islam*, because Muslims could now have their dead buried there.[36] Second, the same year, the Defence Ministry took steps to provide containers with halal food for Muslim soldiers who requested them. Finally, in 1990 and 1991, the CORIF's united approach led to a more or less general consensus about the date of the beginning of Ramadan. Before then, imams aligned with Algiers, Mecca or Istanbul had dated the beginning of the fast from the time when the Ramadan moon was seen in one or other of these cities, whereas others went by the appearance of the moon in France's skies. The divisions this caused among believers in France were temporarily healed, only to resurface with the crisis of the CORIF following Haddam's departure.[37]

The CORIF's detractors judged these achievements disappointing, given the efforts devoted to it by three successive ministers of the interior. In the opinion of its supporters, however, it enabled France to get through the Gulf War without being torn apart by the sympathy shown for Saddam Hussein by many Arabs and Muslims in France at a time when the French army was fighting against Iraq on the Saudi front. Once the war was over, the President of the Republic thanked the Muslim 'community'[38] for its 'dignity' and 'sense of responsibility' during the conflict, and later met the members of the CORIF at the Elysée Palace on 26 March 1991. By recognizing the CORIF, the President seemed to be saying that the body, the supreme representative of the 'community', had played an eminent part in the preservation of civil peace during the months of 'Operation Desert Storm'.

However, the CORIF's members had expressed diverging views as soon as Iraq invaded Kuwait in August 1990. The Algerian head of the main Marseilles mosque in the rue du Bon Pasteur, M. Alili, attended the Islamic conference in support of Saddam Hussein organized in Baghdad on 9–11 January 1991, which ended with a call to jihad. Alili constantly railed in the press at the Saudi and Kuwaiti regimes and at the American soldiers whom he accused of desecrating Muslim holy sites.[39] At the opposite end, the head of the Evry mosque, M. Merroun, and the leader of the Federation of Islamic Associations of Africa, the Comoros and the West Indies, M. Dramé, criticized Iraq for its 'treacherous aggression [which] does not fit in with Islamic logic' and its 'secular nationalist ideology, condemned by Islam'.[40] M. Haddam of the Mosque of Paris, who along with his Marseilles colleague had attended the Baghdad conference (whilst reminding the public that he had also taken part in a CORIF delegation to Saudi Arabia a month earlier), adopted a more nuanced stance, showing sympathy for the Iraqi president and the dangers facing his country, but also placing his hopes for a settlement in President Mitterrand's standing in the Arab world.[41] As for the UOIF leaders, they emphasized that they had 'always wanted peace during this war', whilst simultaneously taking care not to offend either grassroots support for Iraq and/or the monarchies of the Arabian peninsula, who in return showed their generosity in the following months.

Despite its members' widely differing views, the CORIF survived the Gulf War without being torn apart. The conflict had indirect effects on Islam in France, as the Saudis held back their financial support for those organizations which had been incautious in their public statements. But the Group itself remained unaffected by these changes. However, another external crisis dealt a fatal blow to the CORIF's work: the 11 January 1992 *coup d'état* in Algeria. President Chadli Benjedid was replaced by Muhammad Boudiaf, who had been living in exile in Morocco, and a five-member transitional government (High Committee of State) was formed. One of the members of the new government was the rector of the Muslim Institute of the Mosque of Paris, Tedjini Haddam, also a member of the CORIF. This meant that a member of the Algerian government was now in charge of the Mosque of Paris. The appointment was a terrible snub to the French government, which had originally formed the CORIF as a means of cutting links between Algiers and the Mosque of Paris.

Since his arrival in France in June 1989, Haddam had adopted a cautious approach, constrained by the growing weakness of the Algerian government and the rise of the FIS and popular protest. Although nominated rector by Algiers, with the consent of the Society of Habous and the Boubakeur family which controlled it, Haddam took part in the talks leading to the creation of the CORIF, and thereby abandoned his predecessor's claim to act as exclusive representative of Islam in France. He went even further: in November 1990, Haddam took part in the general assembly of the National Federation of Muslims of France (FNMF), which five years earlier had been set up precisely to counter the hegemony of the Mosque of Paris, and he was elected to its board of directors. By following this consensual approach, he avoided many of the criticisms which had been levelled at his predecessor Sheikh Abbas.

In 1992, however, his nomination to the High Committee of State and subsequent departure for Algiers opened him up to attack. At a CORIF meeting on 20 January, with nine out of fifteen members present, it was decided that Haddam's new post was incompatible with that of rector of the Mosque of Paris, and with membership of the Group. Some of the CORIF members were keenly aware of grassroots support for the FIS, which the *coup d'état* had robbed of its electoral victory, whilst others anticipated the French state's desire to end the Algerian government's control of the mosque. Following the decision, the Group put forward to the interior minister, Philippe Marchand, the name of Jacques-Yakoub Roty, a Frenchman born into a family of converts, as Haddam's replacement. The move showed the CORIF's intention to take the mosque in hand and set aside the statutes which required approval of the nomination by the Society of Habous.

The CORIF had reckoned without the determination and resourcefulness of the Boubakeur family. Si Hamza Boubakeur, still a formidable character at the age of eighty, cabled Haddam in Algiers to ask him to give up his post on the High Committee and return to head the Mosque of Paris. The Society of Habous met on 6 February and declared that the rector would 'carry on his mission', denouncing the 'rumour-mongers and intriguers'. The same day, Haddam contacted the interior minister to confirm this information. Thus ended the first act of an unfolding drama, marked by theatrical stunts on the part of the Boubakeurs and hesitation on the part of the French authorities.[42]

The surprises were not yet over. On 7 February, Haddam announced his departure from the CORIF, which had 'stabbed [him] in the back', but the same evening, the Algerian ambassador in France stated that Haddam had not given up his post on the High Committee and would be leaving the next day for Algiers for three days. On his return, the CORIF stepped up its pressure on him. Roty, who now saw himself as rector of the Mosque, declared that the 'French solution' represented by him would win general support.

The strange situation of an official rector shuttling back and forth from Paris to Algiers and an unofficial rector making public statements from the wings ended on 12 April, when a general assembly of the Society of Habous unanimously elected Dalil Boubakeur (Si Hamza's son) rector of the Muslim Institute of the Mosque of Paris.

Once again, Si Hamza Boubakeur had decided the fate of the Mosque in his own way. Having handed control over to the Algerian government from 1982 to 1992 during the Mitterrand years, when his family had few influential contacts in the French ruling circles, he took it back again at a time when the right looked set to return to power and his family would have friends in high places.

The CORIF felt badly snubbed, and reacted strongly. Its spokesman M. Dramé called the election a 'put-up job'.[43] At the Interior Ministry, the situation was described as 'transitional', but once again the French government had been faced with a *fait accompli*. Dalil Boubakeur's position appeared difficult for the first few months. But he had strong support behind him. The Algerian government confirmed its backing for Boubakeur (who was originally from Skikda, in Algeria) and continued to finance the Mosque's substantial staff budget. Boubakeur was also strongly supported by various influential associations of former *harkis*. The (Gaullist) RPR president and mayor of Paris, Jacques Chirac, approved a substantial grant from the city council to renovate the Mosque, and inaugurated the renovation project on 7 December, shortly before the legislative elections of March 1993.

For his part, the socialist minister of the interior, now Paul Quilès, sharply criticized the new rector, describing it as 'unacceptable that a religion of this importance should be the vassal of a foreign power' and reasserting his support for the CORIF, which Boubakeur refused to join. In a public show of exasperation, Quilès refused en bloc to grant visas to around thirty Algerian and Egyptian imams invited by the Mosque of Paris to preach in France during Ramadan. In response, the rector complained of the government's 'bullying tactics'. However, after the 1993 elections and the triumphal victory of the right, the new interior minister, Charles Pasqua, threw his weight behind Boubakeur. The CORIF's days were over.

The CORIF had been created at the initiative of the socialist government, with the aim of bringing Islam into line with other religions and calming 'many tensions resulting from many misunderstandings', according to its main architect in the French administration, Raoul Weexsteen.[44] Its principal aim was to free Islam in France from the control of the Algerian government, so that when it lost out to Algiers during the Haddam episode, it did not recover from this blow to its authority. The episode showed the strength of influence Algiers had in France, despite the weakening of the FLN state. It also made it clear that the CORIF had not been able to establish any real legitimacy within the Muslim associative networks in France. The CORIF, a creature of the French socialist administration, fell from grace with it. Pasqua, the new interior minister, adopted a radically different approach and chose to bolster the Paris Mosque, encouraging it to build up a network of movements and associations around it.

France, land of Islam?

Whilst the CORIF was trying to build up a network of Muslim leaders 'of goodwill' around the Interior Ministry, Islam in France was meanwhile undergoing profound transformation. The CORIF found itself unable to influence the course of this change. The rise of the Muslim Brotherhood-inspired Union of Islamic Organizations in France (UOIF) during the veil affair made it the most influential of France's Islamic associations. It success was principally due to the professionalism of its organization, which deployed many young, university-educated, bilingual Arabic–French officers to implement a coherent strategy. The Muslim associative movement – first fragmented into a myriad of tiny local associations, then paralysed in the late 1980s by the conflict between the National Federation of Muslims of France and the Mosque of Paris, and later represented at official level by the CORIF – was now dominated by another type of organization, which carried out several practical and effective initiatives offering services to the whole of the target population, instead of simply engaging in wars of words. Before the veil affair, there were around thirty local associations affiliated to the UOIF. In 1994, its general secretary, M. Ben Mansour, claimed a membership of 207 local associations, most of them pre-existing groups which affiliated to the UOIF in order to benefit from its services without necessarily sharing all of the Muslim Brotherhood's ideology.[45]

According to its statutes, the aim of the UOIF is 'to represent Islam and Muslims in France and defend their interests'.[46] The association strives to organize an 'Islamic community' defined by religious observance, which will gather together all people of Muslim origin and 'bring them back to the faith'. To this end, the UOIF intends to negotiate with the public authorities in order to win various legal concessions which would give the 'community' a form of autonomy within French society compatible with the 'principles of Islam', as defined by the organization.

The UOIF activity which commands the most media attention is the annual Christmas-time gathering, which has been held at Le Bourget since 1988. In 1992, it attracted around ten thousand people. It is rather like a left-wing political festival, with meetings, discussions and stands. The UOIF's own company, Euro-médias, produces and distributes video cassettes, which relay the meeting's Islamist preaching and lectures (in Arabic, but since 1992 also in French) into thousands of homes. The undisputed star of the videos is Hassan Iquioussen, a preacher of Moroccan origin from Lille, who preaches in French and has found an enthusiastic following among the young who are 'rediscovering Islam'. Another popular French-language preacher is Hani Ramadan, a grandson of Hassan el Banna and representative of the Islamic Centre in Geneva.

But the UOIF is also very active on the ground, providing a range of services to local groups needing assistance with specific demands, such as planning permission for a mosque, or negotiations with school authorities over the wearing of the veil: legal support, lobbying (helped by the fact that two of its leaders were members of the CORIF from 1990 to 1993) and media relations. The organization also has a reputation for being able to supply the all-important 'recommendations' (*tazkiyya*) to benefactors in the Arabian peninsula, which are a necessary condition for subsidies to Islamic associations, especially for the construction of mosques. These activities were crowned with the January 1992 inauguration of the first Islamic 'Institute of Theology', in the Nièvre department. However, this expression of the UOIF's power aroused concern among some politicians and sections of the media, who suddenly became worried by the influence of an organization which preached an ideology inspired by that of the Muslim Brotherhood.

Much of the UOIF's organizational and intellectual strength may be attributed to the background of most of its founders, Tunisian students belonging to the urban petty bourgeoisie who were initiated into activism through the Movement of the Islamic Tendency (MTI).[47] The MTI, founded in Tunis in 1979 under the leadership of the philosophy professor Rached el Ghannouchi and the lawyer Abd el Fattah Mourou, was severely repressed towards the end of Habib Bourguiba's regime. After Ben Ali came to power in November 1987, it had two years' respite. Its imprisoned leaders and activists were released, and it even took part in the early elections announced by the new regime in April 1989. The movement then changed its name to Al Nahda.[48] However, it bitterly denounced the rigged elections and went underground, with some of its members turning to armed resistance. Since then, it has been mercilessly suppressed. Most of its leaders escaped abroad, emigrating mainly to France, where many took up postgraduate studies, usually in the applied sciences.

At the end of the 1980s, the movement's spokesman in France, M. Habib Mokni, together with Ghannouchi, who had fled to London, advocated a reappraisal of the Islamic doctrine of the Muslim Brotherhood. In their view, modern Islamist ideology needed to take into account the tremendous changes which had taken place in the world in the twenty years since Sayyid Qotb (incarcerated in a prison camp in the desert before being hanged in 1966) in the repressive conditions of Nasser's Egypt. At the time when communism was collapsing in Eastern Europe, Muslims too put forward a democratic demand: authoritarian colonial states should not give way to authoritarian states based on religion; rather, the future Islamic state should seek to reconcile pluralism and application of the sharia. This was the programme of Al Nahda in 1989, and this was also the ideal which inspired the journal published in Paris from 1991 by Habib Mokni, *Al Insan* ('Man'), as well as Ghannouchi's 1993 book *Al Hurriyat al 'amma fil daoula al islamiyya* (Public freedoms in the Islamic state).[49] Al Nahda's attempt at synthesizing Islam and Western-style democracy, or reforming the Islamist movement from within, resembles in some ways the stance of the Algerianist, 'technocrat' wing which dominated the FIS in the run-up to the 1991 elections in Algeria, but is far removed from the radical anti-democratic stance of Ali Benhadj, who as we have seen advocated 'smashing open the head of the doctrine of democracy'.

According to Habib Mokni, Al Nahda's ideology reflects the antagonism between the 'military' (radical) and 'political' (democratic) options within contemporary Islamist movements. He criticizes Western states for supporting unpopular Arab regimes for the sole reason that they constitute a 'bulwark against fundamentalism', thereby escalating the tension and encouraging the 'military' Islamists. On the other hand, Western countries as hosts to sizeable Muslim populations are themselves an excellent laboratory for the Islamist democratic experiment to develop. The UOIF, far from simply making a virtue out of necessity in its political action, sees itself as forming a central part of this democratic experiment.[50]

In this way, the UOIF embarked on a crucial change of strategy at the end of the 1980s, after long discussions within the organization. France was no longer simply considered a place of refuge and recruiting ground to resume the combat at home for the Islamic state. From *dar al 'ahd* ('land of negotiated peace'), France became a land of mission, where Islam could be preached and organized for its followers – a piece of *dar al islam* ('land of Islam'). Ben Mansour, general secretary of the UOIF, defines *dar al islam* as any territory where 'Muslims are safe and can practise their religion freely', and contrasts France or Britain, where Islamists can pursue their activities unhindered, with certain North African countries 'where Muslims [i.e. Islamists] are persecuted'.[51] Albeit traditionally Muslim, countries like Tunisia cannot in his view be considered as *dar al islam*.[52]

For this reason, the UOIF demands that Muslims in France be granted recognized minority status, on the basis of their religious affiliation, so that they can obey all the injunctions of their religion.[53] In the long term, the Union hopes to become the representative of the Muslim 'minority' and defender of its specific interests, which it intends to stamp with its own conception of Islam. We have already observed how Indian/Pakistani Islamists organized around the UK Islamic Mission applied a similar strategy and objective, to great effect. But in France, where the Republic is held to be 'one and indivisible' (according to the constitution), there is no legitimate space for communalism within the political system. It took a major crisis – the Creil affair, in autumn 1989 – to force the public authorities to reconsider French political identity.

The UOIF was not the first Islamic association in France to reappraise the situation of Islam in France. In the late 1980s, other groups and associations were already involved in internal debates and restructuring. It was in this context that the National Federation of Muslims of France (FNMF) was founded in October 1985, to counter the influence of the Algiers-controlled Mosque of Paris. The Federation, which had some 140 affiliated local associations at the most in 1989, included various different tendencies, and various component sections of the UOIF joined it. In November 1989, the FNMF held its annual congress at the Omar mosque, headquarters of the Jama'at al Tabligh, in the eleventh arrondissement of Paris. The congress was marked by a conflict between the UOIF-affiliated associations and FNMF president-elect Daniel-Youssouf Leclercq, over split lists for election to the executive committee. The real issue was the FNMF's desire to minimize UOIF influence within the association; the UOIF had gained in prestige during the veil affair and was hoping to gain extra seats. The UOIF, for its part, wanted to reduce the Federation to an Islamic association like any other, as it had already tried to do with the setting-up of the *ad hoc* coordinating committee against *The Satanic Verses*, in March 1989.

Following this incident, the UOIF activists withdrew from the FNMF, thus weakening it considerably. At the same time, they served notice that they were now the third contender for control of Islam in France, alongside the enfeebled FNMF and the Mosque of Paris, which now more than ever appeared to be little more than the religious arm of the Algerian embassy. To mark its new strategy in relation towards French society and the French state, the UOIF officially informed the Paris Prefecture of Police of its amended title: it now became the Union of Islamic Organizations *of* (rather than *in*) France.[54] At the Union's annual gathering at Le Bourget, in December, the theme was 'the integration of Muslims into French society' and Ghannouchi as guest of honour gave a speech in which he supplied the ideological justification for the change of strategy. According to Ghannouchi, the presence of Muslims in the West constituted a radically new situation for Islam, forcing it to rethink the binary division between *dar al islam* and *dar al harb*. It was necessary to 'overcome prejudices whilst maintaining the principles of Islam and trying to establish a sincere dialogue in order to achieve a sincere integration.'[55] According to this view, integration does not mean the search for a private, individual relationship to faith, but rather the practical application of Islam-based communalism, in a situation in which Muslims have set up permanent residence on French soil. 'Our desire is for integration,' declared Ben Mansour, 'and instead they try to assimilate us!'[56]

In order to teach these 'principles of Islam' to the Muslims of France, the UOIF carried out an ambitious project – the creation of a private faculty of Islamic theology. Plans were announced for the construction of the institute in a castle in the Nièvre, just a few kilometres away from Château-Chinon, famous for having had François Mitterrand as its long-serving mayor and for symbolizing the President's 'tranquil force' image. Specialists in Islam, among them Professors Mohammed Arkoun and Bruno Etienne, had for some time been calling for the establishment of a faculty of Islamic theology. Since the French law on the separation of church and state meant that faculties of theology could not be created within public universities, they suggested that a faculty of Islamic theology could be set up in Strasbourg, in order to take advantage of the special statutes of the Alsace-Moselle departments, where the separation of church and state had no legal force (as they had come under German rule in 1905, and the omission was not made good when they returned to French sovereignty in 1918). The two academics envisaged the faculty as a means of training French-speaking Muslims with a firm background in the realities of the French situation and dedication to theology and human sciences, as an antidote against the uncontrolled proliferation of imams from North Africa or the Middle East who preached an 'obscurantist' view of Islam. Their proposals met a mixed reception in secular circles, unconvinced of the necessity of spending tax-payers' money to train imams (any more than they should pay to train priests, pastors or rabbis), whilst at the same time arousing the hostility of many Islamic associations which feared that the culturally well-equipped 'republican' imams would marginalize them in the representation of Muslims in France.[57]

Although these plans came to nothing, they nevertheless expressed the aspirations of some observers of Islam and influential groups of academics, journalists and politicians. The UOIF skilfully presented its own project using the arguments laid out in the earlier plans: it too would train imams well versed in the realities of the French situation. The French-language prospectus of the 'European Institute for Human Sciences', as it was called, stipulates that 'an aptitude for science and theory, as well as an ability to assimilate the Western dimension, represent a considerable advantage for the preservation and co-existence of the different components of multicultural European society.'

The Arabic-language prospectus, aimed at a different audience, presents the project in a rather different light. The name itself is changed ('European Faculty of Islamic Studies'). The objective of the institute is to form an elite group of preachers who would be all the more effective because they would be able to speak directly to the younger generations in their own language: 'there is no doubt that such preachers will have much more prestige than those who have no knowledge of the reality of life in Europe.'[58] The faculty's advisory board is composed of fifteen *ulema*, the most famous of whom is the Egyptian sheikh Youssef el Qardaoui, who is intellectually close to the Muslim Brotherhood; five others teach in Saudi Arabia and two in Sudan. The institute plans to take in fifty students each year on a four-year course, all of them boarders. Fees stand at 35,000 francs per annum, of which 10,000 is charged to the student. Students are admitted on the basis that they are 'known for their commitment (*iltizam*) to Islam and their good morals.'[59] Non-Arabic-speaking students (who follow an intensive year-long course in Arabic at the institute) must have the *baccalauréat*, but it is not required of Arabic-speaking students, who go directly into the imam training stream.

The entry requirements reflect the ambivalent position of the UOIF, which addresses French-speaking and Arabic-speaking audiences in different ways.[60] How was the institute to reconcile the 'preservation of Islam' and the goal of 'integration' promised by the UOIF? Thus, in 1990, just as the Nièvre institute was getting off the ground, the brochure circulated at the Le Bourget gathering dedicated to 'integration' included a section presenting its educational project in glowing terms, and contrasting it favourably with that of other Muslim associations: 'Many associations teach, but with limited means at their disposal, and incomplete curricula which do not reach the desired objective and do not succeed in countering the French dominance of language, thought, customs and behaviour which assails Muslim children from all sides.' The implication was that the UOIF sought to go against this French influence, but this does not sit well with its public pronouncements in France justifying the creation of the institute.

It seems to us that the UOIF's goal of countering French dominance of Muslim children's thought and behaviour entails the organization and development of an autonomous space – perhaps a symbolic space – for the *Umma* (community of believers). Muslims in France should form the avant-garde of this *Umma*. This goal means that the UOIF has had to maintain a firm position on 'the principles of Islam', but at the same time avoid direct confrontation with the French authorities, since the *Umma* is still very vulnerable and could be disrupted by any open conflict. In this sense, the Union is caught in the trap of its own success. Its leadership of Islam in France has meant that, in order to further its plans, it has been forced to make promises to the various forces between which it acts as intermediary: the French state, the oil-rich states of the Arabian peninsula, conservative financial backers who provided the funds to set up the Nièvre institute and its ever more radical grassroots constituency. The radicalized grassroots youth, alienated by the unending prospect of unemployment, are French citizens and therefore much more able to express their discontent than most of the UOIF leaders, who as foreign nationals face the risk of expulsion if they go too far in infringing French norms.[61] Thus, we have seen that the UOIF's public statements vary according to the audience or interlocutor, but the main factor the Union must take into account is the extreme youth of its potential supporters, the 'younger brothers of the *beurs*' of the 1980s movements who have been flocking to Islamist meetings since the Gulf War and the civil war in Algeria. In its struggle to win over this audience, the UOIF faces competition from other associations, whose leaders are themselves members of this second generation, have French nationality and see Islam as the bearer of more radical social demands.

The manifesto prepared for the December 1993 gathering at Le Bourget, on the theme of 'the concerns and aspirations of Muslims in France', reflects the Union's desire to reach out to young Muslims. It uses a quasi-Messianic discourse of radical change and upheaval: 'The *Umma*, which sees the whole world – and itself along with it – thrown into convulsions and collapsing under the yoke of political and economic oppression, has a duty, since it espouses Islam as a spiritual and political doctrine, to take upon itself the mission of saving humanity from servitude, misery and absurdity and bringing it out of the darkness of error and deception to let it take in the light of the true path and happiness.' The *Umma*, with its ability to 'resolve the world's problem ... by preaching Islam among peoples and nations, ... by freeing it from the yoke of ungodly capitalism', faces the 'colonialist unbeliever – the eternal enemy'. But, it possesses 'many, powerful strengths which are without equal ... therefore victory is guaranteed'. First, however, the community must arrive at an awareness that 'the Islamic state, the one and only way to liberate the *Umma* and spread the light of Islam in the world ..., is an obligation of Islam.' In this process, the appropriate means are 'ideological struggle' and 'political combat', with 'the application of Islamic law [as] the priority.'

In its style, the 1993 manifesto stands out from the customary French-language publications issued by the UOIF (although it is hard to tell whether the unsigned text was originally written in French or Arabic, since the Arabic version contains several grammatical and syntactical errors). Its main purpose was to mobilize the thousands of sympathizers who had gathered in Le Bourget, who would respond to the idea of a struggle against 'ungodly capitalism'. It does not address issues specific to Muslims in France, but rather general themes which link Islam in France with Islam in the world and appeal to a feeling of social revolt.

At the beginning of the 1990s, then, an important change took place in the Islamic associative movement in France. Organizations originally oriented towards the country of emigration and its domestic struggles turned their attention towards the host country, thus internalizing the process of permanent settlement in France which most of their activists and supporters had experienced. However, until the veil affair and the Gulf War, this change took place within a restricted Islamic network of associations and concerned almost exclusively the older generation of immigrants. At the end of the 1980s, young Muslims were still attracted to the 'anti-racist' movement in its various forms, from SOS-Racisme to the Young Arabs of Lyons and its Suburbs (JALB), in which Islam was at most incidental to identity. From the autumn of 1989, however, the veil affair allowed the Islamist movements to extend their influence beyond their traditional circles and attract young, educated Muslims. The demand put forward at that time was the defence of the specific interests of a community, defined in relation to religion and strengthened by intensive practice of that religion. The meeting of Islamist communalism and the identity crisis and social alienation of second-generation immigrant youth would constitute the major phenomenon of the 1990s. With the veil affair and especially the Gulf War, the 1980s anti-racist movement split apart and lost much of its appeal to Muslim youth. Some of the *potes* ('pals', after the SOS-Racisme slogan 'Leave my pal alone'), *beurs* and JALB of the 1980s and their younger brothers and sisters went on to find in Islamist communalism a means of negotiating their place in the France of the future.

3

The Communalist Challenge

France's involvement in the Gulf War in January 1991 made the politicians in charge of public security uneasy. They feared that support for Saddam Hussein could soar among France's populations of Arab or Muslim origin, as it had in Algeria, Morocco and Tunisia. In the three North African countries, protestors had chanted anti-French slogans and burned effigies of the French President. In Algeria, a French consulate was attacked, and the hit song of the season was entitled 'Strike, O Saddam!' The song was widely distributed in video shops in the Barbès area of Paris; on its cover, the face of Pascal on a 500-franc note had been replaced by that of the Iraqi president. In North Africa, both Islamists and their secular opponents supported the 'new Saladin' who seemed to offer something to all of them. To the nationalists, he was the leader of the secular Ba'ath party and promoter of a modernizing form of Arabism; the Islamists for their part noticed that his flag included the words 'Allah Akbar', that he called his war a jihad and had himself filmed prostrate in prayer.

In France, journalists were dispatched to the deprived urban areas to write report after report on '*beur* unrest'. Some sought to draw parallels with the 1986 situation, when Middle Eastern conflicts hit Paris in the form of bomb attacks; they tried to identify potential 'terrorists' who might bomb France's cities to further the Iraqi cause. Others showed the effects of the atmosphere of suspicion on the 'French system of integration'; Muhammad Mebtoul, the 'only *beur* member' of the Socialist Party's management committee, was quoted as a representative of a disillusioned generation: 'We were trying to be integrated French citizens, suppressing our feeling of being a community. But now, it will come out into the open – and stay out!'[1]

Despite the fears and fantasies of French politicians and journalists, no major incident concerning the Gulf War occurred in France whilst the hostilities were going on. However, the war revealed situations of social discontent which the festive aspect of the great anti-racist demonstrations of the 1980s had often hidden. Setting aside the personal record of Saddam Hussein and Iraq's ambitions in the conflict, the war created an image of the Iraqi leader as an Arab-Muslim hero fighting against Western violence and oppression, whilst George Bush on the other hand embodied the detested figure of the policeman or security guard. The highly abstract and technical war as seen on television, with little flags being moved around army maps and electronic images of 'Patriot' missiles falling on Baghdad and 'Scuds' on Tel Aviv, was experienced by inner-city Muslim youth as another facet of the 'social war' (a new form of the old 'class war') which pitted them against the society that excluded them.

Class warfare in its traditional sense had become redundant with the fall of communism. Saddam Hussein now provided a new focus for the underlying antagonisms and a new rallying cry around which these youth could express their discontent, because he embodied the 'evil Arab' in the eyes of those who held power in the West. He appealed directly to all those who, rightly or wrongly, felt themselves to be victims of the Western order.[2] In one incident, pupils disrupted a PE class in a secondary school in a deprived area of Lyons (where most of the families are of Algerian origin) by repeatedly chanting 'Sad-dam Hus-sein, Sad-dam Hus-sein'.[3] In another, a journalist from *Le Monde* investigating in Roubaix was jostled by a group of unemployed youths shouting 'Long live Saddam'; he commented: 'A revealing scene. The most disadvantaged youth, with no prospects at all, have latched onto the Iraqi President as their figurehead, the symbol of their alienation. For them, integration is just an invention of politicians.'[4] Accounts of such incidents abound. Despite the consensual ideology of integration and intercultural friendship (the 'pals' of SOS-Racisme), the Gulf War gave a voice to all the grievances, frustrations and social anxieties which had hitherto been unable to find expression.

In January-February 1991, an opinion poll of people of Muslim origin living in France showed that 55 per cent of those interviewed were worried about their future in their country of residence, even though 70 per cent stated that it was where they most wanted to live (20 per cent would prefer to live in their family's native country);

82 per cent feared that the Gulf War would mean a police clamp-down on Muslims, 77 per cent thought it would lead to more racism, 74 per cent to greater difficulties finding work, and 63 per cent to more expulsions. These fears were stronger among those with French nationality and those under thirty-five years of age. Only 26 per cent expressed a favourable opinion of Saddam Hussein (as opposed to 61 per cent negative opinions), although it should be noted that in times of conflict leaders' popularity ratings are some-what erratic (President Mitterrand received 67 per cent favourable replies). However, Saddam Hussein's popularity was higher among foreign Muslims (29 per cent) than among French citizens of Muslim origin (20 per cent), and was also conspicuously higher among the sixteen-nineteen age group (31 per cent) and those who defined themselves as 'believers and practising Muslims' (31 per cent, as opposed to 17 per cent for those who declared themselves 'of Muslim origin' only).[5] The rulers of the Gulf states, the great conservative benefactors of Islamic movements, scored fewer favourable opinions than the then prime minister of Israel (20 per cent). The emir of Kuwait received a popularity rating of 14 per cent (the same score as George Bush). King Fahd of Saudi Arabia scored 18 per cent, and even less (15 per cent) among the 'believers and practising Muslims'; despite the efforts of Saudi Islamic bodies, who sent several missions to France during the Gulf War, King Fahd was only half as popular as Saddam Hussein among the most devout Muslims in this survey.[6]

The general feeling of unrest highlighted during the Gulf War went deeper than the conflict itself. As we have seen, the great majority of people expressed a negative opinion of the Iraqi leader at a time of hostility between his country and France. Nevertheless, the support shown for Saddam Hussein by a sizeable fringe group – between a quarter and a third – reveals the breakdown of the 'anti-racist', pro-integration consensus among immigrant youth. The SOS-Racisme leaders themselves, having criticized France's involve-ment in the war as part of the international anti-Iraq alliance, were abandoned by the liberal intellectuals, politicians and financial back-ers who had previously supported them. At grassroots level, many groups which had broken away from the anti-racist movement denounced the 'media disinformation campaign' which presented an 'all-out war by the West against a country with seventeen million inhabitants' as a 'surgical strike'.[7]

Intifada in France's cities?

In October 1990, as the belligerent states were preparing to fight in the Gulf, a riot broke out in Vaulx-en-Velin, in the northeast of the Lyons conurbation. Following the death of a young motorcyclist knocked down by police attempting to carry out a check on his vehicle, the shopping centre was looted and set alight. The area had been targeted for special urban renewal schemes in the 1980s and equipped with new social and sporting facilities. Renovation had changed the physical aspect of Vaulx-en-Velin from the rundown housing projects of the 1960s, but it did little for the local employment situation and the residents' feeling of social exclusion. Of local residents, 55 per cent came from immigrant families. As in the American riots, however, those emerging with their arms full of loot from the burnt-out shops were not just 'coloured' youths looking for Ray-Bans, Reeboks and Nikes; 'native French' housewives also took the opportunity to stock up on household essentials. The scenes of looting seen on television and graphically described in newspapers were striking because the act of theft seemed to be normalized, shorn of moral reprobation. It seemed to be the normal – even legitimate – expression of revenge for poverty through the forcible expropriation of all kinds of goods, from the utilitarian to the most inaccessible designer goods associated with the television world of the rich and famous. The television images of the riots also brought home to viewers the rituals of this new kind of urban violence, with its borrowings from different subcultures: the Palestinian headscarf and the gestures of the stone-throwing youth of the 'intifada', as well as the American baseball cap.

According to philosopher Jean-Paul Dollé, this 'intifada of the cities' is a form of 'war' waged by the poor, 'all those who did not take part in the mass worship of business, the orgies in praise of money' and who, in the eyes of the rich, 'should not just play along, but should give up and acknowledge defeat!' Since the poor are in a minority and have lost their political voice with the collapse of the labour movement and the embourgeoisement of the labour leaders, they no longer count electorally: 'They can be totally discounted.' The only mode of expression left to them is revolt, and if they did not revolt society would not even notice their existence. Alain Touraine, in his analysis of the Vaulx riots, observes that 'national societies are becoming dislocated' in an 'astonishing movement of "demodernization": we had learnt to define human beings by what they did, instead of what they were ...' Now, 'the social and political sphere is breaking up and the individual is faced with the internationalized economy and communities defined by their specific nature, both by their own traditions and by their acceptance or rejection by others.'[8]

The start of the 1990s in France marked an awareness of this 'dislocation of society' in which, to use Alain Touraine's phrase, the central conflict is no longer between 'exploiters' and 'exploited' but 'insiders' and 'outsiders': those who have a paid job and access to social protection, and those who are excluded from the system because of their age, their educational attainment, their origin, the sound of their name or the colour of their skin. Just as riots and joyriding had hit the national headlines ten years earlier and made the name of housing projects synonymous with juvenile delinquence and social problems (notably Les Minguettes, a high-rise project in the Vénissieux area of Lyons), new names gained notoriety in the newspapers: Le Val Fourré (Mantes-la-Jolie, west of Paris), La Cité des Indes (Sartrouville, just outside Paris) and Le Mas du Taureau (Vaulx-en-Velin), among others. The incidents always followed the same pattern: they all started with mishandled police checks, or an altercation with a security guard in the shopping mall, then the death of a youth (often of North African origin) and finally a protest gathering quickly turning into a riot, with attacks on businesses and vehicles and mass battles with the police well into the night, against a backdrop of flames. The police and media, unable to get to grips with the incidents, blamed organized gangs ready to turn residents' anger into looting and destruction. Riots were also often attributed to drugs and the parallel economy they create, turning neighbourhoods gradually into ghettos as businesses and those with the means to escape moved out of the area.[9]

In the early 1980s, the city riots had led to the creation of a new 'urban policy' (and a specific Ministry for Urban Affairs), with important resource transfers to underprivileged areas. Much was made of the difference between France's interventionist approach – where the state mobilized national solidarity and redistributed funds towards the poor – and the *laisser-faire* approach of the United States, where the poor were left to their fate.[10] But the riots of the 1990s occurred despite the state's attempts to improve matters, and therefore aroused a less sympathetic response than the earlier incidents.[11] In a context of economic crisis and recession, the riots met a widespread lack of interest among the public, whilst some politicians proposed a clampdown on young 'foreign' delinquents and even their expulsion.

In this way, the gulf widened between a section of young people and wider society, including its institutions and values such as school and organized social activities. Those who declared their 'hatred' also knew how much hatred, mixed with fear and distrust, they inspired in return. In the United States, the young ghetto Blacks have an intense feeling of dehumanization in which they are trapped by a social system which treats them as potential criminals and drug addicts. The success of the Black Muslims' preaching stems mainly from the fact that they address their audience not just as real human beings, but as the chosen people of Allah. Similarly, in the kasbah or the Eucalyptus district of Algiers, the popularity of the FIS is principally due to the feeling of pride and self-confidence the movement gives to the dispossessed urban youth who see the state as a completely alien and hostile entity.

No doubt the situation in the Algiers kasbah or Chicago's South Side is much more dramatic than in Vaulx-en-Velin or Le Val Fourré, despite local worries about recent developments in the French cities. But in France too, since the decline of the anti-racist movement of the 1980s, we see a clear trend towards radical rejection of the existing social order – described as a mixture of oppression and the 'law of the jungle' – and an aspiration after a better community life to which Islam gives meaning. Thus, in the Paris suburb of Nanterre, interviews with a group of 'new Muslim youth' (carried out in spring 1993) reveal how they came to rediscover Islam following an initial rejection of both the ills of their social environment (unemployment, drugs) and the models of integration offered to them – especially through school – which they saw merely as attempts to 'disintegrate' them.[12]

One of these interviewees, a twenty-five-year-old first-year student, a French citizen of Algerian parentage, who earns his living by working for a security firm, observes that 'the great blight on my community is drugs, especially in Nanterre, especially North Africans ...' He says that 30 per cent of deaths are caused by overdose, and drugs eat away at traditional solidarities: '30 per cent, young people of twenty-four, twenty-five, it was drugs, I know people who died through drugs, an Arab woman, a young Arab mother, it would have been unheard of at one time, she was coming out of the post office, she had her money on her, ... and another Arab, he knew her, he did her over, why? for drugs, nothing's sacred now, he steals from his own mother, it was just too much.' But according to this young man, the situation at Nanterre has improved, unlike in other towns like Sartrouville or the La Corneuve housing projects, 'because there's a bit more solidarity here, there are a few more mosques, Nanterre is trying a bit harder to beat drugs ..., fight aggression with aggression, they've done raids,[13] because they'd had enough of it, the cops did nothing, they knew who was selling, who was buying ..., you'd think they wanted it to stay like that – we used to find syringes in our porch!' He says that some addicts had succeeded in kicking the habit thanks to Islam, although it was only a small minority and there was always a chance they would return to their old ways.

The reference to Islam as the path to salvation away from the jungle of city life is complemented by strong criticism of the institutional framework of integration. This young Muslim placed a high value on education – since the Prophet said that 'the ink of scholars is more precious than the blood of martyrs – but he felt the French education system had failed him. Its aim is to 'brainwash' young Muslims in an attempt to suppress Islam. Another young Frenchman of Algerian origin, holder of a vocational training qualification (CAP), who has 'rediscovered Islam', protests that 'if you have children, French schools will be an obstacle, because they're going to indoctrinate your children ... They study Darwin, for instance, he says A plus B, it's Darwin, but why do they not tell you at school about the Creator? Straightaway, they'll say that's it, that's Darwin, you're indoctrinated.' Similarly, his friend, who has an advanced vocational diploma (BTS), remarks: 'you have to be a double teacher. I do it with my little brothers before they go to school, I tell them: "they're going to tell you this and that: pay attention, because that's what they're going to teach you: you have to learn it by heart to get good marks, but I'll tell you now it's wrong".'

For these young Muslims, school is not a place where neutral knowledge is dispensed. Secularism itself is seen as an anti-religious stance which challenges the foundations of belief.[14] School aims to produce 'integrated' pupils, that is, young people for whom Islam no longer has any meaning or is relegated to the private sphere. The intention is to 'disintegrate' the Islamic personality and assimilate it totally: 'if you want to integrate, you have to become like them', as the young CAP-holder asserts. In his view, assimilation is synonymous with the moral dissolution he associates with French people: 'fornicate, commit adultery, then you'll be integrated!' The first-year student also rejects French-style integration/assimilation, and proposes instead his own interpretation of integration, based on the idea of 'integrity': 'I am integrated, I have integrity: when I fast, I discipline myself ... They're too keen for us to imitate them, have a glass of red wine on the table.'

In order to combat the disintegration of their identity (either by violent means, like drugs, or by 'brainwashing' at school), these young Muslims living in Nanterre want to rebuild the community and unite Muslims around a model for life and education which not only strictly honours Islam but also takes account of the French political system. Their strategy for achieving this goal remains uncertain: some would like the sharia to be applied to Muslims living in France, whilst others believe this is an unrealistic demand in a state governed by non-Muslims. Political participation poses a similar dilemma: should they set up an Islamic party, should they negotiate with electoral candidates? Nothing is excluded at the outset. Meanwhile, the student compares France with what he understands to be the situation in other Western countries: 'The French go out of their way to make life difficult for us, whereas in England, in the United States there are congregations of Black Muslims, there are towns in Great Britain which are run by Muslims.' For him and his comrades, the path to salvation lies in the rebuilding of a community, if possible within a Muslim-controlled district where good morals would be observed.

The assertion of communalist identity, in response to life in France's deprived urban areas, is a new phenomenon which marks the start of the 1990s. But this does not mean that it represents a majority of young Muslims: many young people from immigrant families do not identify with this viewpoint and feel that integration within French society is more important than the desire to be different; in particular, they put their faith in the values and knowledge acquired in the Republic's schools.[15] It is in this context of multiple experiences and views that we must analyse the demand for a communalist identity, by observing the various different meanings given to the concept by rival social and political actors.

The FIS inside France

One of the groups most often mentioned in relation to re-Islamization of young people of Muslim origin is the Algerian Islamic Salvation Front (FIS), which according to rumour has set up strong secret networks in France. One book,[16] several newspaper articles and a spectacular police operation against suspected FIS supporters on 9 November 1993 have lent weight to the idea that the FIS has played a major role in Islamist movements in France. The 'police' view of social movements, reduced to foreign-inspired conspiracies and intrigues, has thus had the upper hand. In fact, the strategy of the FIS in France has undergone considerable change. At first, the Islamist party refused to accept emigration as a permanent fact. Later, its leaders built up a support network, which became more important after the crackdown in Algeria in June 1991 and especially in February 1992. Its contacts with 'new Muslim youth' in France's cities obliged the party, under pressure from the grass roots, to consider the specific situation of Islam in France, although it has not gone so far as to redirect its activities towards the young generations who will no doubt remain in France. This rethinking of strategy created ambiguities with regard to the French authorities, who in the summer of 1993 began to take various repressive measures against the FIS.

When the FIS was officially set up in March 1989, its leaders did not envisage creating a French branch of the party. Just as the FLN had imagined in the euphoria of independence in 1962 that the immigrants would all return home to the motherland, the FIS at first thought that Algerians would not be able to live under a non-Islamic regime in a reviled and sinful country.[17] The party planned merely to open an office in France as the prelude to an embassy at a future date when the FIS gained power in Algeria. Immigrants generally appear to have been viewed with some distrust by FIS activists, who considered them too close to Western culture and too far from their own interpretation of Islam.

However, once the party began to take off in Algeria, some activists in France tried to take advantage by claiming to be FIS representatives, and the FIS was obliged to deny their claims. A few former members of Bouyali's group or Ben Bella's Movement for Democracy in Algeria and two or three Islamist academics who were followers of Malek Bennabi climbed on the bandwagon. It was not until 1990 that the party began to set up its own organization in France, with a view to building support and collecting funds for activities in Algeria, where it had just won the local elections.[18]

In February 1991, the Algerian Brotherhood in France (Fraternité Algérienne en France, or FAF) was created to relay the FIS's message in France, although it was not directly linked to the party structure. It was run by former mathematics, computing and technology students generally held to be close to the 'Algerianist' or 'technocratic' wing of the FIS which was dominant within the party at that time. But representatives of other FIS tendencies also took up residence in Paris. One of the FIS's founders, Sheikh Abdel Baqi Sahraoui, then aged eighty, became imam of the Khaled Ibn Walid mosque in the Barbès quarter of Paris;[19] he was a member of the 'salafist' tendency which was ousted by the 'Algerianists' at the Batna congress of the party in July 1991. Between February and August 1992 (when the FIS was dissolved and its leaders rounded up), Qamareddine Kherbane and Boujemaa Bounoua, former soldiers in the Afghan jihad and organizers of the growing armed struggle in the Algerian underground, both representing the most radical wing of the salafist tendency, set up several support networks in France until they were expelled to Pakistan. The FIS activists in France in the early 1990s therefore represented its various Algerian tendencies; they collaborated with each other but acted independently. There was no organized 'emigrant' branch of the FIS, as there had been a French federation of the FLN during the Algerian war.

The Algerian Brotherhood in France (FAF) proved the most active. In 1991, it organized meetings in France's main cities to persuade Algerians to vote for the FIS in the forthcoming Algerian elections, originally scheduled for 27 June. The president of the FAF, Djaafar El Houari, a statistics student, stood as a FIS candidate in the elections, which took place in December. Following the *coup d'état* in January 1992 which 'suspended the electoral process', the FAF produced a regular weekly newsletter, *Le Critère*, which it distributed free every Friday outside mosques. Consisting of a single sheet like Daniel-Youssouf Leclercq's *L'Index*, which it resembled in many ways, *Le Critère* was produced using Macintosh desktop publishing facilities (thanks to the computing skills of its editor, Moussa Kraouche) and was very modern in its lay-out and its ironic, satirical style which reflected the student culture of its authors.[20]

Le Critère's editor, Moussa Kraouche, was born in Médéa and moved to France at the age of nineteen, where he distinguished himself as a student. In 1990, he was employed by the (Communist) council of Argenteuil (on the northern outskirts of Paris) to reorganize its computer system. During this time, he followed a classic itinerary for a young man rediscovering Islam: he went to Tabligh meetings, then joined the GIF (the Parisian branch of the UOIF), and went on to set up a French-speaking Islamic cultural association, create an Islamic server for Minitel, and so on. In his home town of Taverny (just north of Argenteuil), he helped to give extra classes to young North African schoolchildren. In 1989, he joined the local consultative committee on prevention of delinquence, at the invitation of the town council. In April 1991, he headed negotiations between the Nanterre 'new Muslim youth' and the local sub-prefecture on issues concerning drugs and violence, after a dealer had been stabbed by an anti-drugs vigilante squad. This exemplary career, combining professional success with work in the community, brought him to the attention of Rabah Kebir, the FIS's representative in Europe, who chose him to be 'spokesman for the FIS's supporters in France', as he defined himself in 1991 in a television interview.

The FAF's newsletter was almost exclusively devoted to information on events in Algeria. Having given a detailed account of the Algerian state's repression of the FIS, 'news of the uprising' began to appear from May 1992 under a logo showing a bomb about to explode. These columns later became 'news of the jihad'. The Algerian leaders were painted in the worst possible colours: week after week, the image built up of isolated, bloodthirsty dictators, subject to foreign control and implacably hostile to Islam. On the other hand, the actions of the 'mujahidin' were presented in the upbeat style of a 'war news' chronicle.

The newsletter's coverage of French affairs was limited to criticism of its support for the Algiers regime. Issue number 5 (13 March 1992) carried the headline: 'France's complicity in the massacre of the people and the rule of dictatorship in Algeria'. But such accusations were rare before 1993. France was still seen as an important land of refuge, and until Foreign Affairs Minister Roland Dumas visited Algiers in January 1993 relations between the two capitals remained lukewarm, following President Mitterrand's statement deploring the suspension of elections. French intellectuals who supported Boudiaf's regime or articles criticizing the FIS were, on the other hand, subjected to merciless invective.

In November 1992, the newsletter published an article by Rabah Kebir himself, denying any FIS involvement in trade in counterfeit Lacoste shirts which had been uncovered by police.[21] A group of unemployed youths from Algiers who frequented the Khaled Ibn Walid mosque in Barbès had been arrested. The president of the FAF also wrote a long article, under the heading 'Islamophobia', in response to other accusations that Islamist anti-dealer vigilante squads had really been set up to take control of the drug trade, and a police report published in the press which warned of 'a drift into terrorism by some small groups arising from the Islamist movement'. 'Would they really prefer to see young people devoting themselves to drugs and crime, rather than see them praying in the mosque?' asked El Houari. He denied that the FIS 'finances itself with drug money. All Muslims know that drug-taking and selling are serious crimes.'[22] However, in June 1993, the discovery of weapons alongside pro-FIS leaflets in premises belonging to an association of 'new Muslim youth' in Nanterre raised questions about the link between the vigilante squads and city violence. The leader of the Nanterre association stated: 'we want to defend purity and public morality against drug traffickers.'[23]

Around the same time, the first systematic 'executions' of 'collaborators' with the regime and of 'sons of France' were taking place in Algeria. *Le Critère* related these killings in its 'news of the jihad' column; thus, for example: 'Tuesday 16 March: the mujahidin killed Djilali Lyabès, ex-Minister for Universities, in Kouba ... Wednesday 17 March: in the Kasbah (Algiers), the mujahidin finally killed Laadi Flici, a member of the Consultative Council, set up by the junta to replace the national assembly elected by the people.'[24] The litany of announcements of executions of police officers and informers, attacks on barracks and desertions continued. The last issue of the newsletter contained the news that 'the writer and journalist Taher Djaout, manager of the secular-communist *Ruptures* journal, described by his friends as enemy number one of the Islamic ideology, received two bullets in the head from the mujahidin.'[25]

At that point, the FAF newsletter was banned by the Interior Minister Charles Pasqua. A fortnight later, it reappeared under the title *Résistance* ('Al Mouqawama'), with the same rubric. The second issue contained the usual 'news of the jihad' alongside party announcements and protests against the ban on *Le Critère*: 'Algiers: Professor Mahfoudh Boucebci, a member of the "Truth for Djaout" Committee, was killed on Tuesday 15 June.'[26] The newsletter was banned after its third issue, but reappeared again under the title *L'Étendard* for six weeks, until a further ban, which this time worked. Whilst the FAF was accused of condoning executions of Algerian intellectuals opposed to the Islamists in its newsletter, the first issue of *L'Étendard* published photographs of Abbassi Madani and Ali Benhadj, who had just been sentenced to imprisonment, with the heading 'The fate of our intellectuals: two years' imprisonment and contempt! and what about the other three thousand intellectuals sent to death camps!'[27]

The FAF's problems with the French police worsened in November 1993, when several dozens of its leaders and supporters were arrested. Most of them were released without charge very quickly; some were placed under house arrest, and three detained in custody. The police operation was carried out a few days after the capture of French consular agents in Algiers by the Armed Islamic Group (Groupement Islamique Armé, or GIA). The aim seems to have been to destabilize the FIS's French support networks and to set strict limits to their activities, and in this it succeeded.

On the level of ideas and mobilization of support, the FAF and the various associations close to it introduced a new dimension to the Islamist movements in France. Originally conceived as a simple support organization relaying the FIS message among Algerian emigrants abroad, the FAF gradually adapted to the situation of Islam in France and became one of its components. Through its work in the community and grassroots activism, it gained a strong foothold in various local associations of 'new Muslim youth', including young Muslims with French nationality. But, unlike the UOIF (with which it shared a common reference to the Muslim Brotherhood), which anchored its activities firmly within the French environment, the FAF remained concerned first and foremost with the jihad in Algeria.

By passing on to its youthful French supporters the mental images popularized by the FIS (the demonization of France, secularism and democracy) and glorifying a jihad in which 'secular-communists' were killed by warriors of the faith, the FAF projected them into a binary world divided into Good (the mujahidin) and Evil (everyone else). How would these young Islamist recruits transpose such ideas onto their daily life: through proselytizing, the fight against drug dealers in the city streets, the organization of a miniature *Umma* in France? Certainly, one could expect an exacerbation of the separatist response – somewhere between the model of the American Black Muslims and the Islamic communalism of Bradford or Birmingham.

Coordinating the movement

Unlike in the United States and Britain, the state in France exerts strong pressure on society to prevent the formation of religion-based communities which would weaken the link between the Republic and its citizens. The state's initiatives aimed at organizing Muslim cult worship in France and creating a single interlocutor were on a completely different scale from the *laisser-faire* approach of the British and American states, influenced by Protestant culture and accustomed to a proliferation of sects and groups. For them, Islam was one mode of religious expression among many. Neither the British nor the American state attempted to 'symbolize' Islam as the French state did with the CORIF.

The decline of the CORIF, following Dalil Boubakeur's appointment as rector of the Muslim Institute of the Mosque of Paris in April 1992, did not mean that the state was no longer interested in organizing the Muslim religion in France. On the contrary, Charles Pasqua (minister of the interior from April 1993) encouraged the Mosque of Paris to become the centre of gravity for associations which were disposed to place their goals and activities within the French context – which *de facto* excluded the FIS's support networks. The official responsible for Islamic affairs inside the ministry noted: 'Centrifugal forces should cease to operate, and a national Islam free of any fundamentalism should be formed with the silent majority.'[28]

Despite the government's promotion of the Mosque of Paris, it was associations like the Jama'at al Tabligh (in the form of one of its main French branches, the Association Foi et Pratique – Faith and Practice), the UOIF and the FNMF which took the lead in coordinating the Islamic organizations of France. Whereas the coordinating structures of the 1980s had attempted to bring together local associations, those of the 1990s sought to unite existing federations in an umbrella organization. The initial meeting took place on 5 July 1992, before the dispute over Dalil Boubakeur's appointment as rector of the Paris Mosque and the ensuing collapse of the CORIF. It was held in the Omar mosque, the Paris headquarters of the Tabligh, and was chaired by Sheikh Sahraoui, imam of the Khaled Ibn Walid mosque, who, although a founding member of the FIS, had distanced himself from the party since July 1991. This first attempt to set up a parallel organization to the CORIF (and therefore free of any association with the French state) did not lead anywhere because of Boubakeur's absence. But it did raise a number of important issues, especially among the young: 'For the first time, the weapon of the vote in French elections [was] discussed.'[29]

Having taken note of this initiative Dr Boubakeur invited the same organizations (UOIF, FNMF, Foi et Pratique and AEIF (the Association of Islamic Students in France)[30] to a meeting on 14 April 1993 (three weeks after the new right-wing government came to office in France). The meeting laid the foundations for a National Coordination of Muslims in France. Boubakeur, who was elected president of the new organization, defined its task thus: 'this coordinating structure is the religious "kernel" of the community. It is a forum for discussion of theology and juridical aspects of the coherence, if not the cohesion of religious life and its different aspects ...' In future, 'a community council may be set up' around it.[31]

Until the time when this representative body could be set up, Boubakeur wished to put the Muslim religious personnel in France into order. According to him, 'In France, Islam may drift and slip out of control, because the element of control, coordination – indeed discipline – of imams is missing (self-proclaimed imams, or those of uncertified training).' He deplored 'the anguished state of these abandoned clerics', 'the dubious nature of some of their public statements or homilies', and proposed 'the urgent appointment of regional managers: muftis or imams delegated by the Mosque of Paris in France', in order to 'bring some sense into the incredible disorder which prevails in France in this area.'[32]

To this end, the rector of the Mosque of Paris inaugurated an 'Institute of Higher Education in Religion and Theology' on 4 October 1993, at a ceremony attended by Charles Pasqua and Culture Minister Jacques Toubon. The institute, created in order to train imams practising in France, opened its doors with a lecture by Professor Bruno Etienne, who expressed pleasure at the fact that 'the existence of Islam in France has finally been recognized and above all that the facile association with an extremism that has nothing to do with Islam except the name given to it by ill-intentioned manipulators has been broken.'[33] Classes are provided for male students with a minimum entry level of *baccalauréat*, and the curriculum combines the disciplines of the *'ilm* (Koran, *Hadith*, *fiqh* etc.) and courses in language and civilization. Religious instruction is intended to promote an 'open, tolerant' form of Islam, and uses both traditional Islamic analysis of the Holy Texts and critical commentaries by non-Muslim Orientalists.

Dr Boubakeur's Institute was meant to rival that which the UOIF had established in the Nièvre, but a third contender appeared on the scene the very week of its inauguration. On 9 October, an 'Islamic University of France' opened inside the Mantes-la-Jolie mosque. It soon had to find other premises, because the Moroccan director of the mosque opposed mixed classes. There were approximately two female for every three male students, and some female students (although not many) even attended classes with their heads uncovered. The 'university' finally set up its headquarters in the Parisian office of the Muslim World League. Operating along the lines of the British Open University, it is run by a young teacher who is a French convert, Didier-Ali Bourg.[34] Bourg collected most of the finances needed to set up the 'university' by fund-raising in the Gulf states, where he encountered opposition from the UOIF's Islamic Institute; it opened with a budget of nine million francs. In the first year, the 'university' attracted 150 students, many more than its two rivals (which required at least *baccalauréat* standard at entry). The students were split into three groups and classes took place at weekends. In addition, a further 150 students followed correspondence courses. In contrast, the Institute set up by the Paris Mosque, which claimed forty students on its rolls, seems to have attracted only around ten students who regularly attended classes, and some of these had problems understanding the French language.

The success of Bourg's Islamic University may be attributed to several causes. Since there were no entry requirements, the classes attracted 'new Muslim youth' from the city housing projects, many of whom had been marginalized by the school system, as well as students with a higher level of educational attainment, who helped the others to catch up. The 'university' aimed to train not only imams, but also professionals who would be able to organize the 'Muslim community of France', negotiate with the public authorities, run associations, learn accounting and law and set up 'Muslim businesses'. The aim of organizing the community stands out strongly in the work of the 'university'. In principle, it means a very open approach to wider French society: 'psychoanalysts and Marxists will present their beliefs to the students and representatives of free thinking or Freemasonry, for example, will be able to expound their views on secularism.'[35] In fact, these lectures did not take place during the 'university''s first year, and little attention appears to have been paid to critical analysis in 1993–4. The 'university''s main mission is to strengthen faith and religious observance and to deliver knowledge relevant to this aim. Classes are punctuated with collective prayer. Meals are taken together, and there is an atmosphere of conviviality, which is greatly helped by the presence of so many female students, even though they sit separately and most of them are veiled.[36] The collective spirit also helps to channel some of the aggression of the less educated students from city housing projects, who have only recently rediscovered Islam and for whom regular attendance at the 'university' is a considerable mark of social prestige in their home environment.

Various different initiatives were in competition, then, to build the 'Muslim community of France'. Alongside the Mosque of Paris, whose rector's special links with Interior Minister Charles Pasqua propelled it to the forefront, other movements – some with more radical conceptions of Islam – succeeded in combining a social message appealing to young people of Muslim origin and ambitions to build an Islamic community. As is the case in Muslim countries today, where religious movements have gained ground in the social and political spheres, different tendencies contended with each other for control of the dominant expression of Islam in France. Within Boubakeur's National Coordination itself, the groups associated with the Muslim Brotherhood and the Tabligh had the best deal.

At the other extreme, a movement led by a young imam, Soheib Bensheikh, has attempted to defend a reading of the Koran which marks a radical departure from that of the various Islamist movements inspired by the Muslim Brotherhood and the Tabligh.

Followers of the ideas of several 'modernist' Muslim authors such as
Ali Abd el Raziq, this group refuses to consider the wearing of the
veil as a 'religious sign'. Its objective, according to journalist
Martine Gozlan, who has written a book about the movement, is 'to
rescue [its] community from obscurantism'.[37] A few local Muslim
associations receive the group when it organizes speaking tours in
France, but it does not possess an infrastructure or support networks akin to those built up by the major Islamist associations since
the late 1980s. Nonetheless, whatever its ultimate goal, Bensheikh's
organization and the support it has received show that, whereas in
the 1980s the main debate was between secularists and religious
movements, in the 1990s it has moved squarely into the religious
sphere.

The veil again

As we have seen, following the Creil affair in the autumn of 1989,
the Council of State had issued a ruling confirming that the basic
principle was the freedom of the pupil. The veil could be worn
except under certain specific conditions, such as proselytizing, propaganda or threats to health and safety. However, in the autumn of
1990, at the Jean-Jaurès secondary school in Montfermeil (a
Parisian suburb which had already witnessed several local clashes
over immigration), five veiled pupils were excluded on the basis of
the school's rules, which stipulated that the wearing of 'any distinctive sign, in the form of clothing or any other form, of a religious,
political or philosophical nature' was strictly forbidden. One of the
families appealed to the courts, and as a result the Council of State
quashed the decision, on the grounds that the school's management
had overstepped its powers and the school's rules contravened the
fundamental principle of the freedom of pupils to express their opinion and their beliefs. The head of the school, Ali Boumahdi, then
claimed that one of the pupils, who had worn veils since primary
school and whose elder brother ran the Muslim cultural and sporting association in Montfermeil, had been proselytizing and had
accused her fellow students who did not wear veils of being 'bad
Muslims'.[38] He declared that the Council of State's ruling 'played
into the hands of the fundamentalists'. However, in his original submission to the Council, there had been no mention of accusations of
proselytism;[39] had there been, the outcome of the case might well
have been different.

This judgement had two consequences. First, the Islamist movements which campaigned for the veil to be worn at school as a symbol of communalist identity were able to claim victory. Second, many heads of schools began to fear that every similar case would result in a court ruling against them. They found themselves placed in an uncomfortable position for which they were ill prepared. Most of them sought to find a compromise solution with the families concerned, steering a middle course between 'the freedom of the pupil' and the 'rejection of proselytism' advocated by the Council of State. During the academic year following the verdict, a growing number of veiled heads appeared in schools throughout the country.[40]

The veil itself carried a different significance for different groups of people. For many pupils, classmates of the veiled Muslim girls, school management or teachers' attempts to impose a dress code appeared to be yet another example of adult repression of young people. The Islamic head covering thus became, somewhat paradoxically, the symbol of freedom and non-conformism, rather like the baseball caps popularized by American television series, or punk hairstyles. For many teachers, on the other hand, giving classes in front of veiled students meant the negation of the ideals of intellectual emancipation and the development of critical faculties, which in their eyes constituted the basis of secular education.

In some schools in the Paris region, the most radical Islamist groups saw the Council of State ruling as the first step in a longer-term campaign. In the following phase of the campaign, some schools granted students dispensation from mixed physical education classes, thanks to medical certificates which in some cases were issued by doctors practising a long way from the school concerned.[41] At Sevran, in Nanterre, pupils demanded a prayer-room within the school; meanwhile, they held collective worship in the corridors. In one such case, the head's refusal to grant permission for a prayer-room led to repeated absences in the early afternoon sessions on Fridays, creating discipline problems.[42] In another school in the Hauts-de-Seine department just north of Paris, final-year students who had previously worn the *hijab* (covering their hair) turned up for the new academic year in September 1993 wearing full 'Islamic dress', including cloak and gloves, thus making life uncomfortable for the teachers, who found it difficult to teach them philosophy and similar subjects. Anyone aware of the educational demands of Islamist groups in Britain would not have been surprised to see a replay of the Bradford or Birmingham situation, several years later.

Two of the most famous incidents broke out in the Rhône-Alpes region in the autumn of 1993. The first involved Turkish and

Moroccan secondary school pupils in Nantua (in the Ain department), and the second a French schoolgirl of Moroccan origin in
Grenoble. The latter case, as we saw at the beginning of this section
of the book, was taken up by a 'native' re-Islamizing group based in
Lyons with a large following among young French people of Muslim
origin as well as converts to Islam: the Union of Young Muslims
(UJM). On this occasion, the demand for the right to wear the veil
became part of a specifically French sociocultural context, embrac-
ing all aspects of life within French society, from school and the
local neighbourhood to the tactical negotiation of the 'Muslim vote'
at election time.

Nantua had since the 1960s discreetly welcomed a sizeable population of immigrant workers from Turkey and Morocco, who provided the manual labour for the prosperous local plastics industries
which had earned the area the nickname 'Plastic Valley'. Thanks to
the 1970s immigration policy of 'family settlement', a large number
of second-generation immigrant children had been born and educated in the town. When school resumed in the autumn of 1993,
four girls turned up for classes at the Xavier-Bichat secondary
school (around a quarter of whose pupils are of North African or
Turkish origin) wearing veils. They were allowed to wear their veils
in class, but when they refused to take them off for physical education lessons, they were disciplined for contravening the school's
safety rules. As negotiations between the head and the families pro-
ceeded, the majority of the school's teachers went on strike on 12
October. A statement signed by several of the teachers declared that
'the wearing of the veil undermines the freedom of the pupils, compromises their safety during science practice sessions and sports and
physical education, and is discriminatory in its treatment of girls and
segregationist.'[43]

Although a compromise was thought to have been reached, two
of the four pupils turned up after the November break still wearing
headscarves; the parents of the other two had opted to enrol them
on a correspondence course instead. The school's disciplinary board
excluded the two remaining veiled pupils on 4 December, and this
decision was confirmed by the Lyons administrative tribunal on 11
May 1994, pending a possible appeal to the Council of State.[44] As in
the Creil incident, Islamist activists appeared on the scene to protest
against the decision. A Turkish imam, who had recently arrived
from Germany, adopted an intransigent attitude on the veil question
(although his views were far from widely shared among the Muslim
population of Nantua) and declared, through an interpreter, in an
interview with *Le Figaro* that 'Allah's law must be obeyed before

French law'.[45] In consequence, he was expelled from France by the interior minister. On the side of the Moroccan families, a curious figure emerged to advise them during their negotiations with the head of the school. A stateless person of Tunisian origin and self-proclaimed 'Islamologist', he informed the head of school that according to his analysis of the Koran, Muslim women were bound to wear a veil covering them 'from head to chest': 'the Koran stipulates [the wearing of the veil], codifies it and establishes the conditions in which it can be removed in private and in public.'[46] On the other side of the Mediterranean, where the affair was followed with great interest thanks to satellite transmission of the French television channels, France's 'persecution' of Islam was denounced from the pulpit by numerous preachers.

The Nantua affair had many repercussions. It showed that, four years after the Creil affair, the underlying issues raised by the wearing of the veil had not been resolved, despite the Council of State ruling. In particular, the teachers' strike, supported by most of the school's teaching staff, pointed to their own malaise and the yawning communication gap between two different sets of values: on one hand were the teachers, many of them left-wing and members of trade unions, and some of whom had taken part in anti-racist, pro-integration campaigns; on the other, a section of the pupils and their families who demanded the right to a communalist identity, as expressed in radical form by the Turkish imam. Between these two opposing sets of views, second-generation youth faced with poor job prospects could hardly make much of a secular education system whose values made sense only as guarantees of access to employment and social integration.

The second major crisis of autumn 1993 had as its leading protagonist Schérazade, a final-year pupil at a Grenoble secondary school. In Nantua, the veiled students were very young and under the influence of parents who spoke very little French; both the Turkish imam and the 'Islamologist' operated in a mental universe which was completely foreign to French values. The Grenoble case was quite different. Schérazade was in charge of her own destiny. It was she who brought her father back onto 'the path of Allah'; he had nothing to do with her decision to wear the veil. Schérazade conducted her campaign for the *hijab* – symbol of communalist identity – within the legal and intellectual framework of the Republic, around the issues of freedom and citizens' rights.

According to her own account, Schérazade rediscovered Islam in 1993, during the month of Ramadan (which fell during the February school holidays). Wanting to know more about her religion, she accompanied her grandmother to the mosque and quickly became convinced that Islam was her blueprint for life:

> Within a week, I had joined Islam, everything became normal and automatic. I prayed five times a day and began to read the Koran with what was available, that is, in French, although really you can only fully understand it in Arabic, literary Arabic, which is much lovelier than Arab dialect. The Koran is the instructions God our Creator gave us for living on earth. When you buy a washing machine, if you don't have the manufacturer's instructions, you can't get it to work properly. The Koran is the same. . . . The veil was part of my duty as a Muslim, it was natural to wear it, it didn't bother me at all.[47]

Schérazade's story resembles other accounts by adolescents of their discovery of a faith (whatever faith it is): through religious observance, they find a haven of inner peace at a difficult time in their lives. In her case, the feeling is heightened by problems of identity resulting from the social environment.[48] The image of the Koran as a set of 'manufacturer's instructions' is a powerful one, and is not without echoes of the 'Little Red Book' which supplied all the answers on life to French adolescents in the early 1970s.[49] From this initial bedazzlement, which she describes with obvious sincerity, Schérazade's life followed a new course. First, she joined a group of her peers, a microcosmic community defined by strict religious observance, and became its standard-bearer. In the summer of 1993, she spent most of her free time in the company of other girls who had 'returned to Islam' in Lyons, and she attended an Islamic summer camp in Savoie. At the same time, she decided to make a symbolic break with her daily environment, notably by covering her head in school, which would lead her to be excluded and to respond by embarking on a hunger strike. She thereby became an exemplary martyr for the Islamic cause and galvanized the Muslim community. Her actions earned her the praise of the Saudi press and a demonstration in her support brought 'new Muslim youth' from all over France.

At school, Schérazade's determination to wear her veil created friction with several teachers, but it was not until the start of the school year in 1993 that the conflict intensified. As in Nantua, physical education classes provided the *casus belli*. At the end of a complex disciplinary procedure, Schérazade was excluded from school on 18 December for refusing to wear the required PE kit. She and her support committee contested the decision, but it was confirmed on appeal to the rector of the Grenoble Academy in January 1994. Her support committee was formed initially by friends in the Union of Young Muslims, a movement based on the demand for Islamic communalist identity, which was inspired by the ideology of the Muslim Brotherhood and in particular by two charismatic young preachers based in Geneva, Tariq and Hani Ramadan (grandsons of the founder of the Muslim Brotherhood, Hassan el Banna). At Christmas 1993, Schérazade took part in the UOIF gathering at Le Bourget, where she spoke to great acclaim; describing the incidents leading to her exclusion, she declared: 'Even if they put the sun in my right hand and the moon in my left hand, I would not take off my veil.' As she said later, 'When I'd finished speaking, even the men were crying. The beginning of the sentence about the sun and the moon was the words the Prophet spoke on the day people from Mecca came to ask him to give up his religion.'[50]

Schérazade's account shows her to have followed the typical path of the 'young new Muslims' who formed the backbone of the re-Islamization movements. But at the end of December, together with a French convert 'sister', she took an initiative which was previously unheard-of in Islamist activism in France: she went on hunger strike. The tactic had been used frequently by all kinds of protest movement in France since the 1970s. Schérazade's hunger strike showed the acculturation of Islamist movements to the norms of French activism, although of course the specific communalist objectives of the movement remained intact.

Schérazade and Sandra, her convert 'sister', spent twenty-two days on hunger strike. Now living in a camper-wagon parked in front of the school, they received the world's press. The Saudi weekly *Al Muslimoon* ('The Muslims', devoted to promoting Wahhabite Islam throughout the world) gave over pages of space to coverage of the two girls' campaign. Under the headline 'They want to pull off Schérazade's veil to discover the secrets of six million [*sic*] Muslims', the publication enthusiastically (and somewhat imaginatively) described France as a country where each village had its own mosque or prayer-hall, where the chant of 'There is no God but Allah and Muhammad is His messenger' could be heard everywhere, where ten French people convert to Islam every day and the proportion of Muslims reached 75 per cent in some areas. The article focused on the 'new Muslims' who, from being Muslims only in name, truly embraced the faith after listening to preachers like F. Maulaoui (the 'spiritual guide' of the UOIF) or Youssef el Qardaoui (president of the academic panel of the Nièvre Islamic Institute): these 'new Muslims' 'discovered the value of Islam after years of floundering in secularism, communism or moral dissolution'. Contrary to the image of violence and terrorism associated with

Islam in the French press (which was 'dominated by Zionists'), 'official French statistics show that as soon as a mosque is built in France, the number of thieves and drug addicts goes down.' Hence, in this context,

> when Schérazade the Muslim wore her veil, and when the headteacher ordered her to remove it, they represented in real terms the history of Islam against its enemies, Good against Evil, tolerance and mercy against racism and violence ... Her friend Sandra converted to Islam, along with Rose and Caroline; Fatima, Aïcha, Bathina and Naoual returned to Islam, whereas before they were Muslims only in name; truly, something beautiful for those who appreciate beauty, and something terrible for those who prefer to remain in darkness...'[51]

Schérazade's action thus lent itself to a Saudi interpretation of the world where Good and Evil are clearly identifiable, but it was also attuned to French styles of protest. The end of the girls' hunger strike on 5 February was marked by a rally in Grenoble which saw Muslims organizing in a completely new way. Responding to a call from the Union of Young Muslims, the FNMF, the Islamic Foundation in Geneva and a few other associations, around 1,500 'young new Muslims' arrived by coach from all over France. The boys and girls (nearly all veiled) marched in separate sections, shouting classic Islamic slogans like 'Allah Akbar', but also slogans which expressed their specific identity as French citizens: 'France is my freedom, so is my veil', or 'French, yes, Muslim too'. All the marchers wore an armband showing a yellow crescent and the words: 'When will it be our turn?', thus drawing a parallel between official attempts to prevent girls from wearing veils in school and the Nazi persecution of the Jews.

The demand for French recognition of Muslim communalist identity thus used two arguments: first, it was presented as a simple extension of individual freedom, a citizenship right to which 'young new Muslims' were entitled; second, it posed as the emblematic victim of oppression, substituting the yellow crescent for the yellow star of the Jews. Setting aside the deliberate hyperbole of the image, we can see at work a logic similar to that of Farrakhan's disciples in the United States: in the case of the Black Muslims, the replacement of the Jews as historical victims of oppression with the Black people through their subjugation and enslavement. At the Grenoble demonstration, the comparison between the Holocaust and the 'persecution' of veiled Muslim girls was too extravagant to make much impression on French society. But its capacity to mobilize the faithful and unite the embryonic 'Islamic community', under the leadership of the various movements set up to promote it, should not be underestimated.

Re-Islamization and political activism

The Union of Young Muslims (UJM), the main organizer of the Grenoble rally, is probably the organization which in the early 1990s has most effectively combined Islamic communalist demands and the rhetoric of citizenship. It espouses a strategy of 'bottom-up re-Islamization', focusing its activities on the local level. It has worked solidly on the ground in the immigrant quarters of Lyons, building up community links in daily life. The UJM was formed in June 1987 around a bookshop/library in the centre of Lyons, *Al Tawhid* ('The Oneness of God'), following early movements to re-Islamize young *beurs* in the regional capital (in 1985–6). Unlike the Islamic associations of that time, which were run either by older North African workers with pietistic tendencies, or by North African or Turkish students with little in common with the second-generation youth born in France, the UJM was from the outset a movement for and of young people of French nationality living in French cities and it addressed the social problems they faced in their daily lives. Up to the beginning of the 1990s, its role was overshadowed by the better-known JALB (Young Arabs of Lyons and its Suburbs), whose leader Djida Tazdaït was elected to the European Parliament in 1989 (on the ecologist party list). The JALB's reference to the ethnic background ('Arabs') of its members, too, bespoke the intention of building a community identity, albeit secular.

With the decline of the anti-racist movement, including the *beur* associations, the UJM gradually moved in to occupy the free space. It was only with its first congress, held in 1992, that it started to attract wider attention. Before this, however, it had already made headway among the disaffected youth of Vénissieux, Villeurbanne, Vaulx-en-Velin and other troubled areas of the Lyons conurbation. Its activities covered several areas. The most important, Islamic teaching and preaching (*islah wa da'wa*) gave youth of Muslim origin (or their non-Muslim companions, who also began to convert along with them) renewed strength to endure often extremely difficult living conditions. Prayer, fasting during Ramadan and moral rectitude meant both an assertion of identity and a positive self-image, in a context of urban degradation and low self-esteem reinforced by the media and the institutions with which they came into contact. This feeling of belonging to a community and positive self-image helps to explain the accounts given by young 'native French' of their conversion to Islam. Life in the city housing projects is already to all intents and purposes 'Arab' because of the large number of residents of North African origin, so by adopting Arab names the young 'Gauls' facilitate their integration into the local peer groups: François becomes 'Abdel', Frédéric 'Kader' and so on. Although the total number of such conversions is small, it is rare not to find at least one convert among associations of 'young new Muslims'.

Alongside its preaching, the UJM developed the various social and educational activities characteristic of grassroots Islamist movements: for example, extra tuition or financial support funds for families in need. The Union also devotes energy to promoting marriage and encouraging sexual abstinence among the youth, to whom life in the housing projects offers so many temptations. This also provides the opportunity to put 'good Muslim' veil-wearing women, whose contacts with men are strictly regulated, in touch with young 'new Muslims', thus strengthening community cohesion and preparing future Islamic generations.[52] Marriages are often celebrated in front of an imam at UJM congresses, in a festive community atmosphere (the UOIF similarly holds wedding ceremonies at its annual gatherings). Community cohesion and self-esteem are further reinforced by the organization of social activities on Muslim religious festivals, celebrated with a sense of the importance of the occasion. Summer camps, weekend outings, conferences and seminars all help to develop the community and inculcate the principles of Islam.

At first, the social and charitable aspect of the UJM's activities earned it the recognition of the French institutions. For several years, it received subsidies from the Social Action Fund for Immigrant Workers (a state body), but these were discontinued on account of the 1905 law prohibiting state funding of religious associations. At the time, the UJM was engaged in organizing demonstrations (which were banned) against *The Satanic Verses* and in support of the right to wear the veil at school.[53] Since then, relations between the UJM and the state have deteriorated. The Union fiercely attacked the CORIF (of which leaders of the UOIF, the UJM's sister organization, were members), and the association's newsletter *Jeunes Musulmans* singled out the minister of the interior, Charles Pasqua, for particular criticism.[54]

In contrast, the UJM has maintained good links with the communist town council of Vénissieux. For three years running (1992–4) council premises were made available to the Union for its annual congress (attended by some 1,500 people in 1992 and 3,000 in 1994). In 1993, representatives of the Socialist Party were invited to speak at the congress; in 1994, the mayor of Vénissieux (also the local parliamentary representative) gave a long speech to delegates. In cultivating links with the communist council, the UJM has been trying to build a local electoral force and organize a Muslim communalist vote, on the strength of which it would negotiate with the local authorities on a reciprocal basis, in exchange for the satisfaction of its own demands.

The theme of the Muslim vote was first raised at the 1993 congress, and it was the subject of a long address by the association's treasurer at the 1994 congress. Responding to the question which had arisen in discussion of whom Muslims should choose in the 1995 presidential elections, he declared:

> Next year, whether it's Mitterrand or another candidate, nothing will change. If we want change, it has to happen within our neighbourhoods ... We should first direct our efforts to the municipal elections, there's no political choice to make, it's a negotiation, it's not just the Muslims: Jews in particular, all communities do it. You go to see the mayor, it's clear, and it's a question of give and take: they mustn't take us Muslims for fools! Non-Muslim French people don't even believe in all this stuff about left and right any more ... You have to talk to local councillors, see what they offer you, and the one that offers the most, insh'Allah, that's the one you elect.[55]

The UJM's spokesman also spoke from the platform on the same subject. Reminding his audience of the inseparable link between Islam and politics ('intrinsic to Islam') and the need to view politics on the basis of the Prophet's teachings, he described the contemporary situation of young Muslims in France as 'serious', and presented three alternative responses. The first, that of the parents' generation, the 'immigrants', consisted of suffering in silence: '"I bow my head, I shut up, and I go and hide in a corner"; you can judge for yourselves how effective that attitude is!' At the other extreme was all-out revolt: '"I've had enough, I'm going to wreck the place." What good does that do you? ... If you rise up, you get beaten down again and you don't help the Muslim cause.' Between the two alternatives, 'the solution we advocate is activism'. But this activism was not the same as that of the 'token Arabs' who became involved in politics on an individual basis in the 1980s; 'since they had no solid feeling of specific cultural identity, they were swallowed up by an ideology, by a system.'

The political activism advocated by the UJM must be preceded by the acquisition of a strong sense of local community identity, in order to deal with local politicians. Negotiations should proceed in stages, just as the Prophet had to deal tactically with the 'ungodly' authorities of Mecca when he was in his 'phase of weakness' at the beginning of his preaching. The first step is to sign up on the electoral list, since 'the mayor consults the list, they're not stupid, the councillors, they're going to see whether it's worth dealing with people like that. "Are you on the list? Are your children? You have eight children, Ma cha' Allah, and seven of them can vote? Well, let's see what we can do ..." Then they come round: "Hello, M. Muhammad, how are you?" They come into your home ...'

The UJM's political action thus seems to be geared towards politicians already in office (or candidates for office) rather than fielding Muslim candidates. They want to avoid the trap of becoming 'token Muslims'. In this, their strategy resembles that of the Islamic associations in Bradford, which found it more useful to lobby a 'native English' councillor than to put up an Indian or Pakistani councillor, who would know the system less well and therefore be less effective in delivering the associations' demands. Indeed, if politics is a means to be used along the lines advocated by the Prophet, it would be blasphemous to regard it as an end in itself. According to the UJM's spokesman, 'the end-goal is to win Allah's approval, *soubhanouhou wa ta'ala*, it's not to be elected to the National Assembly or the local council, it's to win God's approval by defending justice on earth.'

The UJM's primary reference is to the Prophet; in the speech quoted above, France is likened to Arabia of the early days of Muhammad's preaching, brought to a world where Islam did not previously exist. The UJM's speakers thus revive the days of the 'first Koranic generation' (in the words of the Islamist thinker Sayyid Qotb), when Muhammad and his followers moved cautiously in their dealings with the authorities. 'In a society of *kuffar* (ungodly people), when the *kuffar* attack the Muslims, you must join the *kuffar*'s spheres of power in order to alleviate the Muslims' burden,' explained the UJM spokesman at the end of his speech on activism. Thus, values and ideas belonging to a radical form of contemporary Islam are deployed within a strategy of community-based negotiation with local politicians in the non-Muslim ('ungodly') environment.

Vénissieux's communist parliamentary representative and mayor, André Gérin, addressed the congress after the debate following this speech by the UJM spokesman. A little taken aback by some of the remarks he had heard, he began by saying that, 'in the eyes of the people', there were differences between 'the young Muslims from working-class areas' and 'the emirs of the sixteenth *arrondissement* of Paris', revealing a certain amount of distance from the political logic of Islamic communalism. But he went on to emphasize that common action could emerge, 'as far as values, the struggle against colonialism, social struggles, progressive ideas are concerned'. 'We are in a phase', he explained,

> when there is a great political change, very serious things, the spread of underdevelopment in the less well-off city areas, you are among the most vulnerable groups in respect of this situation: but there is one positive thing, there is what you are doing, how you have developed over the last three years, I think it is positive, I don't agree with everything, but I consider it my responsibility as mayor and parliamentary representative to go along with you on what seems to me to be positive.

Various interpretations of Gérin's speech are possible. The UJM's treasurer interpreted it one way when he spoke of the mayor visiting 'M. Muhammad' to secure his vote and his children's vote at the next elections. But leaving aside this cynical attitude where electoralism and communalism complement each other as much as they do in Birmingham, the attitude of the communist notable is worthy of attention, revealing as it does the 'important changes' he mentions in his speech. Gérin, mindful of the growing popularity and effectiveness of the movement and its future potential, is keen to attract it into the camp of 'progressive forces' and distance it from the 'emirs of the sixteenth *arrondissement* of Paris'. His attitude reflects the ambivalent stance of the French Communist Party (PCF) to the social movements emerging from Islam over the last twenty years. In 1977, the Confédération Générale du Travail trade union (close to the PCF) had approved the establishment of mosques in factories such as the major Renault or Citroën works as 'progressive'.[56] But in 1991, in the northern town of Libercourt, it was a communist mayor who organized a 'municipal referendum' to prevent the extension of a local mosque.[57] *L'Humanité*, the communist daily, has devoted much attention to the FIS's establishment in city areas; it considers the FIS a terrorist movement, like the Algerian communists who consider it a fascist party and consequently have become favoured targets for the armed Islamist commandos.

These, in broad outline, are the principal changes which the demand for recognition of an Islamic communalist identity have undergone in the first half of the 1990s. It is now expressed by young people from North African families, born in France's cities and in most cases possessing French nationality. The Islamist activists have

successfully combined their religious message with the social disaf-
fection of underprivileged *beur* youth and with educated youth's
aspirations after a respected identity. In the mid-1990s, the movement is not yet dominant among populations of Muslim origin in
France. But it is a new movement, with considerable potential for
development, especially as the social situation in France looks set to
worsen and the institutions which formerly served as integrating
mechanisms (mainly school and the labour movement) continue to
lose their grip. It aims to act as both the mouthpiece and the regula-
tor of social conflict, by expressing social grievances through the
prism of Islam in the hope that the local and national authorities,
themselves unable to control the situation and eager to secure peace
at the least cost, will subcontract regulation of the social problems
to them.

In many ways, the situation recalls that of Britain and the United
States, but there are marked differences because of the absence of a
culture of communalism in the French political tradition. The state
remains hostile to communalism. Moreover, unlike the British and
American situations, the populations of foreign origin in their
majority have until now rejected any reconstruction of identities
inherited from pre-immigration experiences. The anti-racist and *beur*
movements of the 1980s helped to strengthen the impression among
second-generation immigrants that they were all working towards
the same end, and to unite them in a future French identity rather
than divide them into separate national identities. The process to
some extent echoed the mixed cultural environment of the societies
of the North African countries of origin, which had appropriated
elements of French culture. In contrast, after 1989, the radical
Francophobia expressed by the FIS in Algeria, its insistence on a
strict division between 'pure' and 'impure' (the latter being France
and 'her sons') and its reference to a community identity defined by
strict religious observance and an exclusive and intransigent interpretation of Islam, mark an important shift in the range of cultural
symbols available to the Islamist movements in France. This change
tends to make the use of Islam as a means of distancing followers
from the integrationist model of the Republic more credible than it
has been in the past, especially for those young people of Muslim
origin who are deeply affected by their marginalization in French
society. Although they are full citizens, the Republic does nothing to
guarantee their social integration and give them access to the labour
market. It is still too soon to judge whether the new movement has
just been a passing phase attracting only minority support, or
whether it is the precursor of trends to come. In any case, it is clear

that whether the state is centralist and 'assimilative' as in France, or liberal and 'pluralist' as in Britain and the United States, the demand for communalist identity gathers force with the spread of systematic social exclusion in postindustrial society.

Conclusion

We have seen how, in three major countries whose political traditions have played a large part in spreading the variants of the 'Western model' they represent, demands for the recognition of an Islamic communalist identity have developed, highlighting unprecedented contradictions and cleavages within postindustrial societies. At the same time, modes of Islamic expression in the United States, Britain and France depend on the national context and combine the cultural codes of the country with conceptual categories which can be traced back to the Koran along more or less orthodox routes. Even in their heterogeneity, they reveal a series of common themes, and by comparing these themes we can assess the extent of the restructuring of cleavages within our societies at the end of the twentieth century.

First and foremost, the emergence of communalist movements forces us to re-examine the notion of citizenship, which has been at the heart of Western political thinking since the Enlightenment. The new movements react to a perceived 'denial of citizenship' (formulated in their own vocabulary) which affects their followers and their target audience to different degrees, by transposing their demands for social and political recognition onto a religious register. It is in the United States that this process has been pushed the farthest. The world view of the Black Muslims, as expressed by Farrakhan and his disciples, is the deliberate negation of the identity attributed to Blacks by American society. Hence, membership entails a change of name: at an individual level, the adoption of X whilst awaiting a new, Muslim surname; at the group level, the rejection of the label 'negro' and the choice of a new group identification –

'Black', then 'Muslim'. The casting-off of old identities has culminated in Black separatism and the desire to build 'a nation within a
nation', even if this goal has not been achieved in reality. In consequence, Black identity is rebuilt as the negative image (in photo-
graphic terms) of the identity attributed by white America. An
idealized form of citizenship based on a radical alterity (an imagi-
nary other world, both in spatial and transcendental terms) replaces
citizenship marked historically by racial segregation and later by
'hyperghettos' combining both spatial ghettoization and labour-
market segregation. In order to guarantee this new identity, the
movement turns to Allah in a deliberate rejection of the white man's
God. The universality of the Christian culture is in their eyes simply
ethnocentrism and an attempt to legitimate the crimes perpetrated
by the West – in Farrakhan's words, a 'gutter religion'. At this stage
in the construction of a community identity, there is nothing left to
share with non-Muslim society, not even conflict between social
groups, since the new community is constructed as a harmonious
whole. Sealed off from outside society, it is conceived as a total, disciplined system: hence, in the case of the Black Muslims, the emphasis on strict dietary rules, dress code and physical appearance, and
sexual behaviour. Here, too, we see the 'negative image' of the sexual permissiveness and other excesses of ghetto life. Citizenship
means belonging to the strictly disciplined community, within which
democratic expression is prohibited.

In the British case, the Rushdie affair erupted in a context where
citizenship posed a curious problem for the immigrant populations
of the Indian subcontinent. These immigrants more or less automati-
cally possess the attributes of citizenship, such as voting rights and
the right to stand in elections, but the exercise of citizenship is
affected on one hand by differential legal status which gives more
rights to 'patrials' ('native Britons') than to other groups and on the
other by statistical monitoring based on race and ethnicity which
provides a mechanism for 'positive discrimination' in favour of
minority groups (job quotas and so on). In this context, the expression of a community identity does not, as in the United States, result
from the violent rejection of racist segregation embedded in the
national political tradition, but rather constitutes a response to a
system which perpetuates in mainland Britain the colonial norms of
indirect rule. Communalism was originally conceived of in consensual terms. It suited the British state because it marked the proletar-
ian populations of Muslim origin off from the native working class,
thus making class solidarity between the two groups more difficult
and so helping to maintain social peace through the recognition of

specific cultural and religious identities. Mosques and Islamic charitable associations sprang up during the first years of immigration, encouraged by the British state. They helped to stabilize the immigrant populations from the Indian subcontinent and make them into a more efficient and compliant workforce. Thus, not only the British state but also industry was satisfied.

Formed at a time of full employment, for a mainly adult male population, the system would remain in place in a radically different context after the mid-1970s, characterized by structural unemployment and the entry and settlement of immigrant families with children. As the immigrants' children grew up surrounded by British culture and attended British schools, communalism continued to develop in this new context. Demands for separate treatment of Muslim children in British schools increased: dispensations from certain subjects, special foods, a rejection of multiculturalist religious education. The Muslims' campaigns won the support of several local authorities, whilst the Honeyford affair and later the Swann report and the Education Reform Act of 1988 reflected the contradictions of state policy, which remained in favour of religious segmentation in schools but had not worked out how to cope with community demands which undermined the basic social values of state education. The Rushdie affair and the power struggles within the Islamic movement it provoked illustrate the contradictions of social segmentation. In a context where unemployment had eaten away at the traditional paths to integration through work and wage income, Islamic communalism expressed new objectives; instead of promoting consensus and social peace as in the 1950s and 1960s, it became the vehicle for the expression of frustration and anger, which it channelled into a heightened sense of difference and separate identity.

French political tradition has actively combated any form of regional, ethnic or religious identity which could weaken the link between the individual and the state. In France, the state has tried to contain religious expression within a legal framework controlling worship and has refused any form of differential legal treatment. Citizenship is, in principle, granted only to those foreign nationals who have lived on French soil for a lengthy period, which implies acculturation, knowledge of the French language and acceptance of the fundamental values of the Constitution. The French case thus differs markedly from the British situation, which has been the object of a wide consensus at least until the late 1980s. In France, from the mid-1970s until the Creil affair in 1989, the expression of Islamic identity served as a transcendent reference beyond the space between the far-away native land and an impenetrable and silently hostile host society. It was limited to the older generation. To all intents and purposes it did not affect the prevailing definition of French citizenship, for few of these former 'immigrant workers' were French; if anything it provided spiritual and solidaristic comfort to alleviate the lack of citizenship rights. In contrast with Britain, which provided compensation for the distinction between 'patrials' and 'non-patrials' in the form of 'positive discrimination' in favour of certain ethnic groups, there was no room in the French system for differential treatment of citizens. Once acquired, citizenship meant the same rights and duties for everyone.

Starting from very different situations, France and Britain faced the same problem at the end of the 1980s. Citizenship, whatever its original significance, had lost its meaning for large numbers of young people from immigrant families, victims of social disintegration and labour-market exclusion yet officially citizens of a country where most of them were born. In this difficult social context, a new form of assertion of Islamic community identity has emerged in France, in the various veil campaigns and later in the growth of associations of 'young new Muslims' in city housing projects, and demanded recognition from the public authorities. Reacting, as in Britain, to a denial of social and economic citizenship which formal citizenship could not offset, these 'new Muslims' demand a greater say in political life not as individuals but as a community. For them, the Muslim community provides more freedom than does 'anti-religious secularism'. Communalist activism expresses a rejection of social marginalization. In comparison with Britain or the United States, demands for differential recognition have remained relatively free of separatist tendencies or external ties which would bring the movements into direct conflict with the Republic. The Turkish imam expelled from Nantua in late 1993 for proclaiming that Allah's law had precedence over French law learnt to his own cost the consequences of breaking the taboo.

However, if the social situation in France's deprived urban areas continues to deteriorate, there is every chance that a movement which until now has remained cautious in its attitude to French institutions and limited in its appeal will both spread and become more radical, as hundred of thousands of 'little brothers' and 'little sisters' leave school and find the labour market as closed to them as it was to their elder siblings. Moreover, the situation in Algeria increasingly threatens to sharpen the tensions underlying the expression of Islam in France. If the radical tendency within the FIS comes to power, propagating the discourse of Ali Benhadj repudiating

France and all its values, it is unlikely that Islam in France will remain unaffected. The exacerbation of tensions between pro- and anti-FIS tendencies among the two million or so people of Algerian origin living in France, and between Muslims and wider French society over events in North Africa, could prove an explosive cocktail if mixed with youth unrest in the cities. Within the latent cleavages and antagonisms in postindustrial society lies the complex interrelationship between national and international issues exemplified in the events of the Rushdie affair in Britain.

Notes

Introduction

1 (*Translator's note*)   The term *'beur'* is widely used in France to designate children born in France of immigrant (or pre-independence Algerian) parents. They usually have French nationality but many of them claim an identity independent of both their parents' and the dominant French culture.

I 'In the Wilderness of North America'

1 Mike Davis, 'Burning All Illusions in LA', in *Inside the LA Riots* (New York, Institute for Alternative Journalism, 1992), p. 99.
2 Blue is the colour of the Crips, red is the Bloods' colour. On American gang culture, see Martin Sanchez Jankowski, *Islands in the Streets: Gangs in American Urban Society* (Berkeley, Cal. 1991).
3 Interview published in *Against the Current*, no. 39, July–Aug., 1992.
4 See Loïc Wacquant, 'The Zone', in Pierre Bourdieu (ed.) *La Misère du monde* (Paris: Seuil, 1992), pp. 181–204.
5 Quoted by Salim Muwakkil, 'Leaders Lacking in a Black and White World', in *Inside the LA Riots*, p. 107.
6 See especially the ADL Research Report, *Louis Farrakhan: The Campaign to Manipulate Public Opinion. A Study in the Packaging of Bigotry* (New York, 1990).
7 Jonathan Kaufman, *The Broken Alliance: The Turbulent Times Between Blacks and Jews in America* (New York, 1989), p. 248.
8 The Nation of Islam, *The Secret Relationship between Blacks and Jews (Vol. I)* (Chicago, 1991).
9 *Los Angeles Times* survey, cited in Lucius J. Barker, *Our Time has Come: A Delegate's Diary of Jesse Jackson's 1984 Presidential Campaign* (Chicago, 1988), p. 84.
10 Cited by Robert G. Newby, 'The "Naive" and the "Unwashed"', in Lucius

J. Barker and Ronald W. Walters (eds) *Jesse Jackson's 1984 Presidential Campaign* (Chicago, 1989), pp. 170–1.

11 Kevin Pritchett, 'Malcolm X, Conservative Hero', *The Wall Street Journal*, 8 Nov. 1992.

12 Claybourne Carson, *Malcolm X: the FBI File* (New York, 1991), pp. 29, 203, and Malcolm X, *The Last Speeches* (New York, 1989), pp. 118–20.

13 *The Final Call*, 27 July 1992, pp. 7–11.

14 *The Final Call*, 10 Aug. 1992, p. 35.

15 *The Final Call*, 22 Nov. 1992, p. 5.

16 *The Final Call*, 29 July 1992, p. 5.

17 On the representation of Blacks as three-fifths of a white person, see Denis Lacorne, *L'Invention de la République: le modèle américain* (Paris, 1991), pp. 34–5.

18 See James E. Laue, 'A Contemporary Revitalization Movement in American Race Relations: the Black Muslims', *Social Forces*, vol. 42, Mar. 1964, pp. 315–23.

1 The Birth of an American Religion

1 Erdmann Doane Benyon ('The Voodoo Cult among Negro Migrants in Detroit', *The American Journal of Sociology*, May 1938, pp. 894–907) gives first-hand information on Fard and his disciples in the early 1930s (p. 896). This account is taken up by C. Eric Lincoln, *The Black Muslims in America* (Grand Rapids, 1994 [first edition 1961]), pp. 11–17.

2 In Arabic, 'Fard' means 'individual' or 'unique, unparalleled' and, by extension, 'God'. It is not used as a surname.

3 On this question, see Wacquant, 'The Zone'.

4 Beynon, 'The Voodoo Cult', p. 895.

5 Compare the practice of the Jama'at al Tabligh, a re-Islamizing movement created in India in 1929, which required each follower (usually uneducated and with little knowledge of Arabic) to recite the Muslim creed and pronounce perfectly the phonemes of learned Arabic which constitute it. See Kepel, *Les Banlieues de l'Islam* (Paris, 1987), pp. 179ff.

6 Beynon, 'The Voodoo Cult', p. 903.

7 In Fard's time, three opuscules compiled by him circulated among disciples: *Teaching for the Lost Found Nation of Islam in a Mathematical Way* and the two volumes of *Secret Ritual of the Nation of Islam*.

8 These archives were used systematically in a book which presents a mass of previously unpublished material, but also puts forward an extremely controversial argument: Karl Evanzz, *The Judas Factor: The Plot to Kill Malcolm X* (New York, 1992). On Fard, see pp. 142–6.

9 See the photograph taken by Detroit police on 26 May 1933, reproduced in Malu Hasa, *Elijah Muhammad: Religious Leader* (New York, 1991), p. 51.

10 See Evanzz, *The Judas Factor*, p. 146.

11 See Eric Foner, *Reconstruction: America's Unfinished Revolution* (New York, 1988).

12 See William Julius Wilson, *The Declining Significance of Race: Blacks and Changing American Institutions* (Chicago, 1980), pp. 42–61, 122–5.

13 Franklin Frazier, *Black Bourgeoisie* (New York, 1962), p. 78.

14 C. Eric Lincoln and Lawrence H. Mamiya, *The Black Church in the African American Experience* (Durham, N.C., 1990), p. 206.

15 See Wilson, *Declining Significance of Race*, p. 125.

16 See Morroe Berger, 'The Black Muslims', *Horizon*, winter 1964, pp. 53ff., for an early discussion of this question in the context of the Nation of Islam.

17 Islamic literature in the United States today emphasizes the role played by Muslim figures in the early generations, but they seem to have been few in number. See, for example, Fareed H. Nu'man, 'Muslim Population in the United States: A Brief Statement', The American Muslim Council, Oct. 1992.

18 Among the various Muslim missionaries in the United States at that time, the Ahmadiyya sects apparently played a part in propagating Islam among Blacks. The movement was founded in India by Ghulam Ahmad (1839–1908), who saw himself as the last of the prophets, contradicting Islamic dogma which states that Muhammad was 'the seal of prophecy'.

19 Apologists for Islam are quick to contrast Christian 'racism' with Islamic tolerance.

20 Lincoln, *The Black Muslims*, p. 53.

21 Lawrence H. Mamiya and C. Eric Lincoln, 'Black Militant and Separatist Movements', in *Encyclopaedia of American Religion* (1987), pp. 756–7.

22 Hasa, *Elijah Muhammad*, p. 41.

23 According to Evanzz, *The Judas Factor*, he had turned to drink.

24 Hasa, *Elijah Muhammad*, p. 45.

25 Preface to Elijah Muhammad, *Message to the Blackman in America* (Chicago, new edition 'under the auspices of the Honorable Louis Farrakhan', no date [first edition 1965]), preface (pp. xxii, xxiv).

26 Ibid., p. v.

27 Ibid., p. 31.

28 Ibid., pp. 110, 112.

29 On the cosmogony of Elijah Muhammad, see his *Message to the Blackman*, pp. 110–22, 294. See also Malcolm X (with Alex Haley), *The Autobiography of Malcolm X* (New York, 1973 [first edition 1964]), pp. 164–8.

30 On this, see Gilles Kepel, *The Revenge of God: The Resurgence of Islam, Christianity and Judaism in the Modern World* (translated by Alan Braley) (Cambridge, 1994).

31 On Malcolm X's view of Freemasonry, see *Autobiography*, pp. 158–60.

32 *Message to the Blackman*, p. 119.

33 *Autobiography*, p. 162.

34 *Message to the Blackman*, pp. 45–6.

35 Carson, *Malcolm X*.

36 Anyone familiar with Islamic cosmogony will find the Nation of Islam's view of the world's creation extremely surprising and heterodox. Malcolm X, who at first believed in Elijah Muhammad's account, later dismissed it as 'tales' after breaking with the Nation of Islam leader and adopting Saudi-style Islam. See his *Autobiography*, p. 168.

37 See D. B. Cruise O'Brien, *The Mourides of Senegal* (Oxford, 1971).

38 Elijah Muhammad, *The Supreme Wisdom*, vol. II (no date or place of publication), p. 43.

39 *The Final Call*, 20 Apr. 1992, p. 27.

40 *The Final Call*, 27 July 1992, p. 27.

41 *The Final Call*, 22 July 1991, p. 33.
42 *The Final Call*, 20 Apr. 1992, p. 27.
43 Ibid.
44 Berger (*The Black Muslims*) mentions that the Salaam restaurant in Harlem, which belongs to the Nation of Islam, displays the word 'kosher' on its window. It is true that some of the dietary restrictions of the Black Muslims are shared by kosher rules: catfish is prohibited (as a fish without scales) as are shellfish (creatures with their skeleton 'on the outside').
45 Beynon, 'The Voodoo Cult'; Michael Parenti, 'The Black Muslims, From Revolution to Institution', *Social Forces*, summer 1964, pp. 185–7; Perry E. Gianokos, 'The Black Muslims: An American Millenialistic Response to Racism and Cultural Deracination,' *Centennial Review*, vols. 23–4, 1979, pp. 445–6.
46 Malcolm X, *Autobiography*, p. 169.

2 The Three Lives of Malcolm X

1 Malcolm X, *Autobiography*, p. 2.
2 Ibid., p. 38.
3 James H. Cone (*Martin & Malcolm & America. A Dream or a Nightmare* (New York, 1991) systematically compares the experience of these two major figures of Black American activism.
4 Malcolm X, *Autobiography*, p. 67.
5 Ibid., p. 150.
6 Cf. Gilles Kepel, *The Prophet and the Pharaoh: Muslim Extremism in Egypt* (translated by John Rothschild) (London, 1985; Berkeley, Cal., 1993), pp. 50ff.
7 After breaking with the Nation of Islam and going on pilgrimage to Mecca, he took the name Malik al Shabazz. But the fame he had attracted under the name Malcolm X meant that he carried this, and not his Muslim name, into posterity.
8 According to a much cited expression of Malcolm X, 'those who talk don't know, and those who know don't talk'. The figure of 100,000 was given by Malcolm X's opponent during a debate at Harvard University on 24 March 1961, and was not contested by him. At his secret meeting with the Ku Klux Klan on 30 January 1961 in Atlanta, Malcolm X apparently claimed to have 175,000 activists. But during a CBS programme on 13 July 1959 ('The hate that hate produced'), the presenter Mike Wallace cited the figure of 250,000 Nation of Islam members.
9 These methods were later condemned by Wallace Muhammad, who radically reformed the organization set up by his father. See Peter Goldman, *The Death and Life of Malcolm X* (Chicago, 1979 (2nd edition)), p. 433.
10 Enfuriated by the carping among the women activists and their sloppiness, Malcolm X ordered them during a meeeting at the Muslim Temple of Philadelphia 'to buy scales and to weigh the women activists every Monday and Thursday; those who are overweight will have two weeks to lose ten pounds, otherwise they will be suspended.' Cited in Carson, *Malcolm X*, p. 120.
11 See the account in Goldman, *Death and Life of Malcolm X*, pp. 55ff.

12 Quoted in ibid., p. 99. The full text of the speech is given in Carson, *Malcolm X*, pp. 220–1.

13 'The hate that hate produced' was the name of a CBS television programme, broadcast in several episodes from 13 July 1959, produced by Mike Wallace, and presented by the Black journalist and essayist Louis Lomax. The programme presented the movement to a wide audience for the first time, and provoked an angry reaction from Malcolm X. See Malcolm X, *Autobiography*, pp. 238ff. By Louis Lomax, see *When the World is Given* (New York, 1963), particularly pp. 191ff. Carson, *Malcolm X*, pp. 159–70, gives transcripts of parts of the programmes.

14 Nathan Glazer, *Ethnic Dilemmas, 1964–1982* (Harvard, 1983), p. 1.

15 On the WUST station (Washington, DC), 12 May 1963: transcript in Carson, *Malcolm X*, pp. 231ff.

16 The 'subversive' organizations targeted by Eisenhower's presidential decree no. 10450 in 1953 (which allowed surveillance of 'suspect' individuals and barred them from certain jobs) were the various American communist parties (such as the Communist Party and the Trotskyist Socialist Workers' Party) and also various Nazi groups. The Nation of Islam was not subject to these measures. See Marie-France Toinet, *La Chasse aux sorcières* (Brussels, 1988).

17 Malcolm X, *The Last Speeches* (New York, 1989), p. 126.

18 Malcolm X's last year has given rise to a sizeable body of literature. The 'socialist' interpretation is put forward mainly by George Breitman, in *The Last Year of Malcolm X: The Evolution of a Revolutionary* (New York, 1967), and George Breitman, Herman Porter and Baxter Smith, *The Assassination of Malcolm X* (New York, 1991). See also *Malcolm X Speaks*, ed. Breitman (New York, 1965), and Malcolm X, *The Last Speeches*. The proliferation of articles and books on Malcolm X in 1992 and 1993 was due to the release of Spike Lee's film.

19 *Mr. Muhammad Speaks*, 14 Mar. 1975, p. 5.

20 See Carol Ohmann, 'The Autobiography of Malcolm X: A Revolutionary Use of the Franklin Tradition', *American Quarterly*, summer 1970, pp. 131–50.

3 Farrakhan in the Looking-Glass of America

1 Interview with Wallace D. Muhammad, in Clifton E. Marsh, *From Black Muslims to Muslims: The Transition from Separatism to Islam, 1930–1980* Metuchen, (New Jersey and London, 1984), p. 113.

2 See in particular *The New York Times*, 6 Dec. 1973, and Louis Farrakhan's replies, in Minister Louis Farrakhan, *7 Speeches*, Newport News, no date [1974], pp. 41–64.

3 See the (unpublished) study by Lawrence H. Mamiya, 'Louis Abdul Farrakhan (1933–): Minister of the Nation of Islam' (1992), which the author kindly allowed me to consult.

4 See Lincoln, *The Black Muslims*, ch. 1.

5 Speech by Louis Farrakhan, 21 Feb. 1993, in Chicago: reproduced in *The Final Call*, 29 Mar. 1993, p. 32.

6 *Mr. Muhammad Speaks*, 14 Mar. 1975, p. 5.

7 'First official interview with the Supreme Minister of the Nation of Islam, the Honorable Wallace D. Muhammad', *Mr. Muhammad Speaks*, 21 March 1975, pp. 3–14.

8 Lawrence D. Mamiya, 'From Black Muslim to Bilalian: The Evolution of a Movement', in *Journal for the Scientific Study of Religion*, June 1982, p. 148.

9 Cf. Raquel Muhammad, 'The Black Muslim Movement after the Death of Elijah Muhammad', thesis, United States International University, San Diego, 1980, pp. 113ff., 146ff.

10 Warith means 'heir', and 'Deen' means 'religion'. Within the movement, his disciples call him 'W. D. Muhammad', while he remains known outside the movement as 'Wallace'.

11 See W. D. Muhammad, 'Evolution of the Nation of Islam' (lecture given 19 Nov. 1978) in *As the Light Shineth from the East* (no date or place of publication [1980]).

12 On the liquidation of the Nation of Islam's assets, see the monthly *Chicago*, Dec. 1991, pp. 110–13, 146–51.

13 *Mr. Muhammad Speaks*, 5 Sept. 1975, p. 5.

14 Reproduced in the first edition of the organization's new monthly publication, *The Final Call*, undated [1981] and numbered vol. I, no. 7 (referring to the six issues published under this title by Elijah Muhammad in 1934), pp. 2–4, 9, 14–26.

15 Ibid., p. 28.

16 Cf. the arguments presented in Kepel, *The Revenge of God*.

17 My definitions of the hyperghetto draw on the works of William Julius Wilson, *The Declining Significance of Race* (Chicago, 1980); *The Truly Disadvantaged: The Inner City, the Underclass and Public Policy* (Chicago, 1987); (ed.) 'The Ghetto Underclass: Social Science Perspective', *The Annals of the American Academy of Political and Social Science*, Jan. 1989. For an analysis of the debates surrounding poverty in the postindustrial city and the notion of underclass, see Michael B. Katz, *The Undeserving Poor: From the War on Poverty to the War on Welfare* (New York, 1989), chs. 4 and 5, and *The 'Underclass' Debate* (Princeton, New Jersey, 1993).

18 'The Conspiracy: Young Gangs, Violence and Drugs', available on two 90-minute cassettes.

19 Interview with Conrad Muhammad, 'Minister for Youth' of the Nation of Islam, Harlem, 2 Nov. 1992.

20 Interview with Ice-T, 1 May 1992, on radio WHYY-FM. Reproduced in *Inside the LA Riots*, p. 127.

21 *The Final Call*, 24 Aug. 1992, p. 21.

22 *Mr. Muhammad Speaks*, 6 June 1975, p. 22.

23 Louis Farrakhan, interview with *The National Alliance*, 13, 20 and 27 Dec. 1985. Reproduced in *Independent Black Leadership in America: Min. Farrakhan, Dr. Fulani, Rev. Sharpton*, with introduction by William Pleasant (New York, 1990), pp. 34–5.

24 See Joseph P. McCormick II and Robert C. Smith, 'Through the Prism of Afro–American Culture' in Barker and Walters (eds), *Jesse Jackson's 1984 Presidential Campaign*, pp. 101–4.

25 Quoted by Kaufman, *Broken Alliance*, p. 243.

26 See Taylor Branch, 'Blacks and Jews: The Uncivil War', in Jack Salzman (ed.), *Bridges and boundaries: African Americans and American Jews* (New York, 1992), p. 65.

27 Quoted in Barker, *Our Time Has Come*, p. 75.
28 Ibid., pp. 77–81.
29 Minister Louis Farrakhan, 'A Warning to the Jews', dated 1985(?).
30 See The *Final Call*, vol. I, no. 7, p. 25.
31 Farrakhan, *Back to Where we Belong: Selected Speeches by Minister Louis Farrakhan*, edited by Joseph D. Eure and Richard M. Jerome (Philadelphia, 1989), pp. 161–2.
32 See an interview with Farrakhan published in *The National Alliance*, reproduced in *Independent Black Leadership in America*, p. 49.
33 *The Final Call*, 31 Oct. 1990, published a picture of Nassif congratulating Farrakhan, whereas an editorial on another page explained that 'the Arab people see the liberation [by Iraq] and unification of Kuweit as a step towards their national survival' ('Why Arab Masses Back Hussein', by Ali Baghdadi, p. 11).
34 *Independent Black Leadership in America*, pp. 43–4.
35 See the hotel brochures reproduced in Salzmann, *Bridges and Boundaries*, p. 174.
36 Kaufman, *Broken Alliance*, p. 29.
37 James Baldwin, 'Negroes are Anti-Semitic because they are Anti-White', *New York Times Magazine*, Apr. 1967.
38 Glazer, *Ethnic Dilemmas*, p. 100.
39 See Clayborne Carson, 'Blacks and Jews in the Civil Rights Movement: The Case of SNCC', in Salzmann, *Bridges and Boundaries*, pp. 36–49.
40 *Independent Black Leadership*, pp. 44–5.
41 The Ocean Hill-Brownsville incident is chronicled in great detail by Kaufman, *Broken Alliance*, pp. 121–56; most of the facts of the case given here are taken from this source. See also Carson, 'Blacks and Jews in the Civil Rights Movement', pp. 47–8.
42 Gorée Island is a small island off Senegal which became a major entrepôt for the Atlantic slave trade until the end of the eighteenth century.
43 *The Secret Relationship*, p. vii.
44 Ibid., pp. 12–13.
45 Ibid., pp. 178.
46 Ibid., p. 207.
47 See P.-A. Taguieff, *Les Protocoles des Sages de Sion: Faux et usages d'un faux* (Paris, 1992).
48 *New York Times*, 20 July 1992.
49 Interview with the author, Harlem, 2 Nov. 1992.
50 451 murders in 1992 and 455 up to 21 Dec. 1993 (Agence France Presse, 21 Dec. 1993).
51 Abdul Alim Muhammad, in an interview with the author, Washington, 8 Dec. 1993.
52 *The Final Call*, 22 Sept. 1992, p. 5; *Washington Post*, 18 July and 20 Aug. 1992.
53 Interview with author, 8 Dec. 1993.
54 *The Final Call*, 15 June 1992, p. 7.
55 Interview with author, 8 Dec. 1993. The arguments in favour of Immunex treatment are presented in a (roneo) booklet, *The Biography of Dr. Abdul Alim Muhammad M.D.* (no date), which contains a section on 'The efficacity of multiple sub-type low dose orally absorbed alpha-interferon therapy in patients with HIV infection: a clinical retrospective analysis'. To the author's

knowledge, these arguments have never been published in a medical science journal.

56 *The Final Call*, 29 March 1993, p. 5.

57 *The Final Call*, 22 July 1991, p. 34.

58 *New York Times*, 19 April 1993, p. C11.

59 This comment appears on the blurb for the second edition of *A Torchlight for America* (Chicago, 1993).

60 *The Final Call*, 8 Dec. 1993: 'We fast the twelfth month of the Christian year to relieve ourselves of having once worshipped that month as the month in which Jesus was born. ... In this month, we should keep our minds on Allah, Who came in the Person of Master Fard Muhammad; my God and your God and my Saviour and Deliverer to Whom be praises forever for giving us life after our mental death for the past 400 years.'

61 See *New York Times*, 16 Jan. 1994; *Los Angeles Times*, 26 and 28 Jan., 4 Feb. 1994; *International Herald Tribune*, 16–17 April 1994. This incident led to considerable press interest in the Nation of Islam in the United States and abroad.

II The Britannic Verses

1 According to interviews carried out by the author with Ishtiyaq Ahmed, spokesperson for the Bradford Council of Mosques (20 Feb. 1993), and Liaqat Hussein, general secretary (15 Oct. 1993). See also Philip J. Lewis, *Islamic Britain: Religion, Politics and Identity among British Muslims* (London, 1994), p. 233 n. 36.

2 *Observer*, 1 Oct. 1989. This idea is also discussed in Reda Bensmaïa, 'Une nouvelle maladie humaine: l'afictionalité', in *Cent intellectuels arabes et musulmans pour la liberté d'expression, Pour Rushdie* (Paris, 1993), pp. 93–8.

3 Ziaudinn Sardar and Merryl Wyn Davies, *Distorted Imagination: Lessons from the Rushdie affair* (London/Kuala Lumpur, 1990), p. 151. This book is one of the most virulent and sophisticated attacks on *The Satanic Verses* and its defenders.

4 These words came from the Indian Muslim MP Syed Shahabuddin, who launched the victorious campaign for *The Satanic Verses* to be banned in his country (*The Times of India*, 13 Oct. 1988). Quoted in Lisa Appignanesi and Sara Maitland (eds), *The Rushdie File* (London, 1989), p. 47.

5 Jorgen Nielsen, *Muslims in Western Europe* (Edinburgh, 1992), p. 41. Among the Muslim population there are around 121,000 Arabs; apart from Yemenis, many of these Arab populations are wealthy Middle Eastern groups who do not experience the settlement problems of disadvantaged individuals and groups. As regards Nielsen's figures, like any estimations of these populations they are disputed by all sides (brochures published by Islamic associations claim two million Muslims), but they at least give some idea of the size of the populations involved.

1 Return to the Empire

1 Anil Seal, *The Emergence of Indian Nationalism: Competition and Collaboration in the Later XIXth Century* (Cambridge, 1968), p. 12.
2 See Yohanan Friedmann, 'Islamic Thought in the Indian Context', in Marc Gaborieau (ed.), *Islam et Société en Asie du Sud* (Paris, 1986), p. 80.
3 Peter Hardy, *The Muslims of British India* (Cambridge, 1972), pp. 1–2. In an identical process, contemporary Hindu movements sharpen the religious difference in an anachronistic way in order to identify it as the essence of Indian history and thus advocate militant 're-Hinduization' today. On this question, see Christophe Jaffrelot, *Les Nationalistes hindous* (Paris, 1993).
4 The question of the status of territories containing Muslim inhabitants which were conquered by non-Muslims was posed in the Middle Ages with the Crusades and especially with the Mongol invasions in the Middle East. It was the subject of a juridical examination by Ibn Taimiyya (1263–1328). See G. Kepel, 'Egypte aujourd'hui: mouvement islamiste et tradition savante', in *Annales ESC*, no. 4, 1984, pp. 667–80.
5 On the doctrine of jihad, see Alfred Morabia, *Le Gihad dans l'islam médiéval. Le 'combat sacré' des origines au XIIe siècle* (Paris, 1993).
6 Sufism (from the Arabic 'suf', meaning wool, the cloth worn by the mystics) emphasizes the immediacy of contact with God and mysticism. Its followers are organized in numerous brotherhoods (*tariqa*) led by sheikhs (or 'guides', known as *pir* in Urdu) to whom their disciples attribute powers of intercession and a certain kind of extra-perception.
7 See Barbara Daly Metcalf, *Islamic Revival in British India: Deoband (1860–1900)* (Princeton, 1982).
8 Francis Robinson, 'Varieties of South Asian Islam', *Research Papers on Ethnic Relations*, no. 8 (University of Warwick, 1988) p. 4.
9 Ibid., pp. 5–6.
10 See Robinson, ibid.; also Kepel, *Les Banlieues de l'islam*, ch. 4, on the movement in France.
11 Louis Dumont, *Homo hierarchicus: Le Système des castes et ses implications* (Paris, 1979), p. 378.
12 The word 'communal' appeared in the 1920s to describe membership of a community, particularly Muslim or Hindu. Since then, it has been used to denote confrontation between religions and its violent consequences. In the context of India, the term had pejorative connotations, both for Indian nationalists (who rejected the fragmentation of the 'nation' they wished to lead to independence) and for various colonial analysts who interpreted it as a local irritation which would be superseded by the emergence of modern national consciousness. See Gyanendra Pandey, *The Construction of Communalism in Colonial North India* (Delhi, 1990), pp. 7–9.
13 Hardy, *The Muslims of British India*, p. 101.
14 Pandey, *The Construction of Communalism*, pp. 198–9.
15 The Congress Party, which took shape as early as 1885, campaigned for the independence of the whole of India, within a secular nationalist perspective. This did not prevent it from using all the mainstays of Hindu culture in order to mobilize sections of the population which were not receptive to the modern vocabulary of self-determination or democracy in its anti-colonial campaign. This of course created a feeling of cultural unease among many Muslims.

16 David Page, *Prelude to Partition: The Indian Muslims and the Imperial System of Control (1920–1932)* (Delhi, 1982), p. 260.
17 Leonard Binder, *Religion and Politics in Pakistan* (Berkeley and Los Angeles, 1961), pp. 102–4, 142–5.

2 'Britishness' and Identity

1 Survey cited by Jacques Leruez, *L'Ecosse: une nation sans état* (Lille, 1993), p. 9.
2 On 'race' and 'citizenship' in Britain within a comparative context, see Catherine Neveu, 'Citoyenneté et racisme en Europe: exception et complémentarité britannique', *Revue Européenne des Migrations Internationales* (1994) and *Communauté, nationalité et citoyenneté. Les Bangladeshis à Londres* (Paris, 1993).
3 Harry Goulbourne, *Ethnicity and Nationalism in Post-Imperial Britain* (Cambridge, 1991), p. 92.
4 On the other hand, the London government was anxious to retain the allegiance of the millions of English, Scottish and Welsh settlers who went to live in the colonies and avoid cutting links between them and the Crown, as the American settlers had done at the end of the eighteenth century. Between 1871 and 1988, there was considerable net emigration from Britain (except for the period between 1931 and 1961). Between 1961 and 1971, Britain lost 320,000 inhabitants through emigration, and 699,000 between 1971 and 1981. This net emigration makes Britain unique among the industrialized nations of Western Europe. See Zig Layton-Henry, *The Politics of Immigration: Immigration, 'Race' and 'Race Relations' in Post-War Britain* (Oxford, 1992), p. 2.
5 Ibid., p. 39. The Labour Party leadership condemned the rioters.
6 The authorities of the Commonwealth nations also issued British passports to their citizens.
7 Nielsen, 'Muslims in Western Europe', pp. 40–1.
8 In 1972, the Ugandan dictator Idi Amin Dada announced the expulsion of 50,000 people of Indian origin carrying British passports. 27,000 of these took up residence in the United Kingdom, amidst a climate of hostility.
9 Didier Lapeyronnie, *L'Individu et les minorités. La France et la Grande-Bretagne face à leurs immigrés* (Paris, 1993), p. 213.
10 See Heather Booth, 'Which "ethnic question"? The development of questions identifying ethnic origin in official statistics', *The Sociological Review*, May 1985, pp. 254ff.
11 Goulbourne, *Ethnicity and Nationalism*, p. 5.
12 Ibid., pp. 12–13.
13 On this, see Kepel, *Les Banlieues de l'islam*.
14 The first mosques to be built on British soil were constructed in Woking, Surrey, in 1889–90 and in Liverpool in the early 1890s. Plans for a great mosque in the capital of the empire, in order to compete with the Paris mosque which was built in 1926 as an expression of France's claim to be a 'Muslim power', came to fruition only in 1977 with the construction of the great mosque in Regent's Park – well after the end of empire. See HM Reference Services, Central Office of Information, *Some Aspects of Islam in*

Britain (1984), p. 2, and Nielsen, *Muslims in Western Europe*, pp. 4–6.

15 Religion has not been the only form of expression of identity. The division of Yemen (until 1990) between the Marxist southern state and the more conservative regime in the north led to the creation in 1970 of a Union of Yemeni Workers, with the aim of promoting socialism and supporting the Marxist government of Aden. See Fred Halliday, *Arabs in Exile: Yemeni Migrants in Urban Britain* (London and New York, 1992).

16 Nielsen, *Muslims in Western Europe*, p. 45. 'Registered' mosques are those enjoying charitable status and the tax advantages it offers. This figure does not therefore include informal places of worship which may be set up in houses, garages, factories etc.

17 Danièle Joly, 'Making a Place for Islam in British Society: Muslims in Britain', *Research Papers in Ethnic Relations*, University of Warwick, 1987, pp. 4, 8. According to 1981 census data, 88 per cent of the Bengali and Pakistani population is concentrated in nine of Birmingham's thirty wards.

18 Jean Ellis, 'Local Government and Community Needs: A Case Study of Muslims in Coventry', *New Community*, Apr. 1991, p. 365.

19 S. W. Harrison and D. Shepherd, 'Islam in Preston' (unpublished paper, no date [1975]), p. 5.

20 Glenda Robson, 'Muslims in Manchester' (unpublished paper, Sacred Trinity College, Manchester, no date [1987]), p. 38.

21 The Punjab spreads from northern India into the northwest of Pakistan (around Rawalpindi); the district of Mirpur in Kashmir borders the Indian-controlled part of Kashmir, where a guerrilla war is being led by Muslim separatists; Pathans come from the northwestern province on the Indian–Pakistani border, which also borders Afghanistan. All three have different vernacular languages. Gujerat is situated in northwest India, north of Bombay; many Gujerati business-people emigrated to East Africa, from where they were later expelled.

22 See Joly, 'Making a Place for Islam', pp. 6–8.

23 Yusuf Qamar, secretary of the committee of the central mosque, Birmingham, interview with the author, 17 Feb. 1993.

24 Mohammad S. Raza, *Islam in Britain: Past, Present and the Future* (Leicester, 1991), p. 49.

25 Lewis, *Islamic Britain*, pp. 89–90.

26 Sher Azam, president of the Bradford Council of Mosques, interview with the author, 16 Oct. 1993. Sher Azam was one of the early immigrants to Bradford.

27 Pakistani worker, interview with the author, Southfield Square, Bradford, 15 Oct. 1993.

28 Lewis, *Islamic Britain*, p. 90.

29 See Muhammad Siddique, *Moral Spotlight on Bradford* (Bradford, 1993). The author is a follower of Pir Mahroof. His book, which displays on its cover a map of Bradford with the words 'Freedom–Pornography–Aids–Divorce–Politics–Drugs–Abortion–Prostitution–Racism', includes a very detailed chapter on prostitution in Lumb Lane, illustrated with a plan of the area indicating the street corners where prostitutes stand as well as the mosques and Koranic schools.

30 Note that the World Islamic Mission should not be confused with the Wahhabi-inspired Muslim World League, based in Mecca, or with the UK Islamic Mission, which is the British branch of Mawdudi's movement.

'Grassroots' Muslims themselves are often confused by the similarity between these names.

31 Pir Mahroof, interviews with the author, 12 Feb. and 15 Oct. 1993.

32 Sher Azam, interview with the author, 16 Oct. 1993.

33 Other Islamist activists are more critical of the mosques' teaching, claiming that the imams' outdated methods (rote-learning of the Koran) and use of corporal punishment repel children and put them off Islam: see Raza, *Islam in Britain*, pp. 48–60.

34 This is a summary of the seventeen 'educational problems of Muslims in the UK' listed in Ghulam Sarwar, *Muslims and Education in the UK* (London, 1983), pp. 7–11.

35 Layton-Henry, *The Politics of Immigration*, pp. 110–11.

36 Birmingham city council created 54,000 jobs, which made it the biggest local employer. In 1984, the council circulated a questionnaire among its employees in order to monitor their ethnic origin, and discovered that less than 7 per cent of them were 'black', set against a total 'minority' population calculated at between 20 per cent and 25 per cent. Khurshid Ahmad, head of Birmingham city council's Race Relations and Equal Opportunities Unit, interview with the author, 10 Feb. 1993.

37 Roy Hattersley MP, interview with the author, London, 15 Feb. 1993.

38 See Danièle Joly, 'Immigration, citoyenneté et pouvoir local: les musulmans à Birmingham', in Rémy Leveau and Gilles Kepel (eds), *Les Musulmans dans la société française* (Paris, 1988), p. 197.

39 Lewis, *Islamic Britain*, p. 56.

40 M. Le Lohe, 'The Effects of the Presence of Immigrants upon the Political System in Bradford', in R. Miles and A. Phizaclea (eds) *Racism and Political Action* (London, 1979), p. 197.

41 Lewis, *Islamic Britain*, p. 146.

42 City of Bradford Metropolitan Council, Directorate of Educational Services, 'Education for a multi-cultural society: provision for pupils of ethnic minority communities', Bradford, 10 Nov. 1982, in particular articles 2.7, 3.1, 3.3.4 and 3.4. Extracts from these instructions were printed in Muslim Educational Trust booklets and recommended as a model for other local authorities. In Birmingham, in response to demands made by the Muslim Liaison Committee set up in 1983, the city council's education department circulated heads of schools with instructions on specific provision for Muslim pupils, along the lines of the Bradford document. See Muslim Liaison Committee, City of Birmingham Education Department, *Guidelines on Meeting the Religious and Cultural Needs of Muslim Pupils* (Birmingham, 1988) (published in English and Urdu).

43 Lewis, *Islamic Britain*, p. 149.

44 On the Honeyford affair, see Dervla Murphy, *Tales from Two Cities. Travel of Another Sort* (London, 1987), pp. 103–42.

45 Ray Honeyford, 'Education and Race: An Alternative View', *Salisbury Review*, Jan. 1994.

46 Lord Swann, *Education for All* (London, 1985), p. 8.

47 Ibid., p. 7.

48 The Islamic Academy, *The Swann Committee Report: An Evaluation from the Muslim Point of View – An Agreed Statement* (Cambridge, 1985), pp. 3–4.

49 Swann, *Education for All*, p. 465.

50 The Islamic Academy, *The Swann Committee Report*, p. 5.
51 In a 1991 publication, the Muslim Education Trust insists that Islam prohibits all forms of human representation, and that Muslim pupils may follow art classes only if they deal with Islamic art. Similarly, Muslim pupils
may sing to the glory of Allah in music lessons, but may not play instruments. Dance is seen as an incitation to debauchery and is strictly forbidden.
See Ghulam Sarwar, *British Muslims and Schools: Proposals for Progress*
(London, 1991), pp. 22–3.
52 *The Education Act of 1988* (London: HMSO, 1988), section 7 paragraphs 1
and 2.
53 Ghulam Sarwar, *Education Reform Act 1988: What Can Muslims Do?*
(London, 1989), p. 2.
54 See The Islamic Academy, *Resources for the Teaching of Islam in British
Schools* (Cambridge, 1986).
55 Mustafa Yusuf McDermott, Muhammad Manazir Ahsan, *The Muslim
Guide for Teachers, Employers, Community Workers and Social
Administrators in Britain* (Leicester, 1986 [first published 1980]).
56 The Islamic Foundation, *PCIQ: User's Guide* (Leicester, 1992), p. 4.
57 Darul Uloom, Birmingham, 'Prospectus' (no date), p.1.
58 Her Majesty's Inspectors/ Department of Education and Science, *Darul
Uloom Islamic School in Birmingham: A Report* (London, 26 Nov. 1990),
pp. 10–11.
59 Cf. J. M. Halstead, *The Case for Muslim Voluntary-Aided Schools: Some
Philosophical Reflections* (Cambridge, 1986).
60 *Islamia School Yearbook 1991/1992*, p. 2.
61 *Economist*, 19 Dec. 1992, p. 31, and *Q News* (Britain's first Muslim
weekly), 2/21, 20 Aug. 1993, p. 7.
62 See *White Paper: Choice and Diversity in Education* (London, 1992).

3 The Rushdie Affair

1 Among populations of Bangladeshi origin, religious movements had less
control of political expression than among the Pakistani populations, and
did not develop at the same time. See Younis Samad, 'The Politics of
Cultural Identity among Bangladeshis and Pakistanis in Britain' (unpublished paper, Oxford University, May 1992).
2 Pierre Bourdieu, 'Genèse et structure du champ religieux', *Revue Française
de Sociologie*, XII, 1971, pp. 295–334.
3 In some Islamic circles, the identification of 'minorities' in the United
Kingdom by race or ethnic group rather than religion has been severely criticized. On this issue, see Tariq Modood, 'Muslims, Race and Equality in
Britain', *CSIC Papers No.1* (Selly Oak Colleges, Birmingham, June 1990).
4 *Independent*, 10 Sept. 1988.
5 *Impact International*, 28 Oct. 1988.
6 Quoted in *The Times*, 20 Feb. 1989.
7 The proportion of Muslims in India has risen regularly: 10.84 per cent of the
population in 1971 and 11.35 per cent in 1981. In the early 1990s, there
were 120 million Muslims in a total Indian population of 840 million.

8   See Asghar Ali Engineer (ed.), *Delhi–Meerut Riots: Analysis, Compilation and Documentation* (Delhi, 1988).
9   A selection of such texts can be found in Appignanesi and Maitland, *The Rushdie File*, pp. 35–53.
10 M. M. Ahsan and A. R. Kidwai (eds), *Sacrilege versus Civility: Muslim Perspectives on the Satanic Verses Affair* (Leicester, 1991), pp. 315–16.
11 *The Sunday Times*, 19 Feb. 1989, cited in Appignanesi and Maitland, *The Rushdie File*, p. 56. See also Malise Ruthven, *A Satanic Affair: Salman Rushdie and the Wrath of Islam* (London, 1991), p. 92.
12 The UK Islamic Mission, *An Introduction (Ta'rif al bi'tha al islamiyya fi-l mamlaka al muttahida)* (London, no date, pp. 1–2).
13 Khurram Murad, *Da'wah among non-Muslims in the West: Some Conceptual and Methodological Aspects* (Leicester, 1986).
14 In particular, photographs show the platform at the Mission's annual congresses, with such dignitaries as Mawdudi himself (in 1976), Muhammad Qotb (the brother of the leading theoretician of the Muslim Brotherhood, Sayyid Qotb) and various leading Saudi figures, including the imam of the Mecca mosque.
15 Banna founded the Muslim Brotherhood in Egypt, the model for contemporary Islamist movements. Ibn Taimiyya is the major ideological reference for the Muslim Brotherhood and for Mawdudi and his followers as well as for the Saudi leaders.
16 Interview with the author, Leicester, 11 Feb. 1993. The Refah Partisi is the leading Turkish Islamist party. Founded by Necmettin Erkaban, it is represented in the Ankara parliament and obtains between 10 per cent and 15 per cent of votes in elections.
17 Ahsan and Kidwai, *Sacrilege versus Civility*, pp. 26–7. The UK Action Committee on Islamic Affairs included organizations affiliated to the Jama'at i-Islami, various Deobandi associations and personalities, and groups closely linked to Wahhabism like the Ahl e-Hadith association. All these groups were considered to be close to Saudi views of Islam. The Islamic education lobby had met in similar conditions to respond to the Swann report in 1985.
18 See Richard Webster, *A Brief History of Blasphemy: Liberalism, Censorship and The Satanic Verses* (Southwold, 1990) and 'The Rushdie Affair: A Documentation', *Research Papers on Muslims in Europe* (Selly Oak Colleges, Birmingham, June 1989).
19 This was confirmed by a High Court decision on 9 Apr. 1990. See Akbar Ali Malik, *The Satanic Verses: Was it Worth all the Fuss? A Muslim Lawyer's Viewpoint* (London, 1993), pp. 101–6, 123–33.
20 Lewis, *Islamic Britain*, p. 156.
21 Ruthven, *A Satanic Affair*, pp. 97–8.
22 Lewis, *Islamic Britain*, p. 159.
23 See Yasmin Ali, 'Identity and Community: Young British South Asians in the 1990s', in David G. Bowen (ed.), *The Satanic Verses: Bradford Responds* (Bradford, 1992), p. 68. For a description of the young protesters on the 27 May 1989 demonstration in front of the Houses of Parliament, see *Guardian*, 29 May 1989, and Ruthven, *A Satanic Affair*, pp. 1–3.
24 Religious poetry of Imam Raza, translated by G. D. Qureshi, cited in Bowen, *The Satanic Verses: Bradford Responds*, p. 24.

25 *Bradford Telegraph and Argus*, 14 Jan. 1989, reproduced in Appignanesi and Maitland, *The Rushdie File*, p. 67.
26 Ahsan and Kidwai, *Sacrilege versus Civility*, p. 41.
27 A fatwa is an authorized legal judgement based on the Holy Texts of Islam. The flexible status of the imam has led to the pronouncement of fatwas of all kinds, which have no effect except on their own group of followers. Institutional Sunni Islam has tried, without any great success, to limit the power to pronounce fatwas to muftis (literally: 'he who pronounces fatwas'), who are the subject of attempts at government control in modern Muslim states. In Shiite Islam, only the great ayatollahs, who have the title 'mujtahed' ('interpreter of the Holy Texts'), are authorized to pronounce fatwas, and these have effect only for the believers who specifically follow them.
28 Ishtiyaq Ahmad, interview with the author, 20 Feb. 1993.
29 Ahsan and Kidwai, *Sacrilege versus Civility*, pp. 17–18, and Ruthven, *A Satanic Affair*, p. 152.
30 According to Sardar and Davis, *Distorted Imagination*, pp. 197–8, the Institute was mainly financed by Saudi Arabia in the beginning, but financial quarrels contributed to the breakdown of relations.
31 The Muslim Institute for Research and Planning, *Draft Prospectus* (London, 1974); Dr M. Ghayasuddin (deputy director of the Institute), interview with the author, London, 18 Oct. 1993.
32 Siddiqui seems not to have realized the mobilization potential of the affair in the early stages. The Iranian government, too, reacted only slowly to the publication of the novel. Rushdie's previous novels had been published in Iran, and one had even won an award. *The Satanic Verses* was reviewed unfavourably in the Tehran newspaper *Kayhan Farangi* in Dec. 1988, but at that stage there was no hint of death threats against the author.
33 Kalim Siddiqui, *The Implications of the Rushdie Affair for Muslims in Britain* (London, no date [1989]), pp. 9–10.
34 The Islamic Defence Council, another *ad hoc* group set up to campaign against *The Satanic Verses*, which had organized both the 27 May demonstration and the march on Penguin publishers the next day, protested that 'This is the declaration of those 46 Islamic countries of the world who were either not capable of doing anything or did not wish to do anything.' Nevertheless, the group was fundamentally opposed to Ayatalloh Khomeini and felt that his intervention had prevented the West from modifying its position. Although it recognized the emotional satisfaction felt by many Muslims at the fatwa, it considered that it was ultimately a political mistake to 'dance to the tune of Ayatolla [*sic*] Khomeini'. M. Atiqur-Rahman Sambhli, *Our Campaign against* The Satanic Verses (London, 1991), pp. 21, 25.
35 Siddiqui, *The Implications of the Rushdie Affair*, p. 16. In fact, reliable estimates of the number of people of Muslim origin in Britain put it at around one million.
36 *The Muslim Manifesto: A Strategy for Survival* (London, 1990), pp. 5, 13, 16, 31.
37 Kalim Siddiqui, 'Inaugural Address. The Muslim Parliament of Britain: Political Innovation and Adaptation' (copy of speech, London, 4 Jan. 1992), p. 5.

38 *Independent on Sunday*, 5 Jan. 1992.
39 *Independent*, 4 Mar. 1989.

III France, Land of Islam

1 For an account of Islam in France before 1987, see Kepel, *Les Banlieues de l'islam*.
2 *Politis*, 26 Oct. 1989, p. 24.
3 In 1990, half of the young people of eighteen from Algerian families who had left school without qualifications were unemployed. See Michèle Tribalat, 'Les Immigrés et les populations liées à leur installation en France au recensement de 1990', *Population*, no. 6, 1993.
4 The expression belongs to Georges Lavau, who has used it in the context of the French Communist Party's role in expressing working-class discontent. See Lavau, *A Quoi sert le Parti Communiste Français?* (Paris, 1981).

1 The FIS versus the 'Sons of France'

1 There are divergent accounts of the date and place of this 'first' proclamation (there were several of them). Official accreditation, as required by a new law on political associations, was granted only on 9 Sept. 1989. The following month, on 5 Oct., the FIS began to publish its organ, *Al Munqidh* ('The Saviour'), which soon sold 300,000 copies. It continued to appear until 2 Feb. 1992 (despite six months of censorship between 26 June and 1 Dec. 1991).
2 At the local elections, the FIS obtained 54.25 per cent of the vote (33.73 per cent of the total electorate). In the first round of the legislative elections in Dec. 1991, it gained 47.27 per cent of the vote (24.59 per cent of the total electorate). 118 FIS deputies were elected at the first ballot (sixteen FLN). See J. Fontaine, 'Les Élections législatives algériennes', *Monde Arabe/Maghreb-Machrek*, no. 135, Jan.–Mar. 1992, p. 155ff. The results were challenged by the FIS, which claimed to have won 82.51 per cent of the vote at the 1990 local elections: see *Al Munqidh*, special edition, 28 dhou al qi'da 1410.
3 On this question, see Monique Gadant's pioneering study, *Islam et nationalisme en Algérie, d'après El Moudjahid, organe central du FLN de 1956 à 1962* (Paris, 1988). According to Gadant (p. 11), 'the use of Islam as a symbolic reference cementing the unity of society allowed the FLN to control its ideological borrowings from Marxism and to reduce these borrowings to a simple technique of development. The synthesis of Islam and this "Marxism" constitutes an ideology of national construction which represses in advance (and would repress in reality) all social conflicts in the realm of morality.'
4 See Benjamin Stora, *Messali Hadj, pionnier du nationalisme algérien* (Paris, 1987) and *La Gangrène et l'oubli: La Mémoire de la guerre d'Algérie* (Paris, 1991).
5 On this question, the main reference is Muhammad Harbi's work: see in

particular *Aux origines du FLN* (Paris, 1975), *Le FLN, mirage et réalité* (Paris, 1980) and *L'Algérie et son destin* (Paris, 1992). The latter re-examines the issue in the context of the emergence of the FIS.

6 Interviews with Slimane Zeghidour, *Politique Internationale*, autumn 1990, pp. 180, 156. Similar statements may be found in interviews compiled by Séverine Labat, 'Islamismes et islamistes en Algérie', in Gilles Kepel (ed.) *Exils et royaumes: Les Appartenances au monde arabo-musulman aujour-d'hui* (Paris, 1994), pp. 58–9.

7 *Al Munqidh*, no. 18, p. 1. Note that the term 'mujahaddin' in Arabic means 'soldiers' but etymologically refers only to jihad fighters, that is, fighters in the holy combat for the triumph of Islam. In *Al Munqidh* no. 33 (15 Nov. 1990), Ali Benhadj violently criticizes those who fought the war of independence for a cause other than Islam, referring sarcastically to veterans who were rewarded with a tobacconist's shop or bar, who do not deserve the title of 'mujahaddin'.

8 *Al Munqidh*, no. 18, p. 7.

9 See François Burgat, *The Islamic Movement in North Africa* (Austin, Texas, 1993).

10 Quoted (translated from Arabic into French) by L-.W. Deheuvels, *Islam et pensée contemporaine en Algérie* (Paris, 1992), p. 250.

11 The front page of *Al Munqidh*, no. 52, 27 Mar. 1991, lambasted the Algerian government, denounced as 'Rousseau's heirs', for prohibiting electoral propaganda within mosques.

12 The document is reproduced in M. Al-Ahnaf, B. Botiveau and F. Frégosi, *L'Algérie par ses islamistes* (Paris, 1991), pp. 45–8.

13 Mahfouz Nahnah, who was later to found the Algerian *Hamas* group in 1989, a local branch of the Muslim Brotherhood, attempted in 1976 to organize armed resistance to the regime, on the grounds that it was illegitimate because it did not apply the sharia. He was immediately arrested and imprisoned before he could get any organization off the ground. See Al-Ahnaf, Botiveau and Frégosi, *L'Algérie par ses islamistes*, pp. 26ff, 64ff, and A. Ayyachi, *Al islamiyyun al jaza'iriyyun bayn al sulta wa-l rusas* ('The Algerian Islamists between political power and the bullet') (Algiers, 1992), pp. 206ff.

14 Abdallah Jaballah belonged to the Muslim Brotherhood and had an important following at the University of Constantine. He lent his support to the Algerian Islamist movement in 1982. In 1989, he was to set up his own rival Islamist party, Al Nahda ('Rebirth').

15 On the remarkable popularity of 'Alilou' (diminutive of Ali) Benhadj among the youth of the poor quarters, see Meriem Vergès, 'La Casbah d'Alger, chronique de survie dans un quartier en sursis' (p. 79) and Luis Martinez, 'Les Eucalyptus, banlieue d'Alger dans la guerre civile', both in Kepel, *Exils et royaumes*.

16 Ali Benhadj's brother in *Al Munqidh*, 1 Dec. 1991, p. 22. See also Al-Ahnaf, Botiveau and Frégosi, *L'Algérie par ses islamistes*, pp. 70–3, and Ayyachi, *Al islamiyyun*, pp. 200ff.

17 On the important presence of FIS members among the teaching profession, see Ignace Leverrier, 'Le Front Islamique de Salut entre la hâte et la patience', in Gilles Kepel (ed.), *Les Politiques de Dieu* (Paris, 1993), pp. 51–2.

18 Abd al Hadi Doudi, brother-in-law of Bouyali and the leading intellectual

within his group, was imam of the Al Achour mosque. He escaped the government clampdown in 1987 by taking refuge in Marseilles, in circumstances which remain unknown. He became imam at the the rue Bon Pasteur mosque but left after disagreements with the 'rector', Mr Alili, and since then has run another of the city's mosques. See Burgat, *L'Islamisme au Maghreb*, pp. 159ff, and Jocelyne Cesari, *Etre musulman en France: associations, militants et mosquées* (Paris, 1994), pp. 104, 106.

19 Interview with the author, Algiers, Jan. 1993.

20 Interview with the author, Algiers, Jan. 1993.

21 The 'Algerianists' owe their name to Mahfouz Nahnah, who used it ironically to highlight their refusal to follow the line of the international movement led by the Muslim Brotherhood (of which Nahnah was the leader in Algeria). In most cases bilingual graduates in applied sciences, they were often inspired by Bennabi and saw the heightened pietism of the salafists as unnecessarily extremist. They took over the leadership of the FIS at the Batna congress in July 1991, taking advantage of the imprisonment of Madani and Benhadj to expel the salafists. They triumphed in the first round of the legislative elections in Dec. 1991, but were later marginalized when the armed struggle brought more radicalized activists to the fore.

22 The monthly publication of the Muslim Brotherhood, *Al Da'wa*, identified the four major enemies of Islam as Marxism, Freemasonry, secularism and Judaism, the last being ultimately the root of the other three. See Kepel, *The Prophet and the Pharaoh*, ch. 4.

23 *Al Munqidh*, no. 2, 19 Oct. 1989, p. 12.

24 *Al Munqidh*, no. 3, 2 Nov. 1989, p. 4. The term *mahram* denotes, in Islamic law, those with whom one has a kinship relation making marriage illicit.

25 *Al Munqidh*, no. 75, 2 Feb. 1992, p. 2.

26 *Al Munqidh*, no. 12, p. 8 (reproduced in Al-Ahnaf, Botiveau and Frégosi, *L'Algérie par ses islamistes*, p. 246). The phrase used is 'non à la femme émanchipie' instead of 'émancipée', 'chipie' being a general term of abuse against women. Note that the publication of articles in French, despite the 'language of the colonizer' being anathema to the Islamists, is in itself significant. After issue no. 8, the publication contained some articles in French (usually two pages) 'to satisfy the demand of some of our dear readers', until a separate French-language publication, *Al Forkan*, was created by the FIS.

27 *Al Munqidh*, no. 6, 14 Dec. 1989, p. 12.

28 *Al Munqidh*, no. 18, p. 2.

29 *Al Munqidh*, no. 4, 16 Nov. 1989, p. 16.

30 *Al Munqidh*, no. 26, 20 Sept. 1990, p. 14.

31 *Al Munqidh*, no. 33, 15 Nov. 1990, p. 5.

32 *Al Munqidh*, nos. 23, 24 and 25. The text has been analysed and contextualized by A. El-Disfraoui, 'La critique de la doctrine démocratique par le FIS' in Kepel, *Exils et royaumes*, pp. 105–25. See also, by the same author, 'Le poison des orientalistes' (dissertation, Institut des Études Politiques, Paris, 1992), with a translation of the Benhadj text in appendix. Long extracts are also translated in Al-Ahnaf, Botiveau and Frégosi, *L'Algérie par ses islamistes*, pp. 87–98.

33 Sura XXI, Al-Anbia, Verse 18 (translation by Muhammad Marmaduke Pickthall, *The Meaning of the Glorious Koran*). Note that *Al Munqidh*'s transcription of the quotation from the Koran contained a typographical

error, which is considered blasphemous in Islamist circles due to the holiness of the text. A similar error crept onto the front page of the first issue of *Al Munqidh*. It was corrected subsequently, but it made a very bad impression. Such mistakes would be inconceivable in an Egyptian Islamist publication.

34 For a very detailed analysis of the arguments used by Benhadj, see El-Difraoui, 'La Critique de la doctrine démocratique'. pp. 108ff.

35 Ibid. The concept of *chura* in Islamic legal doctrine denotes the consultation of the *ulema* which governments should in principle carry out.

36 For a discussion of these events, see Leveau, *Le Sabre et le turban*, pp. 128–72.

37 See Martinez, 'Les Eucalyptus', pp. 100–1.

38 This idea has been developed, within a wider perspective, by Olivier Roy in *The Failure of Political Islam* (Cambridge, Mass., 1994).

2 Behind the Veil

1 *Le Nouvel Observateur*, 5 Nov. 1992.

2 See Rémy Leveau and Fatiha Dazi, 'L'Intégration par la politique: le vote des Beurs', *Études*, Sept. 1988, pp. 179–88, and Cesari, *Être musulman en France*, pp. 205–22 and 307–18.

3 Gabteni was later to organize a demonstration in Oct. 1989, in support of the wearing of the veil. Then in Feb. 1990 he hit the headlines again with a fantastic story about his kidnapping. At the same time, he sparked off a public controversy when he alleged on television to have received a state subsidy of 400,000 francs from the Social Action Fund, although he was unable to provide proof of this. As a result, he lost all credibility – and with it, access to television air time.

4 See the contributions of authors living in France in *Pour Rushdie*.

5 In 1969, an IFOP survey showed that 37 per cent of people of Muslim origin felt close to the Socialist Party, but only 1 per cent felt close to the UDF (the liberal right-wing Union for French Democracy) and 3 per cent to the RPR (the Gaullist right-wing Rally for the Republic, led by Chirac). See Paul Balta (ed.), *L'Islam dans* Le Monde (Paris, 1991), p. 113.

6 Statement from the Ministry of the Interior, 16 Mar. 1989.

7 On the complex statutes of the Paris Mosque, see Alain Boyer, *L'Institut musulman de la mosquée de Paris* (Paris, 1992), and André Damien, 'L'Islam en France', *Administration*, no. 161, Oct.–Dec. 1993, pp. 112–18. Damien worked with Charles Pasqua in the Interior Ministry, with responsibility for Islam in France.

8 His claim was rejected by a former council employee who stated that the 'confusion' was deliberate. See *Le Monde*, 27 Aug. 1989.

9 Interview in *L'Express*, 22 June 1990. The FIS's statement appeared, somewhat strangely, in *El Moujahid* (organ of the FLN) on 2 July 1990.

10 For an account of the early mosque plans, see Kepel, *Les Banlieues de l'islam*, pp. 306–10.

11 'L'Heure de vérité', Antenne 2 (French public television channel), 19 June 1989.

12 *Libération*, 31 Aug. 1989.
13 Gaëlle Jullien and Frédéric Charillon, 'Le dossier de la construction de la mosquée de Lyon' (dissertation, Institut d'Études Politiques, Paris, 1990), p. 55.
14 According to Professor Lahnèche, president of the ACLIF, the costs would be financed by Muslims of the region: 'We will of course accept foreign contributions, but we will refuse any contributions from non-moderate countries.' Quoted in *Le Monde*, 26 Sept. 1989.
15 Kamel Kabtane in *La Croix*, 8 Sept. 1990.
16 The mosque project 'received a gift of twenty million francs from Saudi Arabia' (*Regards d'Islam*, no. 9, July–Aug. 1992, p. 5), which was not enough to cover the total costs.
17 See Henri Tincq's account in *Le Monde*, 15 Nov. 1989. For a detailed survey of Islam in Marseilles, see Cesari, *Etre musulman en France*, pp. 63–136.
18 In an IFOP survey for *Le Monde* (30 Nov. 1989), 60 per cent of French people identified the word 'Islam' with 'violence', and 71 per cent with 'fanaticism'.
19 *Le Courrier Picard*, 3 Oct. 1989.
20 *Le Monde*, 17 Oct. 1989.
21 Cf. Kepel, *Les Banlieues de l'islam*, pp. 154–8.
22 On these groups, see ibid., pp. 257–74.
23 *Le Monde*, 24 Oct. 1989.
24 According to the Federation's president, Muhammad-Ayyoub Leseur, in an interview in *La Croix*, 25 Oct. 1989.
25 *Le Monde*, 24 Oct. 1989. His predecessor Sheikh Abbas had said similar things in a press conference given during Ramadan on 2 Apr., two weeks before his death, when he advised 'all those who want to get to know Islam not to trust the books and articles which are published today by authors who claim or are held to be experts on everything concerning Islam, but who unfortunately know nothing or next to nothing about it.'
26 *Le Nouvel Observateur*, 26 Oct. 1989.
27 *Le Nouvel Observateur*, 2 Nov. 1989.
28 David Kessler, 'La Laïcité: du combat au droit', *Le Débat*, Oct. 1993, p. 100.
29 *Le Monde*, 29 Nov. 1993.
30 Interview in *Le Débat*, Sept.–Oct. 1990, pp. 3–16, p. 15.
31 Interview in *Le Monde*, 17 Mar. 1990.
32 'The CORIF's work attempts to be methodical and technical, in order to tackle all the problems one by one . . . so that Islam becomes a religion like any other in France,' wrote the technical counsellor who ran the body for successive ministers (Joxe, Marchand and Quilès), Raoul Weexsteen, 'Approche culturelle de l'islam par l'Etat français', in Gérard Ignasse (ed.), *Islam et politique* (Paris, 1992), p. 103.
33 *L'Index*, no. 28, Nov.–Dec. 1991, p. 2. *L'Index* is a free, two-side newssheet published irregularly, with a sharp edge to its comments.
34 A. Mustapha Diop, 'Le Mouvement associatif islamique en Île de France', (unpublished report for the Ministry of Solidarity, Department of Population and Migrations, Dec. 1990), p. 103.
35 See Frédéric Charillon, 'Le Conseil de Réflexion sur l'Islam en France' (unpublished dissertation, Institut d'Études Politiques, Paris, 1991), pp. 22ff.

Charillon notes that, of the Muslims he interviewed, 'not one knew of the CORIF' – one of them confused it with the Jewish CRIF.

36 Nonetheless, some 'maximalists' were not satisfied with this measure, since Islamic burial practice (without coffins) remained prohibited by law for public hygiene reasons. Mokhtar-Ahmed Weisberg, vice-president of the FNMF, maintained that 'what we want is quite simply Muslim cemeteries, not just plots. In fact, Islamic law does not allow us to be buried in cemeteries for people of the Bible [*sic*], or next to them.' *Regards d'Islam*, no. 2, Apr.–May 1991, p. 20.

37 'A complete mess for the start of the Ramadan fast in France. Some began on 4, others on 5, still others on 6 March . . .' lamented *Regards d'Islam*, no. 5, Mar. 1992, p. 20. *Le Critère* (no. 9, 10 Apr. 1992, p. 1), the publication of the Algerian Fraternity in France (French offshoot of the FIS), accused the Paris Mosque of having 'deliberately misled the community' about the date of Ramadan, and informed 'those who began the fast on Thursday 5 March that they will have to fast an extra day to complete the month'. Note that the determination of the date of Ramadan is an important issue in the political struggle for control over Islam between and within the different states of the Muslim world (particularly since the emergence of Islamist opposition movements).

38 M. Mitterrand also thanked the Jewish 'community'. The President's use of the word surprised those who thought that the French state did not recognize any 'community affiliation' on the part of its citizens or foreigners resident on its soil.

39 See, for example, his statements in *Le Figaro*, 29 Aug. 1990, *L'Express*, 7 Sept. 1990, and *Politis*, 24 Jan. 1991. M. Alili gave Abd al Hadi Doudi, one of the leading preachers of Bouyali's underground movement, the job of imam in his mosque. On 29 June 1992, he reacted to the assassination of the Algerian President Mohammed Boudiaf in the following terms: 'The choice of the people on 26 December [1991] was not respected. That's what you get when you sanction injustice.' The minister of the interior, Paul Quilès, brought him to order, calling on him to 'show more reserve in future'.

40 *La Croix*, 5 and 6 Sept. 1990. On the Evry mosque, see Mounia Bennani, 'L'Association culturelle d'Evry', *Les Cahiers de l'Orient*, no. 16–17 (1989–90), pp. 63–76. According to Merroun, the thirty-five million francs needed for the construction of the mosque (still incomplete at the time of writing in 1994) came from the King of Morocco (six million), King Fahd of Arabia (six million) and a loan of seven million francs from the Saudi-controlled Islamic Development Bank, the rest from private donors, mainly Saudi: see *Regards d'Islam*, no. 9, July–Aug. 1992, p. 7.

41 *Le Monde*, 13 Jan. 1991.

42 *L'Index* (no. 31, p. 3), in an article attributed to the pen-name 'Yakoub Méchoui', noted that the minister of the interior 'would have liked to take advantage of the general confusion . . . to regain control of the building, through his puppets . . . But, unfortunately for him, the Doctor-rector returned. It's good news, because all we are waiting for now is the popular insurrection in Algeria, and we can take over.'

43 See *Le Figaro*, 15 Apr. 1992, for Dalil Boubakeur's response.

44 Weexsteen, 'Approche culturelle de l'islam', p. 103.

45 This figure of 207 includes different categories of member: 'active members', 'supporters' and 'friends', defined according to their involvement in the

UOIF's board of directors (interview with the author). See also UOIF, *Les Musulmans de France: préoccupations et aspirations* (Paris, 1993), p. 2.

46 Article 2:3 of statutes. Note that this is a translation of the Arabic text; the French text is slightly different: 'to defend and represent the interests of Muslims in France'.

47 In contrast, the vast majority of leaders of grassroots Islamic associations in the Paris area are much older, have rarely been educated beyond primary school and have had little religious training. Three-quarters of them are semi-skilled machine operators. Moustapha Diop, 'Le Mouvement associatif islamique en Île-de-France', pp. 59ff. See also Cécile Jolly, 'Les islamistes tunisiens à Paris et en Île-de-France' (dissertation, Institut d'Études Politiques, Paris, 1992).

48 The term, meaning 'renaissance' or 'rebirth', usually refers to the flowering of Arab intellectual and political activity in the Middle East in the late nineteenth century, which formed the basis for resistance to Ottoman domination. The name does not have any specifically Islamic connotation, which was a condition for participation in the elections.

49 Published by the Study Centre on Arab Unity, Beirut (the main publisher of Arab nationalist books), Ghannouchi's book was intended to reach out to the nationalist movement and seek common ground between nationalists and Islamists in the common struggle against the 'despotism' of the newly independent states. See in particular Ghannouchi's definition of the 'fourth generation' of Islamists, for whom political pluralism is an inviolable right in the future Islamic state (pp. 288f).

50 Habib Mokni, interview with the author, Paris, Dec. 1992. The same approach can be seen in the Washington-based United Association for Studies and Research, which publishes the *Middle East Affairs Journal*; activists of the Palestinian Islamist movement Hamas have considerable influence within this association.

51 Interview with the author, Paris, 24 Mar. 1994.

52 Since the writings of Sayyid Qotb, Islamist activists refuse to consider states which do not apply the sharia as 'Islamic'.

53 On the other hand, it does not demand the application of the sharia to society as a whole, since Muslims are in a minority. See Sheikh Fayçal Maoulaoui, *Al usus al char'iyya lil 'ilaqat bayn al muslimin wa ghayr al muslimin* ('The sharia as a basis for relations between Muslims and non-Muslims') (Beirut, 1982) and Sheikh Manna' el Qattan, *Iqamat al muslim fi balad ghayr islami* ('The presence of Muslims in non-Islamic countries') (Paris, n.d.).

54 In Arabic, *fi firansa* became *man firansa*. The change was noted (after an interval of two years) with an ironic comment in *L'Index* (no. 31, p. 2): '... the UOIF, an Islamist organization which portrays itself as conciliatory but whose only, true slogan is "no salvation outside our Church", has now declared itself leader.' It is true that by 1992 the UOIF had left the FNMF trailing.

55 Quoted in *Regards d'Islam*, no. 1, Feb.–Mar. 1991, p. 7. As Muslim societies developed, the original distinction between *dar al islam* and *dar al harb* had changed into a division of the world into *dar al islam* and *dar al kufr* ('land of ungodliness'), itself divided into *dar al harb* and *dar al 'ahd*: 'The latter, recognized some time later by Muslim jurists as constituting an

autonomous political entity, is held to contain peoples or states who enter with the Muslims of *dar al islam* into a state of reconciliation or contractual peace', notes Fahmi Jadaane, according to whom Islamist militants like Sayyid Qotb returned to the original binary division ('Umma musulmane et société islamique', *Pouvoirs*, no. 62, Sept. 1993, pp. 33, 40–1).

56 *La Croix*, 31 Dec. 1991.

57 *Regards d'Islam* (no. 3, Nov. 1991, p. 1), greeting the inauguration of the UOIF's 'Islamic university', expressed pleasure that it had 'overtaken the many projects proposed by the government, the Islamologists such as Bruno Etienne or the "progressists" like Muhammad Arkoun who would like to see imams trained in a secular way, in particular in Alsace ...' Didier-Ali Bourg, the managing editor of the journal, would himself later (in 1993) set up a rival institute, the Islamic University of France (UIF).

58 Prospectus, Al kullia al aurubiyya lil dirasat al islamiyya (European Faculty of Islamic Studies) (Château-Chinon, no date [1993]), p. 6.

59 Ibid., p. 15.

60 On behalf of the French government, Kofi Yamgnane, secretary of state for integration, declared the government's acceptance of the principle of religious freedom in France, but expressed doubts about the compatibility between secularism and the 'ideological ties with the Muslim Brotherhood movement and subsidies from countries which are to say the least remote from French republican values' (*Libération*, 10 Jan. 1992). Most of the Eastern European students enrolled at the institute had their application for visas turned down.

61 Of the twelve members of the UOIF's board of directors in 1990, only one had French nationality; four were Tunisian, four Moroccan, two Algerian, one Syrian and one Iraqi.

3 The Communalist Challenge

1 *L'Express*, 30 Jan. 1991. In fact, this 'feeling of being a community' had already found expression within the Socialist Party, with the publication in Apr. 1990 of an 'appeal from socialists of Muslim culture' in response to the 'outburst of anti-Muslim feeling for which the Creil affair served as a pretext'. The text defended 'the rights and identity of our community', described as 'a victim of social exclusion and cultural devaluation': *Lettre des socialistes de culture musulmane*, no. 1, Apr. 1990, p. 12.

2 See Bruno Etienne, 'Cherche héros positif désespérément', *Pouvoirs*, no. 62, pp. 73ff. Etienne sets 'Western arrogance in talking about "negative Arab heroes"' against the way in which 'the Arab-Islamic typology of the hero' is constructed.

3 Interview with the head of the school in Bourdieu, *La Misère du monde*, p. 686.

4 Philippe Bernard in *Le Monde*, 14 Mar. 1991.

5 IFOP poll of 614 people of Muslim origin, conducted between 29 January and 1 Feb. 1991, for the Information and Broadcasting Department of the Prime Minister's office (unpublished).

6 Ibid. In Aug. 1990, Abdallah Turki, vice-chancellor of the University of Riyadh and a notable intermediary in the 'recommendations' needed to

finance Islamic associations abroad, made a trip to Paris to defend the Saudi position. On 23 Sept., the leading Wahhabi thinker Abou Bakr Al Djazairi, an Algerian theologian who taught at the University of Medina, gave a talk at the Institute of the Arab World in Paris, where he attacked the 'atheism' of the 'infidel' Saddam Hussein.

7 N. Cherif, president of the 'Génération Beur' movement, quoted in *Le Point*, 4 Mar. 1991. See also Bruno Etienne, *Ils ont rasé la Mésopotamie* (Aix-en-Provence, 1992).

8 Both authors presented their analysis of the Vaulx-en-Velin events in *Libération*, 15 Oct. 1990. Alain Touraine's arguments were developed in his 1992 book *Critique de la modernité*.

9 On the problems of French 'banlieues' (suburbs: in contrast to the British or American situation, where poorer and immigrant areas are usually situated in the inner city, in France urban redevelopment in the 1960s and 1970s meant that these areas were moved out to the suburbs, while inner cities were reserved for businesses and upmarket housing), see F. Dubet and Didier Lapeyronnie, *Les Quartiers d'exil* (Paris, 1992), Adil Jazouli, *Les Années banlieues* (Paris, 1992) and two very good journalistic investigations, Farid Aïchoune, *Nés en banlieue* (Paris, 1991) and Anne Giudicelli, *La Caillera* (Paris, 1992).

10 See the report *Ville et sécurité: un regard américain* (Paris: Fondation franco–américaine, 1993), which compares the two approaches.

11 See *Panoramiques*, no. 12, 1993, special issue on 'Intégration ou explosion? Banlieues ...' (guest editors Catherine Wihtol de Wenden and Zakya Daoud).

12 The accounts which follow are compiled from these interviews: A. Blom, J. Cahen, A. Rakkah, 'Les Jeunes Musulmans dans la société française. Analyse de 21 entretiens' (dissertation, Institut d'Études Politiques, Paris, 1993).

13 In Mar. 1991, during the first month of Ramadan after the Gulf War, young people identifying themselves with the cause of Islam wrecked a café in Nanterre which had been the centre of the drugs trade. It was the first 'anti-drugs action' associated with Islamism; others followed, notably in the Biscottes project in the south of Lille.

14 Compare these views with the critique of Darwinian teaching by American Protestant fundamentalists or the Loubavitch Jews: see Kepel, *The Revenge of God*.

15 The research by Blom, Cahen and Rakah, 'Les Jeunes Musulmans dans la société française', identifies three very different groups of young people: the first group they call the 'young new Muslims', the second the 'integrated', and the third the 'young secularists'. The first group (from whom the interviewees cited here come) would like to live in an exclusively Muslim area; the second are indifferent to the ethnic and religious composition of their living environment; the third explicitly refuse to live in an 'Arab' or 'Muslim' area, which they see as a potential ghetto.

16 By former police chief Charles Pellegrini, *Le FIS en France: mythe ou réalité?* (Paris, 1992).

17 See Leverrier, *Les Politiques de Dieu*, p. 62, footnote 50.

18 See Hervé Terrel, 'L'Enclave islamique de la rue Jean-Pierre Timbaud', in Kepel, *Exils et royaumes*, pp. 360–2.

19 See Guillaume Coudray, 'L'Intégration au tissu urbain de Khaled Ibn Walid,

"mosquée de fortune" piétiste à la Goutte d'Or' (dissertation, Institut d'É-tudes Politiques, Paris, 1993), who notes that the mosque 'plays down its symbolic function, so as not to disrupt the regulation of the local environment by too strong an assertion of identity', and that Sheikh Sahraoui does not allow the FAF newsletter *Le Critère* to be distributed inside the mosque.

20 Thus, the president of the Algerian High Committee of State, Mohammed Boudiaf, is usually referred to as 'Boudiable' ('Boudevil'), Ali Haroun (a member of the High Committee whom they accuse of having a fondness for alcohol) as 'Ali-vrogne' ('Ali-inebriated') or 'Ali Aaron' (to make his name sound Jewish).

21 *Le Critère*, 20 and 27 Nov. 1992. On the affair, see F. Aïchouine, 'Les Contrebandiers d'Allah, *Le Nouvel Observateur*, 12 Nov. 1992, and Terrel, 'L'Enclave islamique'.

22 *Le Critère*, 20 Nov. 1992.

23 *Le Figaro*, 13 June 1993. See also Guillaume Malaurie's investigation into 'anti-drug squads' in a housing project in the Hauts-de-Seine department, *L'Événement du Jeudi*, 17 June 1993, pp. 40–1.

24 *Le Critère*, 19 Mar. 1993. The assassination of Lyabès and Flici, well-known intellectuals, aroused deep emotion. Dr Flici worked as a doctor to the poor in the deprived kasbah quarter of Algiers.

25 *Le Critère*, 28 May 1993.

26 *Résistance*, 18 June 1993. Dr Boucebci was a well-known psychiatrist in Algiers, who did not hide his opposition to the Islamists.

27 *L'Étendard*, 9 July 1993. The fourth issue of *L'Étendard* carried an 'open letter to Pierre Bourdieu, president of the support committee for "Algerian intellectuals"', expressing surprise at this 'belated and selective awakening of intellectuals on the other side of the Mediterranean' and presenting him with a list of ten names (two Islamist lawyers and eight doctors) of 'independent-thinking intellectuals from this RESISTANT people ... imprisoned in the gaols of the dictatorship'.

28 Damien, 'L'Islam en France', p. 118.

29 Terrel, 'L'Enclave islamique', p. 358. See also *Regards d'Islam*, no. 9, July-Aug. 1992, p. 4.

30 The AEIF, founded in 1963, follows the doctrine of the Muslim Brotherhood, but is independent of the UOIF. It holds its annual congress at Christmas, at the same time as the UOIF gathering in Le Bourget, but attracts a smaller audience. See a report on its 1990 congress in Strasbourg, which attracted 'more than 800 participants', in *Regards d'Islam*, no. 1, Feb.–Mar. 1991, p. 9.

31 Dalil Boubakeur, 'L'État et ses cultes: le cas de l'Islam', *Administration*, no. 161, Oct.–Dec. 1993, p. 145. In this article, Boubakeur outlined his plans for the structure of future community organization in a diagram.

32 Ibid., p. 143. Damien, 'L'Islam en France' (p. 113), estimates that there are some 500 imams practising in France, of whom 4 per cent are French nationals. At the time when Damien's article was published, a number of imams were being expelled from France.

33 Bruno Etienne, 'Convergences et divergences des trois monothéismes en France' (unpublished paper kindly passed on to the author by Professor Etienne), p. 1.

34 Didier-Ali Bourg founded the European Centre for Research and Information on Islam, which published the journal *Regards d'Islam* (fifteen

issues appeared between Feb. 1991 and Feb. 1993). He wrote a postgraduate thesis (equivalent to MPhil) on modes of transmission of religion from Algerian Muslim immigrants to their children (Université de Paris X, Nanterre, 1993) (kindly sent to the author by M. Bourg).

35 *Regards d'Islam*, no. 9, July–Aug.1992, p. 2. See also, 'Dossier de l'Étudiant de l'UIF' (student handbook) (no date [Paris, 1993]).

36 The coeducational nature of the classes, and the seduction strategies it produces, are the subject of ironic comment by Daniel-Youssof Leclercq in *Intégrité Gazette* (a stable companion of *L'Index*), no. 4, Feb. 1994.

37 Martine Gozlan, *L'Islam et la République. Des musulmans de France contre l'intégrisme* (Paris, 1994). Abd el Raziq, a disciple of the reformist thinker Muhammad Abduh, interpreted his thought as a dissociation of religion and the socio-political order. His book, published in 1925 (published in French as *L'Islam et les fondements du pouvoir*: Paris, 1994), caused a scandal in the more traditional Islamic circles. See A. Hourani, *Arabic Thought in the Liberal Age* (London, 1962), pp. 183–92. Soheib Bensheikh is one of the sons of Sheikh Abbas Bensheikh Lhoussine, rector of the Paris Mosque from 1982 to 1989.

38 *Le Monde*, 7 Nov. 1992.

39 According to Kessler, 'La Laïcité', p. 96.

40 Estimates of the number of veiled pupils vary from the low figure in the tens given by the Ministry of Education and the claim of several hundred made by a group of RPR deputies hostile to the veil (in a parliamentary question to Education Minister François Bayrou, 20 Oct. 1993). The organizers of the Union of Young Muslims rally held in Vénissieux in April 1994 put at around a hundred the number of veiled 'sisters excluded in the name of secularism' in the Rhône–Alpes region alone. If we add up the number of isolated cases reported in the national press, they alone came to around a hundred by the autumn of 1993.

41 *Libération*, 30 Oct. 1993.

42 *Le Parisien*, 10 Jan. 1994.

43 *Le Monde*, 13 Oct. 1993.

44 The grounds for the tribunal decision referred mainly to the disciplinary problems created by the pupils' attitude and statements made by their father: see *Le Figaro*, 12 May 1994. The following week, the Orléans administrative tribunal ordered the re-admission of two pupils who had been excluded from a secondary school in Vendôme for wearing veils, on the grounds that 'no one should be harassed for his/her opinions, including religious opinions, provided that their expression does not disrupt the public order laid down by the law': see *Le Monde*, 22–3 May 1994. Disruption of public order seems thus to have become the major issue determining whether administrative tribunals judge the wearing of the veil licit or not.

45 *Le Figaro*, 6 Nov. 1993. According to the newspaper, the imam in question was in charge of the local branch of the 'National Tendency – Islamic Union in France' organization, linked to the main Islamic party in Turkey, Refah Partisi (which won the Mar. 1994 local elections in Istanbul and Ankara).

46 Extracts from his letter published in *Le Figaro*, 16 Nov. 1993.

47 'Moi, Schérazade, combattante de l'islam', interview compiled by Anne Fohr, *Le Nouvel Observateur*, 24 Feb. 1994.

48 Cf. Danièle Hervieu-Léger, 'Renouveaux émotionnels contemporains', in Danièle Hervieu-Léger and Françoise Champion (eds), *De l'émotion en*

religion (Paris, 1990), pp. 217ff.

49 See Virginie Linhart, *Volontaires pour l'usine* (Paris, 1994).

50 *Le Nouvel Observateur*, 24 Feb. 1994.

51 *Al Muslimoon*, 28 Jan. 1994, p. 3. See also an interview with Schérazade and Sandra, written in the same impassioned tone, in the women's pages of the 4 Feb. issue.

52 Such match-making activities are widespread in all movements which aim to build religious communities. See Kepel, *The Revenge of God*, for similar examples among American Protestant evangelism or Hassidic Judaism. See also, above, the importance placed by the Black Muslims on marriage between followers in order to combat the disintegration of family life and resulting 'deviant' behaviour.

53 *Le Monde*, 14 Apr. 1993.

54 The first issue of *Jeunes Musulmans* (Jan. 1994) carried the headline 'Has Charles Pasqua declared war on Islam?', in response to the police operation against suspected FIS sympathizers on 9 Nov. 1993, described as a 'roundup among the Muslim community in France'. The CORIF ('the so-called Muslim body which is supposed to deal with the religious affairs of the Muslims of France') was denounced by a speaker at the UJM's 1994 congress.

55 *Libération*, 13 Apr. 1993.

56 See Kepel, *Les banlieues de l'islam*, pp. 154–9.

57 83.5 per cent of the local electorate voted against the extension. Minister of the Interior Philippe Marchand called the mayor to order by reminding him that the fundamental principle of religious freedom 'may not be undermined by popular consultation'. See *Libération*, 29 Apr. 1993, and *Le Monde*, 2 and 3 May 1993.

Index